PROSPE

What can prosperity possibly mean in a world of environmental and social limits?

The publication of *Prosperity without Growth* was a landmark in the sustainability debate. Tim Jackson's piercing challenge to conventional economics openly questioned the most highly prized goal of politicians and economists alike: the continued pursuit of exponential economic growth. Its findings provoked controversy, inspired debate and led to a new wave of research building on its arguments and conclusions.

This substantially revised and re-written edition updates those arguments and considerably expands upon them. Jackson demonstrates that building a 'post-growth' economy is a precise, definable and meaningful task. Starting from clear first principles, he sets out the dimensions of that task: the nature of enterprise; the quality of our working lives; the structure of investment; and the role of the money supply. He shows how the economy of tomorrow may be transformed in ways that protect employment, facilitate social investment, reduce inequality and deliver both ecological and financial stability.

Seven years after it was first published, *Prosperity without Growth* is no longer a radical narrative whispered by a marginal fringe, but an essential vision of social progress in a post-crisis world. Fulfilling that vision is simply the most urgent task of our times.

Tim Jackson is Professor of Sustainable Development at the University of Surrey, UK, and Director of the Centre for the Understanding of Sustainable Prosperity (CUSP). For seven years he was Economics Commissioner on the UK Sustainable Development Commission, where his work culminated in the first edition of this book. He was awarded the Hillary Laureate for exceptional international leadership in 2016. In addition to his scientific work, Tim is a prize-winning dramatist with numerous radio writing credits for the BBC.

Praise for the second edition of *Prosperity without Growth*

'It is hard to improve a classic, but Jackson has done it... a clearly written yet scholarly union of moral vision with solid economics.'

Herman Daly, author of *Steady-State Economics*

'I remember exactly where I was when I first read *Prosperity without Growth*. It cuts through the intellectual clamour with clarity, courage – and hope.'

Naomi Klein, author of *This Changes Everything: Capitalism vs. The Climate*

'Tim Jackson's *Prosperity without Growth* systematises and renders tangible an essential project few believed to be practical: recovering the dream of shared prosperity and human development through decoupling it from the bandwagon of growth. Essential reading for those refusing to succumb to a dystopic future.'

Yanis Varoufakis, Professor of Economics, University of Athens

'One of the most important essays of our generation: both visionary and realistic, rooted in careful research and setting out difficult but achievable goals, it gives what we so badly need – an alternative to passivity, short-term selfishness and cynicism.'

Dr Rowan Williams, 104th Archbishop of Canterbury, UK

'This challenge to the prevailing growth-based economic paradigm confronts an inescapable dilemma: how to reconcile "our aspirations for the good life with the limitations and constraints of a finite planet". Its thoughtful and penetrating critique is enriched by an outline of credible programs to achieve this end. A very valuable contribution to urgent concerns that cannot be ignored.'

Noam Chomsky, Institute Professor & Professor of Linguistics, MIT, USA

'With much of the world in turmoil, calling for higher economic growth is every politician's comfort blanket of choice. But Tim Jackson compellingly urges those politicians to give up their comfort blanket, to re-think our continuing dependence on economic growth, and to start preparing – urgently – for a world where such growth is no longer viable as its environmental cost massively exceeds its benefits. *Prosperity without Growth* remains the single most important book addressing this most critical of contemporary challenges.'

Jonathon Porritt, Founder Director of Forum for the Future

'Tim Jackson spearheads the obvious truth that GDP growth is not necessary in order to achieve higher well-being in the rich world. Government intervention can produce the desired result, namely full employment, less inequity and reduced greenhouse gas emissions.'

Jørgen Randers, author of *2052: A Global Forecast for the Next Forty Years*

'Tim Jackson has brought his groundbreaking book bang up to date and substantially deepened its arguments. This extensively revised edition sets out more clearly than ever the dimensions of a new and different economics – working for people, planet and prosperity. There isn't a better exposition out there of why and how we need to move beyond growth.'

Caroline Lucas, MP for Brighton, Pavilion

Praise for the first edition of *Prosperity without Growth*

'Bold and provocative.'

The New York Times

'One of the most outstanding pieces of environmental economics literature in recent years.'

Le Monde

'One of the best books of 2009.'

Financial Times

'We live in a finite world but with infinite demands. Human wants, political convenience and intellectual inertia trump planetary limits. Tim Jackson makes headway in setting signposts towards a more sustainable future.'

Camilla Toulmin

'This is one of the most brilliant analyses I've seen. It is a thoughtful and action-oriented masterpiece, with an eye open to how to overcome resistance to the task ahead.'

Arnold Tukker, Professor of Industrial Ecology, Leiden University

'It's easy to lament the unsustainable nature of growth economics. It's slightly harder to re-imagine it on the other side. Hardest of all is to detail the transition, how you get from growth to a steady state without breaking the economy. That's the missing piece, and Tim Jackson has boldly stepped into the breach with a book that is clear, balanced and free of political bias ... *Prosperity without Growth* has got to be one of the most important books of the year.'

Jeremy Williams, Make Wealth History

'[Tim Jackson] has done us a tremendous service in putting the debate into practical and comprehensible language ... This book will be a widely read and influential basis for practical exposition of many of our underlying concerns and ideas for their solution to the broader public.'

Ecological Economics

'Jackson's analysis is truly unique in meticulously disentangling the interdependencies between the economic logic of production, the social logic of consumption, and the conflicting position of the state that keeps the unsustainable machinery of growth moving. Jackson also provides an original perspective that identifies leverage points for change that hold the prospect of eventual effectiveness. I have not encountered such a bright and insightful analysis since the path-breaking work of Donella and Dennis Meadows and Herman Daly.'

Journal of Industrial Ecology

'*Prosperity without Growth* gets my "twice read" honour ... the book reads something like a novel ... Finally, I asked my wife Angie to read the book and summarise it for me. Her conclusion? "This is a good book that will change your life. Read it."'

Vinod Bhatia, JIE

'I thought the book was splendid. Jackson's writing is lucid and well organised. He has a gift for the telling sentence.'

Bryan Walker, *Hot Topic*

'[A] revolutionary text ... whose time has come.'

George Monbiot, *The Guardian*

PROSPERITY
WITHOUT
GROWTH

FOUNDATIONS FOR THE
ECONOMY OF TOMORROW

SECOND EDITION

TIM JACKSON

 Routledge
Taylor & Francis Group

LONDON AND NEW YORK

Second edition published 2017
by Routledge
2 Park Square, Milton Park, Abingdon, Oxon OX14 4RN

and by Routledge
711 Third Avenue, New York, NY 10017

Routledge is an imprint of the Taylor & Francis Group, an informa business

First edition published by Earthscan 2010

British Library Cataloguing in Publication Data
A catalogue record for this book is available from the British Library

Library of Congress Cataloging in Publication Data
Names: Jackson, Tim, 1957- author.
Title: Prosperity without growth : foundations for the economy of tomorrow /
Tim Jackson.
Description: 2nd edition. | Abingdon, Oxon ; New York, NY : Routledge, 2017.
| Includes index.
Identifiers: LCCN 2016027418| ISBN 9781138935402 (hardback) | ISBN
9781138935419 (pbk.) | ISBN 9781315677453 (ebook)
Subjects: LCSH: Sustainable development. | Wealth. | Globalization--Economic
aspects.
Classification: LCC HC79.E5 J298 2017 | DDC 338.9/27--dc23
LC record available at https://lccn.loc.gov/2016027418

ISBN: 978-1-138-93540-2 (hbk)
ISBN: 978-1-138-93541-9 (pbk)
ISBN: 978-1-315-67745-3 (ebk)

Typeset in Bembo and Scala Sans
by Saxon Graphics Ltd, Derby

Printed and bound in the United States of America by
Edwards Brothers Malloy on sustainably sourced paper

This edition is dedicated to Zac, Tilly and Lissy: in recognition of the times when this book took me from you; and in the hope that you will one day take something from it.

'It's your world now, use well the time. Be part of something good; leave something good behind.'

The Eagles ('Long Road out of Eden', 2007)

CONTENTS

FIGURES

Acknowledgements

I owe a huge debt of gratitude to the many people who generously gave me their help and support during the writing of this book: both in the original and in the revised editions.

The initial idea for the book came from a conversation I had with Jonathon Porritt, who was for ten years chair of the Sustainable Development Commission (SDC). Shortly after I was appointed as Economics Commissioner to the SDC in 2004 he and I sat down together to discuss what my role in the commission might be.

We met in a café in Westminster, both of us rushing between other engagements. It was a very short meeting, maybe twenty minutes at most. But it established the course of my work for over a decade. His support for a report that would challenge the foundations of the prevailing economic paradigm was immediate and unwavering. To this day, I continue to benefit immensely from his insight and experience.

Equally vital was the camaraderie of colleagues at the Commission both during the writing and after publication. Commissioners and secretariat alike gave generously of their time, attending workshops, offering critical commentary and reviewing drafts for me. Victor Anderson, Jan Bebbington, Bernie Bulkin, Lindsey Colbourne, Anna Coote, Peter Davies, Stewart Davis, Sue Dibb, Sara Eppel, Ian Fenn, Ann Finlayson, Tess Gill, Alan Knight, Tim Lang, Andrew Lee, Andy Long, Alice Owen, Elke Pirgmaier, Alison Pridmore, Anne Power, Hugh Raven, Tim O'Riordan, Rhian Thomas, Jacopo Torriti, Joe Turrent, Kay West and Becky Willis were amongst those who provided a constant source of encouragement and advice, throughout this time.

Special thanks are owed to those who contributed directly to a series of workshops on prosperity hosted by the Commission between November 2007 and April 2008. Contributors included: Simone d'Alessandro, Frederic Bouder, Madeleine Bunting, Herman Daly, Arik Dondi, Paul Ekins, Tim Kasser, Miriam Kennet, Guy Liu, Tommaso Luzzati, Jesse Norman, Avner Offer, John O'Neill, Tom Prugh, Hilde Rapp, Jonathan Rutherford, Jill Rutter, Zia Sardar, Kate Soper, Steve Sorrell, Nick Spencer, Derek Wall, David Woodward and Dimitri Zenghelis.

The thesis in this book has been informed immeasurably by the warm collaboration I have enjoyed over the last decade with numerous academic friends and colleagues. It is a particular privilege to have led three large research collaborations at the University of Surrey during the time this work was progressing. The Research Group on Lifestyles, Values and the Environment (RESOLVE), the Sustainable Lifestyles Research Group (SLRG) and most recently the Centre for the Understanding of Sustainable Prosperity (CUSP) have provided the intellectual foundation through which so much of my understanding has been forged.

My personal thanks are owed to numerous colleagues at the University of Surrey and elsewhere who participated in and supported these projects. Alison Armstrong, Tracey Bedford, Kate Burningham, Phil Catney, Mona Chitnis, Ian Christie, Alexia Coke, Geoff Cooper, Will Davies, Rachael Durrant, Andy Dobson, Angela Druckman, Birgitta Gatersleben, Bronwyn Hayward, Lester Hunt, Aled Jones, Chris Kukla, Matt Leach, Fergus Lyon, Scott Milne, Yacob Mulugetta, Kate Oakley, Ronan Palmer, Debbie Roy, Adrian Smith, Steve Sorrell, Andy Stirling, Sue Venn, David Uzzell, Bas

Verplanken and Rebecca White are amongst those with whom I shared not just a common agenda but an intellectual bond that was always open and fruitful, even when we disagreed on specifics.

Our research collaboration would not have been possible without the tireless and good-natured assistance of our various support teams: Wendy Day, Marilyn Ellis, Claire Livingstone and Moira Foster all deserve a mention. Particular thanks must go to Gemma Birkett for her central role in managing what was at times a frankly impossible diary and maintaining an unlikely calm in the face of various storms.

In the wake of the first edition, I received such widespread support from so many colleagues and friends that it would be impossible to make mention of them all here. People contacted me from the most unlikely places, and the warmth of their reception remains a vital resource for me in setting this work in perspective

From the hospice manager who drew parallels between my critique of consumerism and the challenge of those entering his care, to the Augustinian sister who wrote to me about Thomas Aquinas' views on the common good; from the economics professor who thanked me for breaking a taboo he had never understood to the grandmother who in the 1960s already brought up her children in accordance with the principles of 'living lightly' on the earth; from the school kids and university students who invited me to give lectures to the investment managers who were prepared to listen and change: these personal responses probably meant more to me than the many thousands of academic pages devoted to analysing and critiquing the limits of 'decoupling'.

It would be remiss of me not to mention by name some at least of those whose intellectual input has been indispensable in the six years since the first edition was published. Amongst those with whom I shared ideas, platforms and time were: Charlie Arden-Clarke, Alan Atkinson, Mike Barry, Nathalie Bennet, Catherine Cameron, Isabelle Cassiers, Bob Costanza, Ben Dyson, Ottmar Edenhofer, Marina Fischer-Kowalski, Duncan Forbes, John Fullerton, Ralf Fücks, Connie Hedegaard, Colin Hines, Andrew Jackson, Giorgos Kallis, Astrid Kann Rasmussen, Roman Krznaric, Satish Kumar, Michael Kumhof, Christin Lahr, Philippe Lamberts, Anthony Leiserowitz, Caroline Lucas, Joan Martinez-Alier, Jacqueline McGlade, Dennis Meadows,

Dominique Meda, Peter Michaelis, Meinhard Miegel, Ed Milliband, Frances O'Grady, Kate Power, Fabienne Pierre, Paul Raskin, Kate Raworth, Bill Rees, Johan Rockström, François Schneider, Petra Pinzler, Juliet Schor, Thomas Sedlacek, Gerhardt Schick, Gus Speth, Achim Steiner, Pavan Sukhdev, Any Sulistyowati, Adair Turner, Barbara Unmüßig, Adam Wakeling, Joan Walley, Steve Waygood, Ernst von Weizsäcker, Anders Wijkman and Rowan Williams. It goes without saying that their views have not always entirely coincided with mine. But their intellectual passion has been such a tremendous resource that they deserve my sincerest thanks.

I am grateful to Tommy Wiedmann, Tomas Marques, Neeyati Patel, Janet Salem, Heinz Schandl and colleagues at CSIRO, SERI and UNEP for their generous inputs to my revised chapter on decoupling. It is interesting to reflect on how much has changed in this debate during the last decade. When I think back on the struggle to pull together useful material footprint data seven or eight years ago, it's an extraordinary testament to an incredibly valuable international research programme. Today, the arguments about the role of trade in obscuring the resource dependencies of affluent nations are widely accepted, due in no small part to this body of work.

I owe a very personal debt of gratitude to Peter Victor, whose intellectual companionship has been a vital ingredient to my own development over the last seven years and a source of inspiration for this second edition. That Peter and I should have found common vision in developing a 'post-growth' macroeconomics was a real co-benefit from his early participation in my SDC work. That we shared so many other common interests was an unexpected bonus. Special thanks also to Peter's wife, Maria Paez Victor, whose quiet tolerance of our week-long conversations was interrupted only by her deliciously incisive critiques of western capitalism.

I have been lucky enough to work with not just one but three separate editorial teams during the production of *Prosperity without Growth*: first with Kay West, Rhian Thomas and Andy Long at the SDC; second with Jonathan Sinclair-Wilson, Camille Bramall, Gudrun Freese, Alison Kuznets and Veruschka Selbach at Earthscan; and now with Neil Boon, Andy Humphries, Cathy Hurren, Rob Langham, Laura Johnson, Umar Masood, Adele Parker and Nikky

Twyford at Routledge. I owe them all sincere thanks for their expertise, attention to detail and patient understanding.

Finally, I'd like to reflect an enduring gratitude to my partner Linda, whose personal and professional support has sustained me immensely through the unanticipated challenges of the last few years. I am particularly grateful for our shared delight in the simple act of walking: along rivers, through woods, across valleys, up mountains. As Satish Kumar once told me (I think he might have taken it from Nietszche), the very best thoughts are those that arrive while you're walking.

FOREWORD TO THE FIRST EDITION

CLARENCE HOUSE

How should we prosper? This is the simple question at the heart of Professor Jackson's lucid and remarkable account of the economics of sustainability in which he asks what it might mean for us to live well within the limits of a finite planet.

One cannot deny that our industrialized techniques and mastery of science have bought us enormous benefits. We live longer and healthier lives, with a diversity of opportunity undreamed of only decades ago. Revolutions in agriculture, nutrition, healthcare, in education, communication and information technology have all opened out our horizons and made possible things that would simply have been unimaginable to our ancestors – all kinds of benefits that no one would willingly forego.

It goes without saying that we surely have a moral duty to share these benefits with those in the poorest parts of the world. There remains an urgent need to improve nutritional health for the two billion people who are still chronically undernourished; to increase access to fresh water for the one billion people who still have no access to safe, uncontaminated water supplies; to provide decent livelihoods for those still struggling to survive in rural sub-Saharan Africa, in parts of South East Asia, in the favelas of Latin America. *Prosperity without Growth* acknowledges at the outset these overwhelming development needs.

The question is, can we meet those needs by following the same path that has also created such a disturbing situation, where we are already consuming the Earth's resources faster than Nature can replenish them? Unfettered consumerism comes at a high price; one that the Earth is finding increasingly difficult to pay. The evidence is very clear: modern progress depends inherently on the exploitation of the extraordinary bounty of Nature; on the wealth of her natural resources, the stability of her climate, the resilience of her ecosystems. But Her bounty is necessarily limited and we have failed to respect those limits. We have taken Nature too much for granted, seemingly leaving her out of the equation altogether as we pursue headlong our desire for convenience in everything.

Professor Jackson seeks to examine whether today's dominant, conventional economic model can help the situation or whether it hinders our chances of establishing a more balanced approach which sustains the Earth's precious life-support systems in the long term. In an effort to tackle the whole issue of full (environmental) cost analysis, I established a project called Accounting for Sustainability which encourages businesses to include in their accounting everything that counts by measuring everything that matters – that is, Nature's essential 'capital contribution'.

Prosperity without Growth is both a radical and a challenging book, but its vision for a shared and lasting prosperity conveys a message full of hope. It is a vision that deserves to be considered seriously. The health of our ecosystems and, thereby, the future prosperity of our children may well depend upon it.

PROLOGUE TO THE SECOND EDITION

Economists are tellers of stories and makers of poems.

D. McCloskey[1]

On the evening of Friday 27 March 2009, a cold wind was blowing and a light drizzle was falling as I walked home from work. It had been a long week and when my phone rang I was tired enough to contemplate not taking the call. But I was also aware that a couple of journalists were still trying to reach me to talk about my report for the UK Sustainable Development Commission (SDC). It was due for release the following Monday.[2]

Prosperity without Growth? (I'll come to the question mark in a moment) emerged from a long-running inquiry I led for the SDC into the relationship between prosperity and sustainability. At the heart of the inquiry was a very simple question. What can prosperity possibly mean in a world of environmental and social limits?

The conventional view is that economic expansion will lead to rising prosperity. Higher incomes mean a better quality of life. This equation seems both familiar and obvious. But it's also clear that, on a finite planet, there must be some limits to material expansion. A rising population with insatiable material aspirations sits uneasily with the finite nature of our earthly home.

In the face of those limits, we're left with just two possibilities. Either we must progressively squeeze the material content out of economic expansion, so that we can continue to grow our economies without trashing the planet, or we must learn to find prosperity without relying on economic growth to deliver it for us.[3]

Neither avenue is easy to deliver. Nor is the choice between them straightforward. Counterfactuality obscures simple logic. Physics, economics, politics, sociology and psychology all lay claim to aspects of the argument. Making sense requires a willingness to question received wisdom and a determined effort to avoid familiar axioms. It also relies on a degree of openness to the possibility of political and social change.

As I walked home that evening I was aware that what had emerged was a complex story. It was also a contentious one. More than 60 years of postwar global policy had insisted that economic size matters; that more is always better. To intimate that quality is sometimes to be preferred over quantity is not exactly revolutionary. But to convey this message was going to be tough at the best of times. And these were surely not the best of times.

The week of our launch coincided with the second ever G20 summit, to be hosted in London by the UK government. The informal aim of the summit was to reinvigorate the economy in the wake of the worst financial crisis in modern history. A press release politely questioning growth might not be the best way for a government commission to win friends in high places.

This sensitivity wasn't lost on us. From the moment we announced that we were to undertake an inquiry into the relationship between growth and sustainability, scepticism rained down on the Commission. I remember a public meeting where a Treasury official, on hearing the news, stood up and accused us of wanting to 'go back and live in caves'.

Faced with this sensitivity, choosing a title had already proven tricky. My fellow Commissioners all highly experienced, independent-minded people, not at all shy about making their opinions heard when contentious issues were on the table. Support for the arguments in the report had revealed a solidarity that was almost unprecedented by the standards of our usual deliberations. But varying degrees of uneasiness attended the title itself.

Without the question mark (as I originally proposed), *Prosperity without Growth* announced a manifesto for change. But in a climate of fear it verged on being inflammatory. Various alternatives were proposed. Could we qualify the word 'growth'? Would 'beyond' be safer than 'without'? Could we live with a different title altogether – something altogether less provocative? None of these suggestions was entirely satisfactory.

The question mark offered a compromise. It had the virtue of softening the tone without entirely dismissing the force of the inquiry. It was, in this form, an invitation to an important debate, perhaps the most vital debate of our time, without actually prejudging the outcome: is it possible to flourish as a society without relentlessly expanding the economy? In the end, our departmental sponsors agreed to accept the compromise so long as we first tested it out on one of the Prime Minister's advisors.

It might seem strange that an arms–length Commission should go to such lengths to appease the sensitivity of its paymasters. But that is realpolitik. If you want complete independence, go publish commercially. If you want influence, you must occasionally heed your sponsors. Clearly, that doesn't necessarily mean simply saying what ministers want to hear. But you should probably avoid waving too much red rag in front of political bulls, if you value your role as advisors.

Our position as a 'critical friend' to the UK government relied on a kind of fragile trust between advisor and advisee. At every stage in the writing of the report, we had presented our findings and discussed the implications with the relevant government departments. At this final stage of proceedings, we effectively gave the Prime Minister's office the power of veto over the title itself.

The answer that came back was reassuring. I don't think it matters what you call it, the advisor told us. Good, we thought. Confident that we had followed due process, we set about drafting our press releases, devising our PR strategy, briefing journalists; conveying the subtleties of the debate so far as we could without taxing the impatience of the media. This too is part of the machinery of policy advice.

By the time the phone rang on that wet March evening, all of this was more or less behind me. And, aside from fielding the odd press inquiry, my weekend stretched quietly ahead, a haven of relative calm before an early start the following Monday for an interview on the BBC's *Today* programme. I decided to take the call.

'Number 10 has gone ballistic,' barked a voice on the other end of the line. The tone was hostile. It was clearly not the journalist I had been expecting, nor a message that I had anticipated. But I recognised the caller immediately. It was the one person who, until that point, had been our closest ally in government, a key political sponsor of the SDC, and a keen supporter of the work that we had been doing. In the space of a few seconds, it was clear all that had changed.

The deceptively simple answer of the Number 10 advisor had been just that: deceptive. As it turned out, the advisor in question was on a plane to China at the moment *Prosperity without Growth?* (with its conciliatory question mark) landed unheralded on the Prime Minister's desk. It was a matter of days before the G20 leaders convened in London to 'kick-start growth again'. 'What on earth had we been thinking?' roared our former ally.

It was a good question, in retrospect. Had we been naïve to suppose such fundamental concerns could be raised with impunity? Possibly. Had we overlooked the ambiguity inherent in the advice we received from Number 10? Evidently. Had we been precipitous in settling on such a sensitive release date? Perhaps. There was clearly an element of bravado involved in launching a report with such a title slap bang into the week of the G20 meeting. But what is the point in having a strong political message and being too timid to convey it to the people to whom it should matter?

Were we wrong to take on the g-word at all, in the context of the financial chaos with which the G20 leaders were grappling? Absolutely not. The moment it stops being permissible to question the fundamental assumptions of an economic system that is patently dysfunctional is the moment political freedom ends and cultural repression begins. It is also the point at which the possibilities for change are significantly, perhaps decisively, curtailed.

Clearly this was not the view of Number 10. And there was little I could do at that late hour to placate our rattled former ally. The embargo was for Monday morning. But the report was already out there. Even if we had wanted it, there was no going back now. I politely excused myself and continued on home. Later I did talk to a journalist. It was a long, surprisingly enthusiastic conversation with a major broadsheet promising a front-page story about the report.

Monday morning, 30 March, I was up at five thirty and shortly afterward on my way to BBC studios at the University of Surrey for the *Today* programme interview. With the word 'ballistic' still echoing in my mind, I remember wondering vaguely what kind of wrath was about to be unleashed.

Once again my reflections were interrupted by a phone call. No angry voices this time, just a simple message. The interview was cancelled. The producer apologised. An important story had come up involving the Prime Minister's own constituency of Kirkcaldy and Cowdenbeath in Scotland. The programme would have to cover this story instead.

Perplexed but not unduly concerned, I made my way to my office on campus, where I searched the morning news. Over the weekend, the government had announced that the Dunfermline Building Society was to be broken up and sold. Despite resistance from the Dunfermline board, who felt they were being sacrificed for expediency, a deal had been rushed through under the provisions of a new Banking Act, passed explicitly to help respond to the financial crisis.

The Bank of England would take on the failing assets and what remained was to be bought by another bank. Job losses were probably inevitable. Some of them (it turned out three and a half years later) would indeed be in Cowdenbeath, the Prime Minister's constituency. This was the story that had stolen our thunder.[4]

As the week wore on, what started out as a frustrating setback became first puzzling and then frankly bizarre. There was no cover story in the enthusiastic major broadsheet. No further pick-up from the *Today* programme. Nothing from any other radio or TV station. No coverage anywhere, in fact. One oblique reference in an article about the green stimulus was the sum total of the impact made by *Prosperity without Growth?* on the national media in early April 2009.

★★★★★

Seven years later, in the warm sunshine of a late May afternoon, I sit down to reflect on the extraordinary journey from there to here. Looking back is always salutary. I'm reminded of the eponymous narrator's opening line in the film *The Go Between*. 'The past is another country,' he says. 'They do things differently there.'

That journey might never have started, I suppose, were it not for the internet. Between an unwilling government and an unwitting media, *Prosperity without Growth?* seemed destined simply to disappear into the void. But at some point following the eerie silence of the 'launch', people began to download the report from the SDC website.

Before long, it had been downloaded more often than any other report in the Commission's history. Invitations to discuss and present the work began to trickle in. Not from our government sponsors, sadly. Or even, at first, from predictable sympathisers. The interest came instead from a curious mixture of somewhat unusual suspects.

Poverty campaigners, asset managers, faith groups, consumer organisations, theatre managers, engineers, archbishops, diplomats, museums, literary societies and the occasional member of royalty. The trickle very soon became a flood – one which, to this day, has not really abated.

Six months after its abortive launch, a revised version of the SDC report was published by Earthscan, a small independent publisher with a long-standing commitment to ecological literature. Jonathan Sinclair Wilson, Earthscan's managing director, had read the SDC report shortly after it came out and saw its potential as a book much sooner than I did.

His confidence was rewarded. Within a few weeks of publication, the first print run had sold out and the first of what would soon become 17 foreign-language translations were being negotiated. By early 2010, *Prosperity without Growth* was no longer a contentious government report languishing under its sponsor's disapproval, but an unexpectedly popular book with a surprisingly receptive audience.

★★★★★

One of the biggest surprises was the international appeal of the book. It may well have been more popular abroad than it was at home. In France and Belgium it fed into the lively debate that surrounded the publication of the Sarkozy Commission's work on measuring social progress. In Germany, it contributed to the formation of an official *Study Commission on Growth, Well-being and Quality of Life.* In 2011, the German government reprinted the book to make it more widely accessible for educational purposes.[5]

Nor was this interest confined to the advanced economies. Amongst the 17 foreign-language translations were Chinese, Korean, Lithuanian and Brazilian Portuguese editions.

A young Indonesian economist asked me if I'd talk with a group of government economists involved in developing a 'one-hundred-year' plan for Papua Province. I had my doubts about questioning economic growth in a country with an average per capita income of less than $3,500 and I said so.

But the idea of contributing to the discussion of a hundred-year plan was somehow too enticing. So I spent half a day in a Skype conversation with the group. Their premises were simple. We have rich natural resources, an enormous development challenge and a desire to create our own vision of prosperity rather than borrow the broken dream of the West. How can we make that work?

At a meeting at the UN in New York in November 2013, I gave a 20-minute keynote talk on the 'growth dilemma' to an international audience. The debate went on for four hours. Following my 'provocation', the moderator turned to a minister from Ecuador. 'Is the growth debate just a luxury of countries that have already grown?' he wanted to know. The response was an emphatic no. 'If growth means to reach a state in society in which selfishness and consumption are the basis, then we don't want to grow,' answered my fellow panellist. 'The model we are proposing is not based on consumption but on solidarity, on sustainable development, on a change in the growth paradigm', she told us.[6]

Ecuador's concept of *buen vivir* has such striking resonances with the concept of prosperity in the original report that I was immediately drawn to it. Perhaps the reverse was also true. In a slightly surreal postmodern moment, four hours later, the entire contingent of

Ecuadorian parliamentarians came up to me and asked if they could have a photograph taken with me to post on Instagram.[7]

The UK government was profoundly unhappy with its troublesome advisors. The Commission itself became an early casualty of the drive for austerity. But what had emerged in place of official approval was an almost insatiable appetite from ordinary people across the world in almost very walk of life to scrutinise the most pernicious myth on which modern society rests: that it's possible for human activity on planet Earth to go on expanding indefinitely. Many of them clearly found this easy fiction wanting.

In the end, I gave up trying to predict or explain the intensity of these debates or the unexpected nature of the responses to the book. I began to understand that this was quite simply a conversation whose time had come. Or perhaps to be more accurate, whose time had come round again.

At a meeting in Lake Balaton in Hungary, a bearded American poked a camera at my face and I heard the shutter click. That's one for the bulletin board, he said. He introduced himself as Dennis Meadows, co-author of the Club of Rome's influential *Limits to Growth* report, published almost four decades earlier. The next day he gave me a signed first edition of the book, declaring that it was the last spare copy he had.

Veterans of those earlier debates were exuberant that a government commission had finally addressed the question they'd spent their whole lives asking. But this was by no means a debate from the past. In lecture halls across Europe, young and old alike turned out in their hundreds, keen to engage with an official report that had dared to speak the unspeakable. I felt humbled; and often slightly overwhelmed.

Particularly moving were the economics students, many of whom would sit patiently on the steps of the auditorium, or sometimes even behind me on the stage, waiting for their chance to participate in the conversation. Afterwards they would confront me in the corridors.

'Where can we get this kind of economics?', they would ask. 'We've been studying for almost three years, and these issues have never even been raised in our courses.' I would point them to the classics: Herman Daly's *Steady State Economics*, Fred Hirsch's *Social*

Limits to Growth, the original *Limits to Growth* report. Texts to which they should surely already have been introduced by their lecturers.

Some of those students took the arguments directly to their teachers. There was both a logic and an irony to this. After all, if there's one thing economics professors ought to understand it's the law of supply and demand; and if these kids were starting to demand a different economics, sooner or later their professors would have to start supplying it.

Most of these discussions were rational, intelligent and good-natured. There was also a mildly lunatic fringe of course. There always is when speech is truly free. And very occasionally there was also rage. The voices of the disenfranchised and the dispossessed rarely speak without a tinge of anger.

To be honest, some of this anger was frightening. There was a sense of menace on the Copenhagen streets one morning. It was the day of a huge public demonstration for 'climate justice'. Angry young activists in black faced off against the assembled ranks of the police, apparently just willing the fragile morning to dissolve into mindless violence.

Five years later, in Chile, where I had been invited to speak at a conference on sustainability in business, I was mugged at knifepoint in a public park by disaffected youths who evidently saw little in Chile's burgeoning economy to improve the quality of their own lives and were willing to resort to violence instead.

In Greece, during the height of 'austerity', I spoke at a public debate that was packed full of angry men and women, railing against 'odious debt' and campaigning for 'forgiveness or default': some respite that would allow Greece to rise from her knees again.[8]

This for me is why the discussion around growth matters so much. Expelling critical discussions from the table and hammering down the nails of the status quo won't solve the ecological, social and financial challenges we face. It is much more likely to generate dissent, anger and eventually violence.

By the time I visited Greece, austerity had become the ugly watchword for a massive tightening of fiscal policy across Europe, in the aftermath of the financial crisis. Businesses were closed; shops were boarded up; litter, torn up cardboard boxes, the discarded bedding of the homeless and angry political slogans disfigured the streets of Europe's capital cities.

On the penultimate day of my Athens trip, I made my way down from the hotel to the port of Piraeus and took a ferry to Hydra, an island I had briefly visited as a student, many years previously. As we came into the sweeping crescent of the island's natural harbour, it seemed momentarily as though nothing had really changed.

The same white houses nestled into the same dry hillside, the same brightly coloured boats danced on the sparkling water. Tourists and locals mingled on the quayside as the ferry discharged its passengers. A slight, elderly woman came forward carrying a cardboard sign offering rooms for the night. It all seemed rather familiar.

On a closer inspection there clearly were some differences. There were more (and bigger) yachts in the marina than I remembered; and a careful attention to the clientèle in the harbourfront cafés revealed the near ubiquity of the mobile phone. But the contrast between the angry chaos of Athens and the surreal beauty of life on the island remained.

From a vantage point high above the harbour I gazed across the terracotta roofs towards the azure brilliance of the Aegean Sea and revelled in the warmth of the November sun on my back. It felt, momentarily, like prosperity.

But the sensation was as ephemeral as the winter warmth. The quest for real utopias is strewn with innumerable dead ends and this was clearly one of them. As an icon of Hellenic beauty, Hydra still holds a certain poetic fascination. But as a model for prosperity it is deeply flawed.

The barren hills that rise above Hydra port were once lush with vegetation from the natural springs that gave the island its name. The wealth that flowed from its position as a maritime stronghold was also drying up.

Even my initial impression of continuity was wrong. The population of Hydra had declined by almost a third since I had last been there and the island's continued existence as anything more than a playground for the rich depended heavily on the run-down ferry which an hour or so later would carry me back to Athens across the cold, moonlit sea.[9]

★★★★★

The past is another country. They do things differently there. The confidence with which world leaders assumed it would be possible to 'kick-start' growth again. The belief that business as usual was waiting to return, just round the corner. Even the righteous anger that confronted me on the telephone on that rainy March night has a quaint, other-worldly quality to it now.

It's become much clearer in the interim how far out of balance our economies were. How burdened with debt. How reliant on bankrupt dreams. How at odds with the fragile ecology of the planet. How mired in inequality. And how devastating the political and social consequences of this inequality could be. In my own country, the Brexit vote was a howl of anguish from those who had been left behind.

It's not as though some efforts weren't made to fix things. At first, through financial stimulus and bailouts. And then through austerity and monetary policy. But rewarding the architects of chaos while withdrawing social investment from the poorest and most vulnerable had only exacerbated the problems. Where we looked for renewed prosperity, we found increased fragility, deepening debt and rising inequality.

Not all those efforts were dedicated to maintaining the status quo. Some took the world in a more positive direction. Global investment in renewable energy has increased by almost 60 per cent since the crisis and more than tripled in the last decade. A whole new set of sustainable development goals was negotiated to measure progress towards a better world. And against all odds, the Paris summit in December 2015 reinforced a political determination to tackle climate change.[10]

Some of this gives grounds for hope. Some of it provokes even deeper fears. On the one hand, our conversations about progress have become more open and more thoughtful than we might even have imagined possible seven years ago. On the other hand, the tensions across society have become more palpable. Sometimes, it seems, a new barbarism is lurking just around the corner, already gnawing at the core of society and undermining our humanity.

What can *Prosperity without Growth* say in this changed and more uncertain world? Are its challenges at all pertinent to the politics of today? Are any of its prescriptions still relevant? Or was the government report that caused its sponsors so much anxiety just a quirk of circumstance, a passing feature from another, now more distant land?

These were amongst the questions I asked myself, as I sat down to contemplate this revision. My initial assumption was that the book could more or less stand as it was. I anticipated just a light-touch revision, updating some graphs, expanding some references, leaving most of the rest pretty much intact. After all, I had rehearsed the arguments countless times. I'm still rehearsing them. I knew them inside out.

But I was wrong. As I read over the old text, I realised how much had changed. The sense that I had been presenting the same arguments over the intervening years wasn't entirely accurate. I had adapted them as I went along. The case itself had evolved and changed. I had changed. The world had changed. There was no simple light-touch revision that would do justice to this new landscape. And so I found myself rewriting and rewriting again.

One of the most obvious changes has been the geographical frame. I had written the original report for the UK government. I had never expected its wide international audience. This time I have written for that audience. The implications are still mainly related to the advanced economies of the west. But the analyses and the anecdotes are now more international.

I rewrote the opening chapter because I felt that it needed deeper arguments on the question of limits. I had had too many conversations with people who felt I had skipped over the importance of limits or with those who rejected the concept of limits entirely. I wanted to be clearer about where we should take limits seriously, and where our opportunities are to escape them.

I found I had to rewrite Chapter 2, on the financial crisis, almost completely. So much more water has passed under the bridge. Strangely, my original conclusion – that the ultimate cause of the crisis lay in the pursuit of growth itself – has stood the test of time.

But the evidence for it is, if anything, even stronger than it was seven years ago. And the implications are more powerful than ever.

Some things haven't changed. It gradually dawned on me that almost every conversation I'd had in the intervening years was an exploration of one abiding feature of the book: what I had called the 'dilemma of growth'. Even if it is true that economic growth is unsustainable, isn't it self-evidently true that its opposite or its absence is far from desirable, too?

Wasn't this the story of the launch itself? The story of the crisis? The visceral fear of the politicians? The menace on the streets in Copenhagen? My experience in Chile? The anger in Greece? An anger that was to intensify even since my own short visit. Neither I nor Greece could have foreseen that worse was to follow.

The Hydra marina would itself very soon be part of the €50 billion fire-sale agreed with the troika as a condition of the third bailout, along with Greece's postal service and its network of thermal springs. If this was the punishment inflicted on a nation for failing to grow, how could anyone doubt that growth was an urgent and real necessity? [11]

In reality, of course, a much more complex set of circumstances was responsible for Greece's unhappy fate, not the least of which is a web of money and debt that has systematically rewarded a minority and punished the majority. But here, writ large, was the dilemma for those ensnared in that web. The spoils are to the creditor and the devil takes the hindmost.

Nothing I saw along the way, or during any of the myriad debates in which I participated, has relegated the power of this dilemma – nor robbed it of its importance to our common future. If anything, the different circumstances under which I have seen it played out have only served to intensify its importance in my mind. It remains the foundation for the exploration in this second edition.

On the other hand, I have completely overhauled the work on decoupling in Chapter 5. Scientific consensus itself has moved on. It took me close to a month to update the data and redo the calculations. What emerged was fascinating. The logic was similar, but the challenge was deeper. In contrast to those who thought I had overemphasised the degree of decoupling needed, the science of the intervening years suggested I had underemphasised it. Green growth is not going to be easier than I had previously suggested – it's going to be harder than anyone had ever thought.

This new edition isn't just about recalibrating scale and re-establishing the challenge. It has also been about reframing the logic, and clarifying the proposals for change. This latter task was always the aim of the book: not just to diagnose problems or bemoan catastrophe, but to set out clearly the dimensions for a different economics built around a more coherent vision of prosperity. In the intervening years, inevitably, some of that original intention has been forgotten.

A book often becomes reduced to its title. Those two simple words 'without' and 'growth' – so innocuous on their own, so devastating put together – attracted a lot of attention to the book. They also occasionally distracted attention from its prognoses.

Clarifying and expanding these proposals has been the most significant revision in this second edition. In doing so, I've been fortunate to draw extensively on new research. Some of this has come from my own rich collaborations, in particular with Peter Victor, and more recently through the new Centre for the Understanding of Sustainable Prosperity. Some of it has come from new insights into finance, into macroeconomics and into the nature of money itself.[12]

I've been able to employ these new understandings to elaborate more clearly what I have begun to call (Chapter 8) the economy of tomorrow: clearer and more constructive roles for enterprise, for investment, for work, for the money supply and for the public sector. And I've made a better fist than I was able to before (Chapter 9) of establishing the outlines of a new macroeconomic synthesis; one capable of taking us beyond our structural reliance on ever-expanding consumption and delivering a more sustainable and more equitable prosperity.

The revisions took me longer – much longer – than I had anticipated, but the book is a better book because of them. Its fundamental insight remains the same: living well on a finite planet cannot simply be about consuming more and more stuff. Nor can it be about accumulating more and more debt.

Prosperity, in any meaningful sense of the term, is about the quality of our lives and relationships, about the resilience of our communities and about our sense of individual and collective meaning. What this revision shows, even more clearly than before, is that the economics for such a vision is a precise, definable and meaningful task.

Prosperity itself – as the Latin roots of the English word reveal – is about hope. Hope for the future, hope for our children, hope for ourselves. An economics of hope remains a task worth engaging in.

Tim Jackson
June 2016

1

THE LIMITS TO GROWTH

Anyone who believes that exponential growth can go on forever in a finite world is either a madman or an economist.

Kenneth Boulding, 1973[1]

Prosperity matters. To prosper is to do well and to be well. It means that things are going well for us and for those we care about. 'How's life?' we ask our friends and acquaintances. 'How's things?' Casual exchanges convey more than frivolous greeting. They reveal a mutual fascination for each other's wellbeing. Wanting things to go well is a common human concern.

What these 'things' are that should go well often isn't spelled out. 'Good. How are you?' comes the instinctive reply. We rehearse a familiar script. If pushed we'll talk about our health, our family, our work. Success is often paraded. Disappointments are sometimes revealed. Occasionally, to trusted friends, we might be tempted to reveal our dreams and aspirations for the future.

It's certainly understood that this sense of things going well includes some notion of continuity. We aren't inclined to think that life is going swimmingly, if we confidently expect things to fall apart tomorrow. 'Yes, I'm fine, thanks. I'm filing for bankruptcy in the morning.' It wouldn't make sense. The future matters to us. We have a natural tendency to care what will happen there.

There is a sense, too, in which individual prosperity is curtailed in the presence of social calamity. That things are going well for me personally is of little consolation if my family, my friends and my community are all in dire straits. My prosperity and the prosperity of those around me are intertwined. Sometimes inextricably.

Writ large, this shared concern translates itself into a vision of human progress. Prosperity speaks of the elimination of hunger and homelessness, an end to poverty and injustice, hopes for a secure and peaceful world. And this vision is important not just for altruistic reasons but often, too, as reassurance that our own lives are meaningful.

The possibility of social progress brings with it a comforting sense that things are getting better – if not always for us, then at least for those who come after us. A better society for our children. A fairer world. A place where those less fortunate will one day thrive. If I cannot believe this prospect is possible, then what can I believe? What sense can I make of my own life?[2]

Prosperity in this sense is a shared vision. Echoes of it inhabit our daily rituals. Deliberations about it inform the political and social world. Hope for it lies at the heart of our lives.

So far so good. But how is prosperity to be attained? Without some realistic way of translating hope into reality, it remains an illusion. The existence of a credible and robust mechanism for achieving progress matters. And this is more than just a question of the machinery of doing well. The legitimacy of the means to live well is part of the glue that keeps society together. Collective meaning is extinguished when hope is lost. Morality itself is threatened. Getting the mechanism right is vital.

One of the key messages of this book is that we're failing in that task. Our technologies, our economy and our social aspirations are all badly aligned with any meaningful expression of prosperity.

The vision of social progress that drives us – based on the continual expansion of material wants – is fundamentally untenable. And this failing is not a simple falling short from utopian ideals. It is much more basic. In pursuit of the good life today we are systematically eroding the basis for wellbeing tomorrow. In pursuit of our own wellbeing, we are undermining the possibilities for others. We stand in real danger of losing any prospect of a shared and lasting prosperity.

This book is not, however, a rant against the failings of modernity. Nor is it a lament on the untenable nature of the human condition. There are undoubtedly some framing conditions that circumvent our prospects for a lasting prosperity. The existence of ecological limits and resource constraints may be one of these. Aspects of human nature may turn out to be another. Taking heed of these conditions is central to the spirit of the investigation in these pages.

The overriding aim of the book is to seek viable responses to the biggest dilemma of our times: reconciling our aspirations for the good life with the limitations and constraints of a finite planet. The analysis in the following pages is focused on finding a credible vision of what it means for human society to flourish in this context. And establishing the dimensions of a credible economics to deliver this aim.

Prosperity as growth

At the heart of the book lies a very simple question. What can prosperity possibly look like in a finite world, with limited resources and a population expected to exceed ten billion people within a few decades?[3] Do we have a decent vision of prosperity for such a world? Is this vision credible in the face of the available evidence about ecological limits? How do we go about turning vision into reality?

The prevailing response to these questions is to cast prosperity in economic terms and to call for continually rising incomes as the means to deliver it. Higher incomes mean increased choices, richer lives, an improved quality of life for those who benefit from them. That at least is the conventional wisdom.

This formula is cashed out (almost literally) as an increase in what economists call the gross domestic product (GDP) per capita, that is, the average national income per person. The GDP is broadly speaking a measure of the overall 'busyness' of the economy; or, in more precise terms, of the monetary value of the goods and services that are being produced and consumed within a given nation or region. Economic growth takes place when the GDP is rising – usually at a given 'rate of growth' – across the economy.[4]

It's worth pointing out that a rising GDP will lead to rising income (per capita GDP) only if the economy grows faster than the population does. If the population expands but GDP remains constant, then income levels will fall. Conversely, if the GDP rises but the population stabilises (or declines) then incomes will rise even faster. In general, the GDP must rise at least as fast as population just to conserve the average level of people's income.

As we shall see, there are good grounds to question whether such a crude measure as the GDP per capita is really sufficient to the task of reflecting real prosperity. But for now it's a fair reflection of common understanding. In broad terms, increasing prosperity is regarded as virtually synonymous with rising incomes, which are delivered, in the conventional vision, through continued economic growth.

This is of course one of the reasons why economic growth has been the single most important policy goal across the world for most of the last century. And this prescription clearly still has an appealing logic for the world's poorest nations. A meaningful approach to prosperity must certainly address the plight of more than 3 billion people across the world still living on less than $5 a day.[5]

But does the same logic really hold for the richer nations, where subsistence needs are largely met and the cornucopia of consumer goods adds little to material comfort and may even impede social wellbeing? How is it that with so much stuff already we still hunger for more? Would it not be better to halt the relentless pursuit of growth in the advanced economies and concentrate instead on sharing out the available resources more equitably?

In a world of finite resources, constrained by environmental limits, still characterised by 'islands of prosperity' within 'oceans of poverty',[6] are ever-increasing incomes for the already rich really a legitimate focus for our continued hopes and expectations? Or is there perhaps some other path towards a more sustainable, a more equitable form of prosperity?

We'll come back time and again to this question and explore it from a variety of different perspectives. But it's worth making quite clear, as Boulding's comment at the top of the chapter also suggests, that to most economists the very idea of prosperity without growth is a complete anathema. Growth in the GDP is so much taken for granted that reams and reams have been written about what it's based on, who's best at making it happen and what to do when it stops happening.

Far less is written about why we might want it in the first place. But the relentless quest for more that lurks within the conventional view of prosperity is not without some claim to intellectual foundation.

In short, the argument goes something like this. The GDP counts the economic value of goods and services exchanged on the market. If we're spending more and more money on more and more commodities it's because we value them. We wouldn't value them if they weren't at the same time improving our lives. Hence a continually rising per capita GDP must be improving our lives and increasing our prosperity.

This conclusion is perverse precisely because prosperity isn't obviously synonymous with income or wealth. Rising prosperity isn't obviously the same thing as economic growth. More isn't always better. But it does at least provide some explanation for the tenacity with which we cling to the 'little big number': GDP.[7]

Perhaps strangely, prosperity has only recently been cast primarily in terms of money. Its original meaning was just about things going well: in accordance with (pro- in the Latin) our hopes and expectations (speres). Prosperity was simply the opposite of adversity or affliction.[8] The elision of rising prosperity with economic growth is a relatively modern construction. And it is a construction that has come under considerable criticism.

Amongst the charges against growth is that it has delivered its benefits, at best, unequally. The poorest half of the world's population earn less than 7 per cent of the total income. The top 1 per cent by contrast earn about 20 per cent of global income and own almost half of global wealth. Huge disparities – real differences in prosperity by anyone's standards – characterise the gap between rich and poor. Such disparities are dreadful from even the most basic humanitarian point of view. They also generate rising social tensions: real hardships in the most disadvantaged communities which have a spill-over effect on society as a whole.[9]

Extraordinarily, these disparities appear to be worsening. According to the UN Development Programme, incomes today are more unequal than at any time since the middle of the last century. In the space of less than half a century the richest 1 per cent of the population have more than doubled their income share. Income inequality within developing countries increased by 11 per cent in the last two decades. Even within the advanced economies, inequality is 9 per cent higher than it was 20 years ago.[10]

While the rich got richer, middle-class incomes in Western countries were stagnant in real terms long before the financial crisis. Indeed some have argued that rising inequality was one of the causes of the crisis. Far from raising the living standard for those who most needed it, growth let much of the world's population down over the last 50 years. In the last few years in particular, wealth trickled up to the lucky few.[11]

Fairness (or the lack of it) is only one of the reasons to question the conventional formula for achieving prosperity. Another is the recognition that, beyond a certain point at least, the continued pursuit of economic growth doesn't appear to advance and may even impede human happiness. Paradoxical though it may seem, this contention draws support from a long history of philosophical, religious, literary and artistic ideas. And it has experienced a surprising political revival in the last decade.

Even before the financial crisis, when the economy still appeared to be carrying us all towards a brighter and better future, there was disturbing evidence of a growing 'social recession' in advanced economies. A new politics of wellbeing or happiness began to challenge conventional views of social progress, within both richer and poorer economies. In Ecuador, it was formalised in the concept of *buen vivir*, which was embedded in its national constitution. *Buen vivir* has its roots in the indigenous concept of *sumak kawsay*, which translates broadly as 'good life' or 'living well'. It denotes 'a system of knowledge and living based on the communion of humans and nature'.[12]

Ecuador's 2008 constitution was also the first formally to enshrine the 'rights of nature' into law. And this points us towards the third, and perhaps the most important challenge to the conventional equation of continual economic growth: the finite nature of the planet on which we live. Any credible vision of prosperity must hold a defensible position on the question of limits. This is particularly true of a vision based on growth. How – and for how long – is continued growth possible without coming up against ecological and resource constraints?[13]

Simple logic suggests that industrial activity must at some point be bounded. Global economic output is now almost ten times bigger than it was in 1950. If it continues to expand at the same average rate – a prospect that economists and politicians almost universally hope for – the world economy in 2100 would be more than 20 times bigger than it is today: a staggering 200-fold increase in economic scale in the space of just a few generations.[14]

Common intuition suggests that this kind of expansion cannot continue indefinitely. For the most part, as Boulding's satirical comment to the US Congress in 1973 (cited at the top of this chapter) suggests, economists reject this intuition. Some reject entirely any notion of limits. Their rejection is not entirely mad. But as we shall see it is fundamentally flawed.

Confronting limits

Concern for limits is as old as the hills. But like prosperity itself, meanings have changed over time. Ancient wisdom often saw limits not as the obstacle but as the foundation for prosperity. Limitations are equated directly with success, for instance, in the Chinese *Book of Changes* (the *I Ching*), whose origins go back almost 1,000 years BC. By contrast, a life lived without respect for limits was seen as foolhardy and destructive.

'Limitations are troublesome, but they are effective,' wrote Richard Wilhelm in his 1923 translation of the *I Ching*. 'If we live economically in normal times, we are prepared for times of want.' Most often, the analogy used to convey the role of limits in human affairs was taken from nature itself. 'In nature there are fixed limits for summer and winter, day and night, and these limits give the year its meaning,' argued Wilhelm.[15]

Contemporary perspectives are far more likely to view limits as inconvenient or even illusory. The French archaeologist (and Jesuit priest) Pierre Teilhard de Chardin once remarked that our duty as human beings is 'to proceed as if limits to our ability did not exist'. 'We are collaborators in creation,' he said. This view of essentially limitless creativity has been reinforced further by the extraordinary advances in technology since de Chardin was writing. It has begun to seem that almost anything is possible, any resource constraint surmountable, any utopian vision for humanity achievable.[16]

At a seminar I gave in a UK government department shortly after the first edition of this book was published, a government economist insisted that the entire concept of limits was 'economically illiterate'. Former US President Ronald Reagan, appealing to the same *zeitgeist*, once proclaimed that there are 'no great limits to growth because there are no limits on the human capacity for intelligence, imagination and wonder'.[17]

It's worth examining this assertion a bit more closely, precisely because it conveys a partial truth. There are some unlimited aspects to human existence. Ingenuity, creativity, wonder may well be amongst these; and it certainly makes sense to recognise abundance wherever we may find it.

But there's also a fallacy in the claim. The US author Wendell Berry once suggested that our 'human and earthly limits, properly understood, are not confinements, but rather inducements... to fullness of relationship and meaning.' But that doesn't mean, he insisted, that we can pass simply from this abundance of meaning to the assumption that we can overcome all material limits, without risking hubris.[18]

An appropriate relationship between the limited and the limitless turns out to be another central question for the inquiry in this book and we shall explore it in some depth in Chapters 5 and 6.

The struggle for existence

Reagan's remarks were a direct response to the most influential work on limits to emerge from the twentieth century, the Club of Rome's *Limits to Growth*, published in 1972. That report stood in a long legacy of concern for material limits, dating back at least to the late eighteenth century, when Thomas Robert Malthus published his enormously influential *Essay on the Principle of Population*.[19]

At the time it was written, Malthus had just taken up a living as a curate and was staying on his father's estate in Albury, not a million miles from where I now sit writing. One evening in 1797, father and son were sitting together discussing the work of the French philosopher Jean-Jacques Rousseau, who had been a friend of Malthus senior. At the heart of their discussion lay Rousseau's views on social progress and the perfectibility of human society.

Rousseau believed that 'man is naturally good, and only by institutions is he made bad' – a position that stood in stark contrast to the (Judeo-Christian) doctrine of original sin, from which salvation could only be sought through the church. The origin of evil and suffering was to be found, said Rousseau, not in human nature itself but in the corrupting influences of a civilization based on the notion of private property.[20]

Rousseau was later to have a profound influence on Karl Marx, whose arguments against capitalism were also built around a critique of private ownership. According to Marx, the solution lay in common or public ownership. According to Rousseau, the solution was to reject civilization and return to the natural state, 'for savage man, when he has dined, is at peace with all nature and the friend of all his fellow-creatures.' This view in its turn laid the foundation for the romantic movement of the nineteenth century to which many modern environmentalists still appeal.[21]

On that particular evening in 1797, Malthus senior was defending Rousseau's optimistic views about human society; Malthus junior was attacking them. In the aftermath of the argument, Malthus junior felt inspired to set down his case on paper, and the result was the first edition of the *Essay*.

His argument (massively condensed) was that growth in population always runs faster than growth in the resources available to feed people. So sooner or later the population expands beyond the 'means of subsistence' and some people – the poorest inevitably – will suffer a harsh 'struggle for existence' from which ultimately there is no escape.[22]

It's worth remembering that, for Malthus, the import of the population principle lay quite precisely in refuting the romantic view of the savage state as one free from suffering. On the contrary, Malthus argued, suffering is inherent in nature and arises directly from the pressure of population on the means of subsistence.

In destroying the romantics' conception of nature, however, the Parson Malthus was left with a problem in theology: Why should a caring god allow inescapable suffering? Why should an omnipotent god have created a world in which suffering was an integral element in the design?

Malthus dedicated two full chapters in the first *Essay* to these questions. The result was a complex 'theodicy' intended to 'vindicate the ways of God to man'. The divine purpose of creation, said Malthus, is the 'formation of mind'. The world is subject to natural laws that function in such a way as 'to awaken inert, chaotic matter into spirit, to sublimate the dust of the earth into soul, to elicit an ethereal spark from the clod of clay.' The struggle for existence is part of a divine plan to rouse human beings from their natural sloth and achieve a higher purpose.[23]

It's a fairly dismal theology. Much of it was expunged from later editions of the *Essay* and goes virtually forgotten within the environmental legacy of Malthus's work. But it was a critical element in the complex history of ideas from which our modern debates about limits are descended. As we shall see later, these more philosophical aspects remain unexpectedly relevant to modern-day debates about sustainability.

Malthus himself is often roundly condemned for all sorts of reasons. Some of these reasons – such as his jaundiced view of poverty and fierce opposition to the Poor Laws – are entirely valid. It was Malthus, after all, who gave economics the reputation for being a 'dismal science'. So it might as well be said upfront that Malthus was wrong. At least in so far as the particulars of his claims.[24]

That he failed to see (and even defended) the structural inequalities that kept people locked into poverty is one of Malthus' failings. But he was also wrong about the maths. The global population is now over seven times what it was in Malthus' day. And this is partly because the means of subsistence expanded considerably faster than population did – completely counter to Malthus' premise. The global economy is more than 80 times bigger than it was in 1800.[25]

Malthus missed completely the longer term implications of the massive technological changes already taking place around him. Nor could he have foreseen that development would (eventually) slow down the rate of population increase. Over the following two centuries, the means of subsistence more than kept pace with people's propensity to reproduce. Largely because of the easy availability of cheap fossil fuels.

And yet the massive increases in resource use associated with a vastly expanded global economy might still have given a sanguine observer of limits pause for thought. How could such increases possibly continue?

Betting on our future

That was exactly the question posed more than a century and a half later by the Italian industrialist Aurelio Peccei and the Scottish scientist Alexander King. In April 1968, the two men invited a small group of diplomats, industrialists, academics and civil society leaders to a quiet villa in Rome to discuss what they called 'the predicament of mankind': the problem of providing effective short-term governance in relation to potential long-term crises.

The Club of Rome was particularly concerned with the crises posed by exponential increases in consumption in a finite world. In June 1970, they invited Jay Forrester, a professor at the Massachusetts Institute of Technology (MIT) to a meeting in Bern, Switzerland to discuss whether his pioneering work in system dynamics could provide the framework for what they called 'structured responses' to this 'problematique'.[26]

On his way home from Bern, Forrester sketched the outline for what was to become the first system dynamics model of resource dependency in the global economy. In the hands of four bright young scientists at MIT – Donella and Dennis Meadows, Jørgen Randers and Bill Behrens – this sketch became the analytical foundation for the Club of Rome's most famous report. Published in 1972, *The Limits to Growth* ended up selling over 12 million copies worldwide in 30 different languages and provoking a fierce debate that continues unabated to this day.[27]

At the heart of *Limits to Growth* lies a remarkably robust analysis of the relationships between population, technology, industrial capital, agriculture and environmental quality. Though these inter-dependencies are complex, the dynamics are relatively easy to convey. Typically, argued the MIT team, the pattern of industrial development is running along predictable lines.

As more and more people achieve higher and higher levels of affluence, they consume more and more of the world's resources. Material growth cannot continue indefinitely because planet earth is physically limited. Eventually, the scale of activity passes the carrying capacity of the environment, resulting in a sudden contraction – either controlled or uncontrolled. First the resources supporting humanity – food, minerals, industrial output – begin to decline. This is followed by a collapse in population.

It's important to note that collapse doesn't happen in the model because physical resources supporting humanity disappear entirely. It happens because the quality of a resource declines as more and more of it is extracted: it takes more and more investment (both physical and financial) to extract usable high-quality resources from raw materials. Eventually, this process becomes unsustainable, and the amount extracted starts to decline.

Applied to energy, US ecologist Charles Hall has operationlised this dynamic through the 'Energy Return on Energy Invested' (EROI). EROI puts a value on the amount of energy obtained from a fuel like coal or oil, compared to the amount of energy that has to be spent to extract it in the first place. If this value falls far enough, extraction becomes both financially and energetically unviable.

The crucial point is that, as resource quality declines, more and more resources have to be diverted away from production just in order to maintain the flow of resources needed for production. This dynamic not only creates a pressure on output, it also escalates pollution, damaging the resource base itself and threatening basic aspects of society such as food, nutrition and health.

For the most part, the sophistication of this argument was missed. People accused the team of scare-mongering, of scientific illiteracy, of failing to understand the nature of progress. Optimists pointed to the huge technological advances that were being made all around them and the new resource discoveries just over the horizon. But none of this could legitimately counter the *Limits* hypothesis. Nowhere did the MIT team claim that resources were already running out. Nor did they suggest that collapse was imminent, though many people still believe they did.

A famous wager between the population ecologist Paul Ehrlich and the economist Julian Simon illustrates this misunderstanding well. As an economist, Simon knew that if materials were becoming scarcer then their prices should be rising. So he challenged Ehrlich (a long-time sympathiser of the *Limits* hypothesis) to identify five materials whose prices would rise between 1980 and 1990. Ehrlich selected five metals: copper, chromium, nickel, tin and tungsten. The price of all five metals declined over the period and Ehrlich lost the bet.[28]

It emerged later that the result could have been very different in the majority of ten-year periods over the last century. Ehrlich would also have come out richer if he had chosen certain other important commodities. He would certainly have won if the period had been

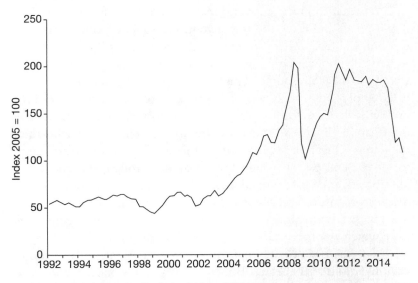

Figure 1.1 Global Commodity Price Index, 1992–2015
Source: Data from the US Federal Reserve (see note 29)

extended to the first decade of the twenty-first century. Between 2000 and 2014, average commodity prices more than tripled (Figure 1.1), leading sanguine observers to talk of a resource price 'super-cycle' and to call for an urgent 'resource revolution'.[29]

A defining feature of this new economic landscape appears to be a significantly greater price volatility. In the two decades before 2003, the oil price fluctuated between around $10 and $30 a barrel. After 2003, it rose dramatically to reach $147 a barrel in July 2008. Since the financial crisis, the fluctuations have continued. Oil prices collapsed through 2015 to reach a low of $30 a barrel at the beginning of 2016, for the first time since 2003. But they have subsequently begun to climb yet again.[30]

The reasons for this volatility are complex. The peak in 2008 coincided with a set of circumstances that included bottlenecks in supply, concerns over climate change and conflicts over land use. The collapse through 2015 was driven partly by new 'unconventional' supplies: mostly from 'fracking' and particularly in the US. But the fall was exacerbated by the response of producers to this sudden glut: an agreement to pump conventional oil even faster in order to drive down prices and force the unconventional suppliers out of business. Geopolitical tensions contributed to this complexity.[31]

Virtually none of this had anything to do with the underlying scarcity of oil as a resource. This fact is seized on by optimists wanting to downplay any suggestion of resource scarcity. But such a claim is problematic. Commodity prices are just too volatile to offer reliable information. Even the threat of scarcity was enough to send them rocketing. Oligarchic behaviour by oil cartels was powerful enough to force a collapse. Through both peak and trough, the underlying physical resource base moved inexorably towards exhaustion. But the market was just too self-obsessed to measure this.

In these circumstances it's difficult to get a handle on the timescale over which resource scarcity will begin to change our world. If the misconceptions about the *Limits* argument were right, collapse should have been obvious already. But that was never what the book said. The team suggested only that such changes would become obvious 'within the next century'.[32]

We are still some way from being able to dismiss (or indeed verify) that projection. Some have certainly argued that 'peak everything' is already visible. Respected observers – including the International Energy Agency (IEA) – had suggested, prior to the crisis, that a peak in oil production would arrive as early as 2020. These estimates clearly underestimated the potential rise in unconventional oil supplies. But the extent of this underestimation remains unclear.[33]

Optimists point to the massive reserves still lying in the tar sands and oil shales. Getting the oil out might be costly and environmentally damaging, but absolute scarcity is still a long way off, they claim. But recent detailed analyses suggest that unconventional oil will at best delay the production peak by a few decades. Some estimates even confirm a peak before 2025 and suggest that fracking will simply slow down the post-peak decline.[34]

In short, we are not in a position either to dismiss entirely or to confirm unequivocally the *Limits to Growth* scenarios. But several recent studies certainly give serious grounds for concern. One of these analysed the extent to which actual data on population, production, resource consumption and pollution reflect the predictions of the Meadows and their team. The findings are clear: the world is currently headed very much in the direction indicated by the *Limits* 'standardised run'. None of the technological change that we have seen since 1972 has caused progress to deviate from the business-as-usual scenario.[35]

Another recent study carried out a range of more specific resource scarcity analyses, using an updated and expanded version of the original MIT model. Analysing production and supply of over 40 essential materials, the authors concluded that most of them have either reached peak production or will do so before 2050. This doesn't mean that we will see absolute scarcity in supply immediately. But it does suggest that more and more of our wealth will have to be directed towards lower and lower grade resources. Peak wealth will arrive around 2017–2022, according to this second study, and from that point on, 'we will no longer be able to take natural-resource fuelled global GDP growth for granted'.[36]

Whether these predictions are right or wrong, two central aspects of the *Limits to Growth* report are hard to dispute. The first is that at some point, the profligate extraction and use of material resources has to stop. The second is more subtle. At the point at which absolute scarcities begin to bite, it is almost certainly going to be too late to make the kinds of changes that will be needed to transform both the resource dependency of the system and its institutional basis. The time horizon for a transformation away from resource intensity has to be some decades in advance of reaching any potential limits.

The MIT team paid particular attention to this second point. The dynamic nature of scarcity is critical in our ability to manage it. *Limits to Growth* highlighted a key distinction between positive and negative feedback loops in the dynamic relationships between technology, resources, consumption and impacts.

Positive feedback tends to lead either to rapid growth or to rapid collapse. Negative feedback tends to suppress or balance such changes and establish the direction of change. Stability depends heavily on the relative strength of positive and negative feedback loops in a dynamic system.

There is a particularly critical relationship between the speed of change of a system and the ease with which change can be managed. In a rapidly expanding system dominated by positive feedback loops, it is harder both to predict and to defend against shocks that arise from accumulating pressure on resources or on ecosystems. By the time the shocks arise, it is already too late to do much about them.

It's not unlike driving a car or skiing down a hill. Our ability to steer safely in the face of unexpected events, depends on dynamic control systems. There is an inevitable lag between our perception of a problem on the road or the slope ahead and our response to it. The magnitude of this delay depends on a mix of factors, some behavioural, some environmental, some technological.

These factors include, of course, our skill and attention, the speed of our muscle responses. They also include the driving conditions at the time: visibility, the state of the traffic, the conditions of the road. And then, of course, there are delays within the technology itself, the responsiveness of the brakes and the steering, for instance.

Some of these things can be improved over time. We can always work on our driving skill and ensure that we have good vision. Improvements in braking systems, for instance, have done wonders for road safety. With the best technology in the world and the response times of a racing driver, we can probably navigate safely through innumerable sudden events at high speed. But typically, control will be much, much easier when things change more slowly.

The problem inherent in systems with strong positive feedbacks is that change is not slow. In the absence of appropriate balancing loops, changes come faster and faster, making control more and more difficult.

Two key lessons flow from this analysis. First, that the faster we drive our economies, the more challenging it will be to respond when scarcities arise. Second, that our best chances for success lie in planning early, long before scarcity arrives. The question we should be asking right now is not whether scarcity is here already, but rather whether there is any prospect at all of it arriving in the foreseeable future. If there is, we should already be acting now. And some kinds of scarcity, it seems, are already upon us.

Running out of planet

In 2015, the Stockholm Resilience Centre published its second 'planetary boundaries' report. The first was published in 2009. For the first time in history, an experienced group of physical scientists (led by Johan Rockström) carried out an extensive audit of our proximity to nine 'critical biophysical boundaries'. Crossing these boundaries, claimed the team, would imply unacceptable environmental change with 'serious, potentially disastrous consequences' for society.[37]

The lessons were salutary. The team discovered that current levels of economic activity already lie beyond the 'safe operating space' of the planet, for four of these critical boundaries. Excess nutrient loading, species loss, ocean acidification and climate change already represent a serious threat to the integrity of ecological systems. In doing so they also threaten to undermine the foundations for human society.

Climate change is probably the most familiar of these threats. Brought to the world's attention in the late 1980s by climate scientist James Hansen and others, climate change has risen inexorably up the political agenda over the last two decades. Its visibility was given a massive boost by the influential Stern review. A former World Bank economist, Nicholas Stern was asked to lead a review of the economics of climate change for the UK Treasury.

It is telling that it took an economist commissioned by a government Treasury to alert the world to things climate scientists – most notably the Intergovernmental Panel on Climate Change (IPCC) – had been saying for years. This is partly a testament to the power of economists in the policy world. But the impact of the Stern report was also due to the seductive nature of its message.

The review concluded that a small early hit on GDP (perhaps as low as 1 per cent of GDP) would allow us to avoid a much bigger hit (perhaps as high as 20 per cent of GDP) later on. Climate change can be fixed, the Stern review concluded, and we'll barely notice the difference. Economic growth can go on more or less as usual.[38]

The idea that it is possible to fix climate change (and presumably all of our other environmental challenges) without much altering the conventional economic model gained an almost perverse momentum in the years following the Stern Review. In 2011, the United Nations Environment Programme declared that green growth (their term for economic growth with lower carbon emissions) could be even faster than 'brown' growth. In 2014, the New Climate Economy report *Better Growth, Better Climate* had a similar message for policy makers.[39]

We'll have occasion to examine this claim more closely below (see Chapters 5 and 6). But the history of climate policy certainly suggests some caution in believing that things will be so straightforward.

The Kyoto Protocol, signed in 1992, committed the advanced economies to reducing annual greenhouse gas emissions by 5 per cent over 1990 levels before 2012. This was supposed to be a first step in combating the threat of climate change. But things haven't quite worked out the way the Kyoto Protocol intended. By 2015, carbon dioxide emissions were over 60 per cent higher than they had been in 1990 and being released into the atmosphere from human activities at a rate 'unprecedented in the last 66 million years'.[40]

The Copenhagen Accord, reached in 2009, established an aspirational goal to restrict global warming to less than 2°C above the pre-industrial average temperature level. Six years later, the global average temperature was still moving inexorably towards that target.

In 2015, temperatures were hotter than in any year since records began in 1850, and the average temperature was for the first time more than 1°C higher than the pre-industrial average.[41]

Despite the imminence of the threat, the Copenhagen Accord failed to agree anything in the way of emission reduction targets, preferring instead to encourage individual nations to come up with their own 'intended nationally determined commitments' (INDCs). In the run up to the 21st Conference of the Parties to the UN Framework Convention on Climate Change (CoP21) in Paris six years later, it became clear that the sum total of these commitments fell some considerable way short of delivering the 2°C goal established in Copenhagen.[42]

In spite of this, the Paris Agreement was astonishingly light in terms of substantive commitments. No emission targets were set and no clear timescale was fixed to achieve them. The thorny problem of financing the low-carbon transition was barely touched upon. But for one extraordinary commitment, it would appear as though the world was paralysed in the face of climate change.

There was one astonishing outcome from the Paris Agreement – a significant strengthening of the Copenhagen goal. Specifically, the deal signed in December 2015 committed its 200 signatories to hold the increase in the global average temperature to 'well below 2°C above pre-industrial levels' and to pursue 'efforts to limit the temperature increase to 1.5°C'.[43]

This goal represented the culmination of over a quarter of a century of intense international policy, and a series of mammoth negotiating sessions in Paris, which ran through the night for several days in a row before the deal itself was signed. But the hard work of actually achieving emission reductions consistent with an aspiration to restrict global warming to less than 1.5°C has scarcely begun.

The IPCC has calculated that to have a better than even chance of meeting this more stringent target, the cumulative carbon dioxide emissions released into the atmosphere since 1870 need to be kept below 2,350 billion metric tonnes. So far, more than 2,000 billion tonnes have been emitted. So the maximum available 'carbon budget' between now and the end of the century is only 350 billion tonnes.[44]

At the current rate of emissions, this budget would be exhausted within a decade. Beyond that point, meeting the target we would have to rely on largely unspecified negative emission technologies; technologies that remove carbon permanently from the earth's atmosphere.[45]

The message from all this is a profoundly uncomfortable one. Global average temperatures are rising. Dangerous climate change is a matter of decades away. And we're using up the climate 'slack' too quickly. It may take decades to transform our energy systems. Yet we have barely started on that task.

What is abundantly clear is that the 'unburnt' carbon locked up in fossil fuel reserves is at least three times the amount of carbon that we can safely burn. Long before we run out of oil, coal and gas, we will have to stop extracting them from the ground and burning them, if dangerous climate change is to be averted. 'Even before we run out of oil,' argues climate change activist Bill McKibben, 'we're running out of planet.'[46]

Beyond the limits

The prevailing economic model relies on a continual, exponential expansion of the size of the economy. Since the middle of the twentieth century, the global economy has expanded on average at around 3.65 per cent each year. By the end of the twenty-first century, if it were to continue to expand at the same rate, the global economy would be more than 200 times bigger than it was back in 1950.[47]

A world in which things simply go on as usual is already inconceivable. But what about a world in which everyone could achieve the level of income expected in the affluent west? In a more equal and considerably richer world, global economic output would need to be 30 times bigger by the end of 2100 than it is today and more than 326 times bigger than it was in the middle of last century.[48]

What on earth does such an economy look like? What does it run on? Does it really offer a credible vision for a shared and lasting prosperity?

This extraordinary ramping up of global economic activity is without historical precedent. It's totally at odds with the finite resource base and the fragile ecology on which we depend for survival. And it's already been accompanied by the degradation of an estimated 60 per cent of the world's ecosystems.[49]

For the most part, we avoid the stark reality of these numbers. The default assumption is that — financial crises aside — growth will continue indefinitely. Not just for the poorest countries, where a better quality of life is undeniably needed, but even for the richest nations where the cornucopia of material wealth adds little to happiness and is beginning to threaten the foundations of our wellbeing.

The reasons for this collective blindness are (as we shall see in more detail later) easy enough to find. The modern economy is structurally reliant on economic growth for its stability. When growth falters — as it did dramatically during the financial crisis — politicians panic. Businesses struggle to survive. People lose their jobs and sometimes their homes. A spiral of recession looms. Questioning growth is deemed to be the act of lunatics, idealists and revolutionaries.

But question it we must. The idea of a non-growing economy may be anathema to an economist. But the idea of a continually growing economy is anathema to an ecologist. No subsystem of a finite system can grow indefinitely — at least in physical terms. Economists have to be able to answer the question of how a continually growing economic system can fit within a finite ecological system.

The only answer available is that growth in dollars must be 'decoupled' from growth in physical throughputs and environmental impacts. But as we shall see more clearly in what follows, this hasn't so far achieved what's needed. There are no prospects for it doing so in the immediate future. And the sheer scale of decoupling required to meet the limits set out here (and stay within them in perpetuity while the economy keeps on growing) staggers the imagination.

In short, we have no alternative but to question growth. The myth of growth has failed us. It has failed the 3 billion people who still live on little more than the price of a skinny latte from the café next door. It has failed the fragile ecological systems on which we depend for survival. It has failed, spectacularly, in its own terms, to provide economic stability and secure people's livelihoods.

The uncomfortable reality is that we find ourselves faced with the imminent end of the era of cheap oil, highly volatile commodity prices, the degradation of air, water and soil, conflicts over land use, resource use, water use, forestry and fishing rights, and the momentous challenge of stabilising the global climate. And we face these tasks with an economy that is fundamentally broken, in desperate need of renewal.

In these circumstances, a return to business as usual is not an option. Prosperity for the few founded on ecological destruction and persistent social injustice is no foundation for a civilised society. Economic stability is vital. Protecting people's jobs – and creating new ones – is absolutely essential. But we also stand in urgent need of a renewed sense of shared prosperity. A deeper commitment to justice in a finite world.

Delivering these goals may seem an unfamiliar or even incongruous task to policy in the modern age. The role of government has been framed so narrowly by material aims, and hollowed out by a misguided vision of unbounded consumer freedoms. The concept of governance itself stands in urgent need of renewal.

But there remains a unique opportunity to invest in change. To sweep away the short-term thinking that has plagued society for decades. To replace it with considered policy capable of addressing the enormous challenge of delivering a lasting prosperity.

For, at the end of the day, prosperity goes beyond material pleasures. It transcends material concerns. It resides in the quality of our lives and in the health and happiness of our families. It is present in the strength of our relationships and our trust in the community. It is evidenced by our satisfaction at work and our sense of shared meaning and purpose. It hangs on our potential to participate fully in the life of society.

Prosperity consists in our ability to flourish as human beings – within the ecological limits of a finite planet. The challenge for our society is to create the conditions under which this is possible. It is the most urgent task of our times.

2

PROSPERITY LOST

The boom, not the slump, is the right time for austerity at the Treasury.

John Maynard Keynes, 1937[1]

The conventional formula for achieving prosperity relies on the pursuit of economic growth. Higher incomes will increase wellbeing and lead to prosperity for all, in this familiar view.

But this vision of progress as a paradise of continually rising consumption has come under serious scrutiny – not just from those who doubt its feasibility on a finite planet or question its desirability from a human perspective, but also from those wondering where on earth economic growth is going to come from in the wake of the worst financial crisis in almost a century.

The fault lines in conventional economics have widened. What once seemed tiny fissures, barely visible to the Western eye, have now become deep chasms threatening to engulf entire nations. The collapse of Lehman Brothers on 15 September 2008 signalled more than the onset of a cyclical liquidity crisis. The pallid light of recession has illuminated crack after crack in the shiny surface of capitalism. It is now apparent that these cracks run right to the heart of the model.

An economy whose stability rests on the relentless stimulation of consumer demand destroys not only the fragile resource base of this finite planet, but also the stability of its financial and political system. Consumer capitalism relies on debt to keep growth going. Burgeoning credit creates fragile balance sheets. Complex financial instruments are used to disguise unsavoury risk. But when the debts eventually become toxic, the system crashes.

Governments committed trillions of dollars to securitise risky assets, underwrite threatened savings, recapitalise failing banks and restimulate the economy in the wake of the crisis. No one pretended this was anything other than a short-term solution. Many even accepted that it was potentially deeply regressive. A temporary fix that rewarded those responsible for the crisis at the expense of the taxpayer. But it was excused on the grounds that the alternative was simply unthinkable.

Collapse of the financial markets would have led to a massive and completely unpredictable global meltdown. Entire nations would have been bankrupted. Commerce would have failed en masse. The humanitarian costs of failing to save the banking system would have been enormous. But government bailouts precipitated further crises. Country after country, particularly across the Eurozone, found themselves negotiating rising deficits, unwieldy sovereign debt and downgraded credit ratings.[2]

Austerity policies, brought in to control deficits and protect ratings, failed to solve the underlying issues. Worse, they created new social problems of their own. The withdrawal of social investment caused rising inequality, deepening unemployment, worsening health outcomes and an increasingly agitated public. The injustice of bailing out the architects of the crisis at the expense of its victims has become plain for all to see. The conditions for wider social unrest remain palpable.[3]

Facing these problems with an economic system still struggling to regain its footing is of course immensely challenging, particularly in the presence of a widely held view that there is no alternative. But it's clear that some serious reflection is in order. Not to stand back and question what happened would be foolhardy. Not to engage in some serious recalibration of the economic model would be to compound failure with failure: failure of responsibility with failure of vision.

And, in principle at least, continuing economic uncertainties present us with a unique opportunity for change. The potential to address both financial and ecological sustainability. The opportunity to confront the limitations of the past with a renewed vision for the future. At the very least, as this chapter argues, it is clear that the task of rebuilding an economy fit for the challenges of the twenty-first century has become more not less essential in the years since this book was first published.

In search of villains

In November 2008, two months after the collapse of Lehman Brothers, Queen Elizabeth II visited the London School of Economics and asked why exactly no one had seen the crisis coming. Feeling perhaps a little caught out by Her Majesty's interest in the matter, the assembled economists went away and did what academics do best: they organised a seminar.

A group of economic heavyweights deliberated long and hard before putting their names to a carefully written three-page letter they hoped would set the record straight. 'In summary, Your Majesty,' they concluded solemnly, 'the failure to foresee the timing, extent and severity of the crisis and to head it off, while it had many causes, was principally a failure of the collective imagination of many bright people, both in this country and internationally, to understand the risks to the system as a whole.'[4]

It was a parsimonious, almost humble letter. But it was also misleading. The truth, as Adair Turner, chair of the former UK Financial Services Authority has noted, was worse than that. This is not to deny that there was a collective failure of the imagination. There clearly was. It's just that this doesn't really answer Her Majesty's question.[5]

How did these system risks arise? Why didn't economists understand them? Why on earth would we leave it to 'collective imagination' to prevent financial disaster? What were the invisible causes of the financial crisis?

A little hindsight is a valuable thing. The proximate cause of collapse of Lehman Brothers is usually taken to be subprime lending in the US housing market. Some have highlighted the unmanageability of the 'credit default swaps' used to parcel up 'toxic debts' and hide them from scrutiny. Others have pointed the finger of blame at greedy speculators and unscrupulous investors intent on making a killing at the expense of vulnerable institutions.

A particularly sanguine take on the set of circumstances leading to the crisis is provided in the documentary film *Inside Job*, which catalogues an extraordinary series of failures of governance that allowed a small minority of already rather rich and powerful people to profit massively from financial collapse by betting cleverly against investments that they themselves had systematically overrated, and by lobbying vociferously against regulation that might have prevented all this.[6]

This clearly wasn't all that was going on. A dramatic rise in basic commodity prices during 2007 and early 2008 (see Figure 1.1) certainly contributed to economic slowdown by squeezing company margins and reducing discretionary spending. At one point in mid-2008, advanced economies were facing the prospect of 'stagflation' – a simultaneous slow-down in growth with a rise in inflation – for the first time in 30 years. Oil prices doubled between July 2007 and July 2008. Food prices rose by 66 per cent, sparking civil unrest in some poorer nations.[7]

A critical factor in all of this was a massively 'over-leveraged' private sector. Households and firms were simply carrying an unsustainable amount of debt. But the most striking aspect of this over-indebtedness was just how long it had been going on. The expansion of domestic private credit across the advanced economies had started already in the 1950s and from that point on continued steadily until the mid-1990s, when the pace of growth even accelerated slightly.[8]

Not all economies were equally susceptible to this trend. Indeed it's a feature of the system of debt that for one part of the global economy to be highly indebted, another part must be saving hard. During the first decade of the twenty-first century, the savers were largely in the emerging economies. The savings rate in China during 2008 was around 25 per cent of disposable income, while in India it was even higher, at 37 per cent.

Even within the advanced economies, there were some clear distinctions between nations. The so-called 'liberal market economies' – mostly the anglocentric ones – led the march towards liberalisation, competition and deregulation during the 1980s and 1990s. The 'coordinated market economies' – the countries of 'old' Europe, Japan and Scandanavia – were much slower to deregulate and tended to depend more heavily on strategic interactions between firms – rather than competition – to coordinate economic behaviour.[9]

But the general trend of a rising domestic private credit amongst the advanced nations was striking. In the US, for example, credit extended to households and nonfinancial companies rose from a little over 60 per cent of the GDP in 1955 to almost 170 per cent of the GDP just before the financial crisis (Figure 2.1). Some of this rise can be attributed to a declining public sector debt. Typically, when

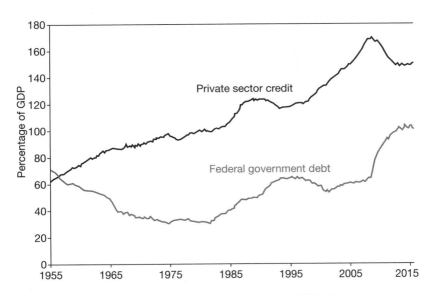

Figure 2.1 US government debt and private sector credit, 1955–2015
Source: Data from the US Federal Reserve and Bank for International Settlements (see note 10)

governments are saving more, the private sector is saving less. This was the trend in the US between the 1950s and the early 1980s, for example, and again during the 1990s. But interestingly there were also periods when private sector credit and public sector debt both rose in parallel.[10]

Particularly notable is the steep rise in federal debt during the crisis itself, a phenomenon mirrored around the world as governments struggled to shore up financial institutions and counteract recession. Generally speaking, public sector debt across the advanced nations increased by over 50 per cent as a proportion of GDP in the space of just a few years as a result of the crisis. In a number of countries – notably Iceland, Ireland, Portugal, Spain and the UK – the debt to GDP ratio more than doubled between 2007 and 2010. By 2015, the sovereign debt of Greece stood at almost 200 per cent of GDP.[11]

The labyrinth of debt[12]

None of this entirely explains the crisis. Debt is not always unsavoury. There is clearly some logic to the claim that the rich economies in particular are (even now) living in a 'debt-fuelled' consumerism and we'll explore that logic later in this book (Chapter 6). But debt is a social institution with a very long pedigree, as anthropologist David Graeber demonstrates unequivocally in *Debt: The First Five Thousand Years*. Debt provided the most primitive means of exchange. Money itself evolved from debt-based exchange.[13]

Lending and borrowing money is certainly an intrinsic feature of the modern economy. A properly functioning financial system plays a vital role in 'smoothing' both our income and our spending patterns over time. We save for retirement, for instance, on the understanding that our earnings potential is higher through our middle years than it will be towards the end. We might also save in pursuit of important 'lumpy' purchases like a car or a holiday.[14]

By far the lumpiest and most important of these purchases is usually our home. In fact, if we had to rely entirely on our own savings to buy a property, it would be almost impossible to achieve for ordinary earners. By taking out a mortgage loan, secured against the home as an asset, we're able to achieve a degree of security in relation to housing that would otherwise be impossible. Always assuming, of course, that house prices are relatively stable, interest rates remain low enough and the financial system remains intact. Under favourable circumstances, the system of extending credit to households performs an important social function in the provision of people's basic needs.[15]

Of course, this sense of security was one of the first casualties of the financial crisis. For as long as the value of homes continued to rise, people's mortgage liabilities were more than offset by the value of their physical assets. Growth in house prices persuaded banks to offer more loans and more people to take them out. More money chasing a limited housing stock contributed in its turn to rising house prices. What looked like a virtuous circle was creating a house price 'bubble' that ultimately couldn't be sustained. When prices collapsed, the virtuous circle became a vicious cycle. Household liabilities were no longer balanced by assets. When this was compounded by falling incomes, ordinary debt began to become unpayable, destabilising not only household finances but the entire financial system.

A well-functioning financial system is also vital for firms, for whom investment represents one of those 'lumpy' purchases that usually cannot be funded entirely from sales revenues. Firms raise money to pay for investment either by selling ownership rights (equity) in the company or else by borrowing money from banks (debt). When things are working properly, this system allows for the renovation and innovation of the productive capacity of the firm.

In fact, there is a sense in which, in a capitalist economy, taking out a loan is the primary act in the 'monetary circuit'. Few private individuals have sufficient resources to finance the building of large factories or the installation of manufacturing plant, without borrowing from somewhere. Before any firm can turn a profit, indeed before it can even make any sales, it must finance its production facilities and pay its workers. Debt is the foundation for production in the capitalist economy.

At the level of the economy as a whole, this leads to an interesting claim that it is loans that create deposits, rather than deposits that create loans. The conventional theory of banking suggests that banks simply intermediate between savers and borrowers. But this is simply wrong. And it is now widely acknowledged that almost all of the money created in modern economies comes into existence through banks first creating loans and then crediting the deposit accounts of those to whom the loans are given.[16]

Governments are, technically speaking, in a slightly different position from households or firms. Since money is denominated in sovereign currency, and because both firms and households must pay taxes in that currency, governments could, in principle, simply spend money into existence by paying public sector wages or by buying goods and services from firms directly in sovereign currency. The most obvious danger in this setup is the potential for governments to 'overspend' and to create inflationary pressures in the economy which then devalue the currency.[17]

Partly because of this danger, but also for what turn out to be ideological reasons, most modern governments only permit themselves to raise money on commercial bond markets, creating interest-bearing debts just as households and firms must do. In some places, this restriction is enshrined in legislation.[18]

The risk of inflation is clearly an important one. But there are also powerful ideological influences at work here, which restrict the room that governments (and central banks) have to manoeuvre in. In fact, as the US linguist George Lakoff has pointed out, the entire metaphor of government as a household is a powerful 'cognitive frame' which has profound repercussions for the power (and powerlessness) of the State. We'll come back to these issues later in the book.[19]

For now, though, we can think of the national debt more or less like household or corporate debt, as the money that government owes to its creditors in the private sector. The national debt increases whenever governments run a deficit, or in other words when tax receipts don't cover public sector spending. Reducing the debt is only possible when the public sector runs a surplus. An increase in the national debt is not unusual during a recession (see Figure 2.1) because incomes and tax receipts are falling and social security outgoings are rising. But a continually rising national debt in a shrinking economy is a recipe for political and social disaster, as countries such as Greece found out to their cost, because the costs of servicing the debt rise even as government's ability to pay them diminishes.[20]

This seems kind of obvious. But assessing the sustainability or unsustainability of debt isn't always so straightforward. Financial assets and liabilities have the curious property that the sum total across the economy always adds up to zero. This becomes clear when you think how financial borrowing and lending works. One person's borrowing is another person's (or firm's) lending. One sector's asset is another sector's liability.

In a closed economy – one without international trade – this would mean that the total outstanding national debt would always be equal to the net financial assets of the private sector. And it wouldn't be possible to reduce public sector borrowing without simultaneously reducing the net lending of the private sector. At the global level, where the economy is of course closed, this must always remain the case.

In open economies, which trade with each other constantly, reducing public sector borrowing can sometimes go hand in hand with increasing the net lending of the private sector, but only when there is a positive trade balance.[21] This is one of the reasons why a country like Germany, with a strong trade balance, was able to reduce its public deficit in the aftermath of the crisis, even as private sector firms were seeking to shore up their balance sheets.

For Greece, on the other hand, which was carrying a negative trade balance, reducing the government deficit could only mean an increase in private sector net borrowing. The push-me, pull-you nature of lending and borrowing creates an uneasy relationship between the public and the private sector. We will see later (Chapter 10) how this can sometimes be turned to the advantage of a canny government. But the strictures it has imposed over the last decade have led to some profoundly unhappy situations.

What transpires from all this is that the distribution of credit and debt across different sectors matters more than the absolute level of either. Figure 2.1 shows that there were periods of time (most notably over the last decade) when the national debt and the credit extended to households and non-financial firms were increasing simultaneously. This can only make sense if financial assets in some other sectors of the economy were increasing over these periods. There are only two possible candidates as the beneficiary sector. Either the financial sector was getting richer, or else the debt the US owed to the rest of the world was increasing.

Some of the debt shown in Figure 2.1 was owned by the US financial sector. But a considerable proportion of it was owned by foreign lenders. This so-called external debt is key to the question of financial sustainability. One of the most striking features of the decades prior to the crisis was an explosion in the external debt of the world's richest economies. Across the advanced nations, the ratio between external debt and GDP rose precipitously from around 25 per cent in 1970 to more than 250 per cent in 2010.[22]

The viability of this external debt depends on a complex mix of factors, including the extent to which it is balanced by productive assets and the relative strength of domestic currency on the international market. Particular pressure is placed on an economy when its economy is shrinking and its currency is losing value. In extreme circumstances, a country may find itself unable to attract investors willing to support its spending and unable to liquidate its assets to compensate for this. At this point the level of external debt relative to the GDP becomes critical. Calling in debts worth more than the national income, for instance, would clearly be catastrophic.

The enemy within

Understanding this labyrinth of debt is a tough grind for the uninitiated. But, as the London economists explained to the Queen, the task isn't much easier for experts, most of whom got caught out massively by the financial crisis.

One of their problems was that economic theory just didn't play out in practice. In theory, expanding the availability of credit should increase real output and make the economy a safer financial place, rather than a more unstable one. And there is a sort of logic to this. Stimulating credit increases the availability of investment capital to firms and at the same time reduces the cost of debt to consumers.

But any number of things can go wrong. One of the earliest signs of imbalance is a rise in inequality. The servicing of escalating debts creates a rising flow of income from debtors to creditors. This is particularly problematic when a relatively small proportion of the population owns a large proportion of the financial assets. It's no surprise to find, as the French economist Thomas Piketty convincingly demonstrated in his bestselling book *Capital in the 21st Century*, that the richest 1 per cent of the US population got considerably richer over the same time-frame in which financial institutions were creating so much more credit.[23]

This isn't the only bear pit. Making credit more widely available doesn't always lead to investment in real physical assets or in the real wealth of households. Sometimes it just leads to speculation. In fact, it's tempting to describe what has emerged in advanced economies in the last decades as a kind of casino economy, where ruthless speculators have used cheap money to gamble on the price of commodities or on property in the hope of making a fast buck before the bubble bursts. Eight years later, the world economy is still reeling from the impacts of this behaviour.

The interaction between these two dynamics is also revealing. Low interest rates lead to easy credit, which creates higher asset prices. Capital gains from these assets favour the richer members of society and increase both income and wealth inequality. Since richer households typically have a higher propensity to save than poorer ones, this leads to a further increase in funds, lowering interest rates further and creating even more cheap credit.[24]

Paradoxically, as inequality increases, poorer households become even less able to service loans. As defaults rise, lenders tend to increase the interest rate on riskier loans. But by this stage it can all be too late; higher interest payments push poor households deeper in debt. Whole asset classes become toxic, dramatically shifting the viability of banks' balance sheets.

Prudent lenders might protect themselves against shocks by maintaining a sufficient proportion of their own capital on the balance sheet to balance their risky loans. The higher the risk, the greater the capital buffer needed to ensure solvency in the case that assets fail. Prudence among households and within banks would have gone a long way to preventing the financial crisis. In fact, attempts to correct the market after the crisis specifically involved provisions to create such buffers. But, at the time, the trends were all in the opposite direction.[25]

So the Queen's question should really be phrased rather differently. Why is it that households, firms and governments more or less dismantled financial prudence in the decades leading up to the crisis?

Some of the answer to this question lies in a kind of natural exuberancy that takes over when things appear to be going well. British economist John Maynard Keynes called this 'animal spirits'. US economist Hyman Minsky described the emergence of financial instability in terms of three stages characterised by three different types of borrower.

The most cautious borrowers, who are also most prevalent in the early stages of the financial cycle, will only take on credit if they are clearly and easily able to pay back both interest and principal within their budgetary constraints. In the next phase, borrowers can pay back the interest easily enough, but rely on new loans to repay the principal. In the final stage, borrowers cannot even service the interest payments on existing debts without taking on new ones. Debts and defaults spiral and instability ensues.[26]

Like Keynes before him, Minsky proposed an absolutely vital role for the State in stabilising an unstable economy. This role favoured prudential oversight and regulation to mitigate the worst excesses of the cycle. Minsky also advocated a form of 'counter-cyclical' spending in which governments became 'employer of last resort' in the event of a crisis: partly in order to offset the inevitable loss of livelihoods associated with financial collapse, and also to provide a much-needed stimulus to get the economy going again.

In the decades preceding the crisis none of this was happening. Oversight was being removed. Regulation was being dismantled. And again, we might paraphrase the Queen's inquiry: why on earth did this happen?

We still don't have an entirely adequate explanation why financial markets managed to destabilise entire economies. Why loans were offered to people who couldn't afford to pay them off. Why regulators failed to curb individual financial practices that could bring down monolithic institutions. Why the expansion of credit had become so dominant a force in the economy. And why governments consistently turned a blind eye or actively encouraged this 'age of irresponsibility'.

This question could partly be answered by saying that policy makers (and indeed many economists) were on the whole painfully ignorant of the work of Hyman Minsky and the small number of economists who might have shed some light on what was going on. Those looking at the profitability of firms and the progress of nations both failed to pay enough attention to the instabilities that were quite clearly emerging in underlying balance sheets.[27]

But even this answer doesn't quite cut it. Because the reality is that, far from exercising or encouraging prudence, governments were deliberately acting in ways that increased fragility. The 1990s and early 2000s were characterised by increasing deregulation of financial markets and a massive innovation in the design of complex financial instruments, all driven (or at least justified) by an ideological assumption that a financial free market would be the best thing possible for the economy.

Way back in 1933, Franklin D. Roosevelt's government passed something called the Glass Steagal Act, a showpiece of US legislation which forced a separation between commercial and investment banking. Basically, it stopped banks taking risks with their depositors' money. In 1999, less than a decade before the crisis, the Gramm-Leach-Bliley Act overturned this separation. Realising that this put deposits at risk, governments began to introduce deposit guarantees. But this simply led to 'moral hazard' – the separation of risk from reward – and encouraged even more speculative behaviour.

Securitisation of mortgage debts – another key element in the invisibility of subprime mortgage risk – compounded these risks. And securitisation was championed at the highest level, spearheaded by Alan Greenspan, former chairman of the Federal Reserve. In *The Age of Turbulence*, Greenspan defends the practice explicitly, arguing that 'transferring risk away from... highly leveraged loan originators can be critical for economic stability, especially in a global environment.'[28]

In testimony to US Congress, Greenspan admitted to being 'shocked' that markets hadn't worked as expected. But this only underlines the point that these interventions were premeditated: deliberate in their intentions to stimulate demand. All along the way, decisions to increase liquidity were made with a view to expanding the economy. 'Amid the crisis of 2008', remarked an *Economist* leader article at the time, 'it is easy to forget that liberalisation had good consequences as well: by making it easier for households and businesses to get credit, deregulation contributed to economic growth.'[29]

For over three decades, in fact, the role of easy credit in stimulating growth had been promoted by the monetarism of Milton Friedman and the influential Chicago school of economics. Reacting against the unwieldy deficits incurred by Keynesian spending programmes in the 1970s, the monetarists believed that monetary policy rather than fiscal policy was the key to economic stability. Paradoxically, Friedman himself didn't believe in a deregulated financial system. But in the hands of policy makers heavily influenced by financial institutions, the deregulation of credit was deemed the best way to boost the economy.

Clearly, a strategy that ended up simply replacing public debt with private debt (Figure 2.1) was always going to be risky one. 'When the music stops, in terms of liquidity, things will be complicated', the CEO of Citibank reportedly remarked, just before the bubble burst. 'But as long as the music is playing, you've got to get up and dance. We're still dancing.'[30]

By the end of 2008, Citibank was no longer dancing. No bank was. The music had clearly stopped – and things were definitely complicated. Just how complicated was indicated by the sheer size of the international bailout. And the fact that even trillions of dollars of taxpayers' money proved insufficient to guarantee stability and avoid ongoing economic uncertainty.[31]

The degree to which this progressive financial deregulation and the surge in private credit contributed to the crisis is now more or less incontrovertible. 'The question arises, then, in the last 15 years: can we identify any sustained stretch during which the economy grew satisfactorily with conditions that were financially sustainable?' asked the former US Treasury Secretary Larry Summers. Hungarian-born financier George Soros linked the emergence of a 'super-bubble' in global financial markets to a series of economic policies designed to increase liquidity as a way of stimulating demand.[32]

And here at last we come close to the heart of the matter. The market was not undone by isolated malpractice carried out by rogue individuals. Or even through the turning of a blind eye by less than vigilant regulators. If there was irresponsibility, it was much more systematic, sanctioned from the top, and with one clear aim in mind: the continuation and protection of economic growth.

Allegiance to growth was the single most dominant feature of an economic and political system that led the world to the brink of economic disaster. The growth imperative has shaped the architecture of the modern economy. It motivated the freedoms granted to the financial sector. It drove the loosening of regulations, the proliferation of unmanageable (and unstable) financial derivatives, and the massive expansion in both public debt and private credit in the decades preceding and during the crisis.

The very policies put in place to stimulate economic growth, Your Majesty, led inexorably towards its downfall. This is the answer the London economists should have given Queen Elizabeth II. The market was undone by growth itself.

A year in the Keynesian sun

This understanding should have led to a profound re-examination of the growth-based economic paradigm. But very little of that actually happened. The mainstream response had more the character of an addict reaching for the bottle to cure a hangover from the night before. Anything, to get growth back again, as fast as possible, no matter what the cost.

Some concessions to a more responsible financial sector were initiated. Practices like short-selling were suspended; increased capital adequacy requirements were called for; there was, briefly, a grudging acceptance of the need to cap executive remuneration (bonuses) in the financial sector.[33]

Admittedly, this last concession was born more of political necessity in the face of huge public outcry over the bonus culture than through recognition of a point of principle. Within only a few months of the crisis, huge executive bonuses were being paid again. As early as December 2008, Goldman Sachs paid out $2.6 billion in end-of-year bonuses in spite of its $6-billion-dollar bailout by the US government, justifying these on the basis that they helped to 'attract and motivate' the best people.[34]

Many such responses were seen as short-term interventions, designed to facilitate the restoration of business as usual. Short-selling was suspended for six months, rather than banned. Capital adequacy requirements were relatively modest and only to be phased in slowly. The part-nationalisation of financial institutions was justified on the basis that shares would be sold back to the private sector as soon as reasonably possible, something that in many cases still hasn't been achieved.[35]

Extraordinary though some of these interventions were, they were largely regarded as temporary measures. Necessary evils in the restoration of a free-market economy. The declared aim was clear. By pumping equity into the banks and restoring confidence to lenders, the world's leaders hope to restore liquidity, reinvigorate demand and 'kick-start' the economy.

Their ultimate goal was to protect the pursuit of economic growth. Throughout everything, this has remained the one non-negotiable: that growth must continue at all costs. Renewed growth was the end that justified interventions unheard of only a few months previously. No politician seriously questioned this goal.

The reasons are not hard to fathom. When spending slows down, unemployment looms large. Firms find themselves out of business. People find themselves out of a job. And governments who fail to respond appropriately very soon find themselves out of office. In the short term, there is a moral imperative to protect jobs and prevent any further collapse. Raising deep, structural questions about the nature of prosperity in such a climate is deemed inopportune if not insensitive.

In fact, those inclined to question the consensus wisdom are swiftly denounced as cynical revolutionaries or modern-day Luddites. 'We do not agree with the anti-capitalists who see the economic crisis as a chance to impose their utopia, whether of a socialist or eco-fundamentalist kind', roared one UK newspaper at the height of the crisis. 'Most of us in this country enjoy long and fulfilling lives thanks to liberal capitalism: we have no desire to live in a yurt under a workers' soviet.'[36]

With that confusingly attired bogey-man looming over the situation, rebuilding consumer confidence to boost high-street spending looked like a no-brainer. And internecine warfare was all saved for arguing over how this is to be achieved.

In the immediate aftermath of the crisis, there were basically two options on the table: expansion of the money supply or a massive fiscal stimulus. The trouble with the first option was that by late 2008 there was already very little room for manoeuvre. Interest rates were already at zero and households were already over-leveraged. The appetite for more and more credit had diminished and the monetary expansion that had protected the consumer boom for so long throughout the 1990s and early 2000s was temporarily unavailable.

Politicians were not yet prepared to indulge in direct injections of money into the economy. These would come later. So bereft of conventional options, policy makers 'quickly abandoned the mantra *markets know better than governments*, blew the dust off their Keynesian textbooks and pumped money and hence demand into the global economy'.[37]

Some of this money was simply emergency funding to shore up ailing financial institutions. 'Governments made available previously unimaginable sums', wrote one set of commentators, 'to bail-out a banking system whose uncontrolled greed and recklessness had brought the global economy to its knees'. But beyond this immediate need, a global consensus quickly emerged around a plan to engage in a full-scale Keynesian stimulus programme akin to the ones put in place in the 1930s.

The closest role model was Roosevelt's New Deal, implemented eight decades earlier as the world struggled to escape the Great Depression. The New Deal had entailed a massive investment in public sector works. It may not have had the short-term effect some claim for it. It didn't in fact achieve a full economic recovery within Roosevelt's first two terms in office. But its long-term impact was enormous. As Paul Krugman, winner of the 2008 Nobel Prize in economics, pointed out: 'The New Deal famously placed millions of Americans on the public payroll via the Works Progress Administration [WPA] ... To this day we drive on WPA-built roads and send our children to WPA-built schools.'[38]

Here was government acting, as Minsky later suggested it should, as 'employer of last resort'. Public sector jobs offer a double dividend. Beyond the obvious benefits in terms of people's livelihoods, these jobs generate a part of what has been called the 'social wage' – a return to households from government spending in the form of lasting infrastructure, improved health and education benefits and better social services.[39]

But public sector jobs are not the only way to mitigate the devastating loss to livelihoods inflicted by an extended recession. Beyond being 'employer of last resort', governments can also inject financial support into specific sectors, or simply aim to stimulate demand (for instance through tax cuts and enhanced benefits) in the hope that this will provide jobs across the economy. All of this fits within the broad idea of a Keynesian stimulus.

The programmes to emerge from the 2008 crisis favoured a mixture of these strategies. There wasn't much in the way of an increase in public sector employment. But specific sectors received direct support from government in a number of places. Most obviously, of course, enormous sums of money were dedicated to rescuing the financial sector itself.

Direct recovery packages were also sought (and sometimes offered) in other sectors. Most notably, the car industry received direct support in both the UK and the US. The US government committed over $23 billion to bail out the ailing giants GM and Chrysler at the end of 2008. Early in 2009, the UK Government promised to underwrite loans to the car industry totalling £2.3 billion.[40]

Perhaps most bizarrely, representatives from the US porn industry approached Congress for support early in 2009, following the car industry bailout. 'Americans can do without cars and such, but they cannot do without sex', argued Larry Flynt, the founder of *Hustler* magazine. Surely more of a publicity stunt than a serious claim, the call nonetheless highlights the profound mess created by the financial crisis, with the vulnerable and not-so-vulnerable alike lobbying for direct support in the matter of their livelihoods.[41]

By far the most interesting variation on the Keynesian theme was the call for a Green New Deal. If the public sector is going to spend money to reinvigorate the economy, argued its advocates, wouldn't it be as well to spend it investing in the new technologies that we know we are going to need to address the environmental and resource challenges of the twenty-first century?

'Investments will soon be pouring back into the economy,' suggested Pavan Sukhdev, the former Deutsche Bank economist leading research on the United Nations Environment Programme's Green Economy initiative. 'The question is whether they go into the old extractive short-term economy of yesterday, or a new green economy that will deal with multiple challenges while generating multiple economic opportunities for the poor and the well-off alike.'[42]

In a report published just after the crisis, the Deutsche Bank identified a 'green sweet spot' for stimulus spending, consisting of investment in energy-efficient buildings, the electricity grid, renewable energy and public transportation. 'One of the reasons that the *green sweet spot* is an attractive focus for an economic stimulus is the labor-intensity of many of its sectors', claimed the Bank.[43]

A study by the University of Massachusetts' Political Economy Research Institute supported that view. It identified six priority areas for investment: retrofitting buildings, mass transit/freight rail, smart grid, wind power, solar power and next generation biofuels. The authors calculated that spending $100 billion on these interventions over a two-year period would create two million new jobs. By contrast, the same money directed at household spending would generate fewer jobs; and directed at conventional sectors like the oil industry fewer still.[44]

The proposal briefly held real political traction. The idea of linking fiscal stimulus with 'green investment' began to take hold. As an HSBC Global Research report remarked at the time, the 'colour of stimulus' was going green. Out of a total commitment of almost $2.8 trillion committed to economic recovery plans at that point, $436 billion (15.6 per cent of the total) could be characterised as green stimulus, according to the HSBC analysis.[45]

But stimulus has to be paid for. The default assumption is that this should come from deficit spending. Temporarily at least, national debts must rise: exactly as we saw in Figure 2.1. The hope is that the stimulus will be effective. Credit will flow, consumers will spend, business will invest and innovate, productivity will return and the wheels of the machine will start turning again. Government will eventually reduce its debt through higher tax receipts. This is the logic of Keynesianism.[46]

After a year in the Keynesian sun, this wasn't quite happening. Or, at least, it wasn't happening fast enough for anxious politicians and unforgiving commentators. The media and opposition parties alike began pointing at burgeoning public sector debt and wagging their fingers in disapproval. With no clear recovery in sight, and with some governments facing national elections, the political rhetoric around stimulus began to change.

The UK was a case in point. The opposition Conservative Party fought the 2010 election almost entirely around the fiscal deficit and the escalating public debt. Framing government as an overspent household, the Tories pitched deficit reduction as a matter of absolute urgency. The metaphor of 'living within our means' was repeated so often that it became the foundation for a widespread political U-turn. The language of stimulus gave way to the language of austerity: a massive scaling back of public spending in an attempt to reduce fiscal deficits.

The argument appeared to gain support from economic evidence. A highly influential paper published by two Harvard economists in 2010 seemed to underline the danger of rapidly increasing national and external debt levels. The paper's most-cited claim was that economic growth rates are 'roughly cut in half' when levels of external debt exceed 90 per cent of the GDP. There was a similar finding for the national debt: with a debt-to-GDP ratio of 90 per cent or more, growth rates were around half of those achievable when the debt-to-GDP ratio was below 30 per cent, claimed the authors.[47]

Extraordinarily, it turned out that the paper itself was riddled with errors, some of them simple coding errors. A reworking of the data revealed that the claims were massively exaggerated. In fact, the frame itself is false. The government is not a household. It doesn't have the same restrictions on borrowing as a household or a firm does. 'It's true that you can't run big budget deficits for ever … because at some point interest payments start to swallow too large a share of the budget', wrote Krugman. 'But it's foolish and destructive to worry about deficits when borrowing is very cheap and the funds you borrow would otherwise go to waste.'[48]

None of this was heard. Governments had already begun to abandon stimulus in favour of austerity. 'Elites all across the western world were gripped by austerity fever, a strange malady that combined extravagant fear with blithe optimism', wrote Krugman. 'Concerns that imposing such austerity in already depressed economies would deepen their depression and delay recovery were airily dismissed; fiscal probity, we were assured, would inspire business-boosting confidence, and all would be well.'

The impacts were as unsavoury as they were predictable. Economies that had been on the verge of recovery were pushed back into recession. With interest rates at zero, and deficit spending outlawed, central banks were forced to turn towards more unconventional monetary policy. They committed even more money – this time in the form of 'quantitative easing' – to try and increase nominal demand and restimulate investment. The sheer scale of these commitments was extraordinary. By 2012, the US alone had committed a staggering $30 trillion – almost twice its annual GDP – to the recovery effort.[49]

But as health economists David Stuckler and Sanjay Basu argue, the 'greatest tragedy of austerity is not that it has hurt our economies. The greatest tragedy of austerity is the unnecessary human suffering that austerity has caused.' *The Body Economic* documents the pernicious effects that cuts in public spending have had on the poorest and most vulnerable in society. Youth unemployment across the world escalated. Job security evaporated. Benefits were decimated. Health outcomes worsened. The incidence of homicide and mental illness rose. In Greece, for example, suicide rates doubled.[50]

There are some profound lessons from all of this for my aims in this book. We'll explore some of these in the coming chapters. But first, there is one more equally important insight to be gleaned from the economic history of the last few years.

Enter the deflationary headwinds...

Prosperity without Growth was born in the midst of the worst financial crisis for eight decades. Its early life was accompanied by a deepening recessionary gloom. Most people assumed this would soon be over.

But as the cries of 'growth at all costs' became louder and louder, the possibility of a 'new normal' gradually began to dawn on economists.

What if, after all the fuss, there just wasn't so much growth to be had any more? What if the capacity of the economy to grow was slowing down? What if the reluctance of businesses to invest and consumers to spend was not just a cyclical downturn but a more entrenched change in economic fundamentals? The term 'secular stagnation' re-emerged — it had first been used in 1939 — to reflect precisely these possibilities.[51]

For the most part, fears of secular stagnation have been directed at the advanced economies. US economist Robert Gordon has suggested that a slowdown in the US economy could come about as a result of a decline in the pace of innovation — many of the big technological advances of the last two centuries are now over — together with six 'deflationary headwinds', which are taken to include: an ageing population, rising inequality and the 'overhang' of consumer and government debt.[52]

Irrespective of precise causes, it is indisputable that labour productivity growth in the advanced economies has been falling consistently for several decades, and was doing so long before the financial crisis. Figure 2.2 reveals the extent of this decline. Growth rates of 4 per cent or more were typical in the 1950s and 1960s. A sharp decline in in the 1970s was stabilised briefly during the 1980s and 1990s, primarily through the productivity gains from the emerging digital economy. But these were not to last. Trend productivity growth has fallen consistently since the turn of the millennium and in 2015 was less than 0.5 per cent.[53]

To be absolutely clear here, per capita GDP (the conventional measure of prosperity) can only rise in this situation by increasing either the proportion of the population in the workforce or the number of hours each of them works in the economy. There are clearly limits to both of these strategies. The first is limited by social factors and the second by human endurance. Beyond a certain point, having more people work longer hours is likely to reduce productivity further.

Not everyone agrees that the problem lies with long-term supply growth. Some attribute it to a persistent slowing down of demand —

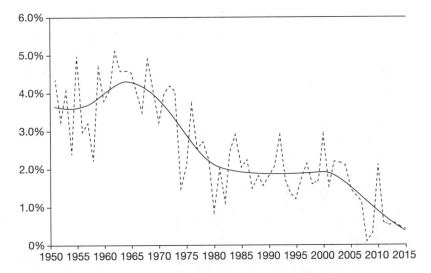

Figure 2.2 Productivity growth in advanced economies, 1950–2015
Source: Raw data taken from the Total Economy Database (see note 53)

the kind of thing that Japan has faced since the early 1990s. But most agree that the process has been going on for some time, masked (prior to the financial crisis) by the huge expansion of private debt and the creation of asset bubbles. In the aftermath of the crisis, as business, households and government all seek to reduce their indebtedness, the long-term weakness of both demand and supply are becoming visible.

Though it started out as a developed world problem, the risks of a global slowdown in growth are increasingly being seen as more widespread. In October 2015, the International Monetary Fund revised its global growth projections downwards for the second time in the year, citing falling growth rates in the emerging and developing economies for the fifth year in succession.[54]

A slowdown in China lies at the heart of this wider problem. Following its decision in 2014 to shift the basis of its economy from export-led growth to an expansion of domestic services, the Chinese economy has been on something of a rollercoaster ride. During 2015, the Chinese government was forced to slash its growth forecast and devalue its currency. Chinese shares plunged 30 per cent in three weeks in the middle of the year and on 24 August 2015 (dubbed Black Monday) over 8 per cent of share value was wiped out in a single day.[55]

The knock-on impacts for the rest of the world are still being played out. But echoes from the past are ominous. Commentators pointing to the likelihood of another financial crash are not hard to find. On Black Monday, it was thought to be so imminent that a former advisor to the UK Prime Minister was infamously warning people to stock up on tinned food and bottled water and make sure they had a wad of hard cash to survive on.[56]

By early 2016, such warnings had become almost commonplace. William White, former chief economist at the Bank for International Settlements, warned the Davos World Economic Forum that the situation building in the global financial system was 'worse than it was in 2007' in a context in which central bankers had 'used up all their ammunition'. The head of Swiss banking giant UBS, Axel Weber, added to the angst by warning that the world was now stuck in an era of low growth.[57]

These comments illustrate the visceral fear that haunts the prospect of an economic slowdown. But the threat of secular stagnation has strange as well as familiar consequences. One of these is that it brings the interests of conventional economists much closer to the concerns of those who have questioned growth on ecological or on social grounds. There now seems to be a distinct possibility that the growth on which we have relied, not only to improve the quality of our lives but also to maintain economic stability, might just not be available any more.

Abandoning, or being abandoned by, growth is still a frightening prospect. But it places at a premium any strategy at all that might protect the quality of our lives and our hopes for a decent life. Seven years after it was first published, *Prosperity without Growth* is no longer a radical narrative whispered by a marginal fringe, but an essential vision for social progress in a post-crisis world.

3
REDEFINING PROSPERITY

Call no man happy until he is dead.

Solon, *c.* 560 BCE[1]

The prevailing vision of prosperity as a continually expanding material paradise has come unravelled. Perhaps it worked better when economies were smaller and the world was less populated. Or perhaps that early utopia was built from the savage imperialism of a few powerful nations. But if it was ever fully fit for purpose, it certainly isn't now.

Climate change, a catastrophic loss of biodiversity and the spectre of imminent resource scarcities compound the problems of failing financial markets and rising inequality. Short-term fixes to prop up a bankrupt system aren't good enough. Something more is needed. An essential starting point is to set out a coherent notion of prosperity that doesn't rely on default assumptions about relentless material consumption growth.

This chapter aims to identify a different kind of vision for prosperity; one in which it is possible for human beings to flourish, to achieve greater social cohesion, to find higher levels of wellbeing and yet still to reduce their material impact on the environment. To live well, and yet to consume less. To have more fun – but with less stuff.

If this seems elusive, even delusional from a modern perspective, it's useful to remember that beyond the consumer paradise lie some strong competing visions of the good life. Some of these hail from psychology and sociology; others from economic history. Some draw on secular or philosophical viewpoints; others are from the religious or 'wisdom' traditions.[2]

Not surprisingly, there are differences between the various approaches. But there are also some striking similarities. Almost all perspectives, even religious ones, accept that prosperity has some material dimensions. It's perverse to talk about things going well, when you lack the basic material resources required to sustain yourself: food and water to be adequately nourished or materials for clothing and shelter.

Security in achieving these aims is also important. Somehow, it's not quite enough to feel satisfied today, if you have no idea where the next square meal is coming from. It's hard to relax when you know the harvest is about to fail. Or your bank account is empty. Or your mortgage payments are overdue.

But, from at least the time of Aristotle, it has been clear that something more than material security is needed for human beings to flourish. Prosperity has vital social and psychological dimensions. To do well is in part about the ability to give and receive love, to enjoy the respect of your peers, to contribute useful work, and to have a sense of belonging and trust in the community.

In a groundbreaking study of poverty, published 40 years ago, the sociologist Peter Townsend found that being poor was never just about the absence of money. People suffer from poverty when they become 'excluded from ordinary living patterns, customs and activities', he discovered.[3]

'Even if we act to erase material poverty,' said the late Robert Kennedy, shortly before his assassination in 1968, 'there is another greater task. It is to confront the poverty of satisfaction – purpose and dignity – that afflicts us all.' Prosperity, it turns out, is in part at least about our ability to participate actively in the life of our society.[4]

Some perspectives — particularly from the wisdom traditions — add in an important moral or ethical component to prosperity. 'Prosperity can only be conceived', writes the Islamic writer Zia Sardar, 'as a condition that includes obligations and responsibilities to others'. My prosperity hangs on the prosperity of those around me, these traditions suggest, as theirs does on mine.[5]

In *The Art of Happiness*, the Dalai Lama takes this suggestion one step further. Those are happiest, he suggests, who show compassion for others and exercise care for them. Perhaps surprisingly, the claim has some support from modern scientific research. 'The very act of concern for others' wellbeing creates a greater sense of wellbeing within oneself', concludes neuropsychologist Richard Davidson.[6]

The recent surge of interest in the science of happiness resonates deeply with the focus of this book. This doesn't mean of course that happiness is the same thing as prosperity. But to the extent that we tend to be happy when things go well and unhappy when they don't, there is clearly some connection between the two.[7]

Using both cognitive and neuropsychology, this emerging science has done much to unravel the complex nature of human wellbeing. It confirms, for instance, that the material conditions of life matter. But they do not exhaust the foundations for happiness. Health, family, friendships and a fulfilment at work are often mentioned ahead of income or material wealth. Freedom and a sense of autonomy seem to matter. So too does a sense of meaning and purpose.[8]

For some, this sense of meaning may entail belief in a higher power. It's fascinating to note that modern psychology has found positive links between religious belief and subjective wellbeing. The link is particularly strong in poorer societies, where the material conditions of life are less secure. But it seems to exist even in richer societies, despite a paradoxical decline in religious participation.[9]

Even in a secular context, it's clear that the human psyche craves meaning and purpose. Without this insight, Solon's strange pronouncement, cited at the top of this chapter, might be entirely incomprehensible, particularly in today's materialistic society.

Success today is synonymous with material affluence. Worth is measured as wealth. Prosperity is cashed out as spending power. How much we have is more important than what kind of person we are.

And who we are today is infinitely more important than how our lives might be seen in retrospect.

Yet there is something immediately recognisable in the idea that, ultimately, we can't take it all with us. The story of our lives, as seen in the round, will not be a record of all the stuff we momentarily enjoyed and ultimately threw away. Nor even of the wealth we managed to accumulate in offshore bank accounts. Neither will it simply be a sum of momentary pleasures.[10]

Rather, the good life is something in which we must invest (to use an economic term) both at the personal and at the societal level. The consumer society may have raised instant gratification to the status of a social good. But the wisdom of ages has always recognised that deeper instincts drive the human psyche and occasionally draw out what might legitimately be called the best in us.

Measuring progress

Fascinating though it is to philosophise on the roots of happiness, the task in hand is to establish a workable vision of prosperity at the societal level. 'The good life of the good person', writes Zia Sardar, 'can only be fully realised in the good society'. The aim of this chapter is to articulate a credible account of prosperity in a world where the global population will approach 10 billion people by the middle of this century.[11]

At least three different candidates emerge immediately from the discussion above and it's useful to distinguish carefully between them. Perhaps the easiest way to do this is to borrow from Amartya Sen, who set out the distinctions very clearly in a landmark essay on 'The Living Standard', first published in 1984.[12]

One of Sen's concepts was characterised by the term *opulence*; another, by the term *utility*; and a third through the idea of *capabilities for flourishing*. It's the third of these in which I'm particularly interested here. But let's start out from the beginning.

Broadly speaking, Sen's first concept – opulence – corresponds to a conventional understanding that prosperity is about material satisfactions. Opulence means a great abundance or extravagance. It refers to the ready availability and steady throughput of material commodities. An increase in the volume flow of commodities represents an increase in prosperity. The greater the throughput, the greater our prosperity. In this view, the more we have, the better off we are.

The logic of abundance as the basis for doing well dates back to Adam Smith. In pre-industrial society, it was quite simply a priority to ensure the provision of the material commodities needed for a decent life. It is still a priority in the poorest countries of the world. Food, water, shelter, sanitation, power: these basic necessities are inherently material in nature. And, for those still living below the subsistence line, some increase in material throughput is unequivocally called for.

But it is pretty straightforward to see that this simple equation of quantity with quality, of more with better, is false in general. Even economic theory recognises this limitation. Economists call it the 'diminishing marginal utility' of goods – and of income itself. Each successive quantity of additional goods (or income) provides less and less in the way of additional satisfaction.[13]

Psychologists sometimes appeal to the concept of 'adaptation' to explain why this phenomenon exists. We become accustomed to (we adapt to) the pleasure something gives us and this leads us to expect the pleasure ahead of indulging in it. Paradoxically, this expectation diminishes the actual pleasure we receive from the indulgence, setting up a dynamic which has us continually striving for more.[14]

But there are other more functional interpretations of the principle of diminishing marginal utility. When you've had no food for months and the harvest has failed again, any food at all is a blessing. When the American-style fridge-freezer is already stuffed with overwhelming choice, even a little extra might be considered a burden, particularly if you're tempted to eat it.

Once my appetite for hamburgers or doughnuts (say) is sated, more of them provide no further joy at all. On the contrary, they may even make me feel ill. And if I'm tempted to ignore these bodily feedback mechanisms against excess I will find myself on the road to obesity, heart disease, diabetes and possibly even cancer: outcomes it is nonsensical to describe as desirable or satisfying.

The sense that more can sometimes be less provides the beginnings of an understanding of the dissatisfactions of the consumer society. 'Just underneath the beautiful surface of affluence', writes the Dalai Lama, 'lies a kind of mental unrest, leading to frustration, unnecessary quarrels, reliance on drugs and alcohol, and in the worst case, suicide.'[15]

There is an even more important lesson emerging from all of this. The suspicion that the richest in the world are consuming more and more of the world's resources in pursuit of less and less additional satisfaction contains a powerful humanitarian argument for redistribution.

Should we not aim to optimise the overall satisfaction associated with our material throughputs rather than maximise the throughputs themselves? And if this is the case, should we not focus our efforts on increasing incomes (and material throughputs) in the regions where this will have the biggest impact on people's quality of life? Interestingly, this idea is also at the core of Sen's second concept: prosperity as utility.

Quantity is not the same thing as quality. Opulence is not the same thing as satisfaction. Sen's second characterisation recognises this. Rather than focusing on the sheer volume of commodities available to us, his second proposal relates prosperity to the uses and satisfactions which commodities provide.[16]

Though it is easy enough to articulate this difference, it is more difficult to define exactly how commodities relate to satisfaction, as many people have noted. The one thing that's pretty easy to figure out is that the relationship is highly non-linear. Even something as basic as food doesn't follow a simple linear pattern in which more is always better.[17]

There's a particularly important complexity here. Increasingly, the uses to which we put material commodities are social or psychological in nature rather than purely material. In the immediate postwar years, it was a challenge to provide for basic necessities, even in the most affluent nations. Today, consumer goods and services increasingly furnish us with identity, experience, a sense of belonging, perhaps even meaning and a sense of hope.[18]

Measuring utility in these circumstances is even more difficult. What is the 'psychic satisfaction' from an iPhone? A new bicycle? A holiday abroad? A birthday present for a lover? These questions are practically impossible to answer. Economics gets round the difficulty by assuming their value is equivalent to the price people are prepared to pay for them in freely functioning markets. It casts utility as the monetary value of market exchanges.

As we have seen (in Chapter 1), the GDP sums up all these market exchanges across the economy. Specifically, it measures the total spending by households, by government and the money invested by businesses.[19] Theoretically, say economists, this sum of market exchanges is not a measure of the volume of stuff, but rather of the utility associated with the throughput of stuff. And this, in a nutshell, is the case for believing that the GDP is a useful measure of wellbeing.

But the equation is deeply flawed. As Robert Kennedy remarked almost half a century ago, the GDP 'counts air pollution and cigarette advertising, and ambulances to clear our highways of carnage. It counts special locks for our doors and the jails for the people who break them. It counts the destruction of the redwood and the loss of our natural wonder in chaotic sprawl.'

And even as it's busy totting up the supposed utility associated with so many dubious or downright destructive practices, there is much that the GDP misses out of its all-consuming account. 'It measures neither our wit nor our courage, neither our wisdom nor our learning, neither our compassion nor our devotion to our country', Kennedy noted. 'It measures everything in short, except that which makes life worthwhile.'[20]

Notice, also, that this comfortable elision of utility with the GDP completely undermines the humanitarian point above. It equates a dollar of GDP for a rich person with exactly the same dollar of GDP for a poor person. Statisticians may do clever things to adjust these dollars for 'purchasing power parity'. But they can't (as yet) adjust for the much higher marginal utility that a dollar represents to a poor person than it does to a rich one.

The formal economics literature is replete with critical examinations of the GDP. But it was to be another 40 years before a senior politician once again dared to articulate its shortcomings. In February 2008, the President of France, Nicolas Sarkozy, set up a Commission led by Nobel laureate Joseph Stiglitz to explore the measurement of economic performance and social progress.[21]

'What we measure affects what we do', reported the Commission late in 2009. 'And if our measurements are flawed, decisions may be distorted ... We often draw inferences about what are good policies by looking at what policies have promoted economic growth; but if our metrics of performance are flawed, so too may be the inferences that we draw.'

Just how far off we are by using the GDP as a measure of social progress has been the subject of some heated discussion. Using a measure first put together in 1989 by US economist Herman Daly and his colleague John Cobb, recent studies suggest (Figure 3.1) that the conventional measure of GDP could be a gross overestimation of social progress, at least since about the beginning of the 1980s.[22]

Bar a couple of short interruptions, per capita income rose more or less continuously between 1950 right up until the financial crisis. But the Genuine Progress Indicator (GPI) levelled off in the late 1970s and even began to decline slowly over the subsequent two decades. The average growth rate of the GDP per capita was around 2.3 per cent over the period. The average growth rate in GPI was barely

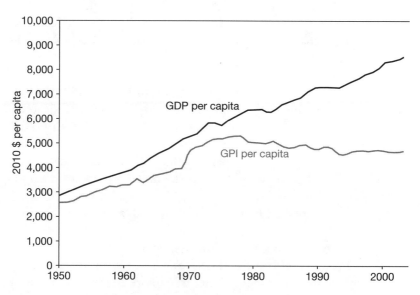

Figure 3.1 Income per capita and the Genuine Progress Indicator (GPI)
Source: Data from Kubiszewski et al. (2013) and World Bank (see note 23)

0.5 per cent. And from the mid–1970s onwards it declined at 0.3 per cent per year.[23]

Such a radical departure from the GDP is a worrying indication that the exchange value is a poor proxy for the overall utility that goods and services provide us with. When we start to subtract out the 'disutility' – the damage caused by the production of those goods and service, for instance – then economic growth can even begin to look a bit like 'uneconomic growth', as Daly has described it.[24]

Happiness wars

The suggestion that income is a poor proxy for utility draws further support from evidence of people's life-satisfaction. This case was argued forcefully by UK economist Richard Layard in a book that was simply called *Happiness*, in which he appealed to the ethics of utilitarianism. Originally developed by the philosopher Jeremy Bentham in the eighteenth century, utilitarianism proposes that 'it is the greatest happiness of the greatest number that is the measure of right and wrong'.[25]

Utilitarianism later provided the foundation for classical economics. But in cashing out utility in terms of income and chasing GDP as a proxy for happiness, argued Layard, economic policy (and economics itself) has lost its way. He suggested that government policy should instead adopt reported life-satisfaction or happiness, rather than GDP, as the appropriate measure of social progress.[26]

In support of this claim, Layard drew on several decades' worth of evidence on the elusive relationship between income and happiness. At the very least, he argued, if GDP really provides a useful measure of utility, then we should expect to see substantial changes in reported happiness in growing economies. Does higher income lead to increases in happiness or does it not?

Perhaps not surprisingly, a fierce controversy surrounds this question in economics. After all, what's at stake here is the authority of the entire economic model. If it turns out that economic growth cannot actually deliver rising levels of happiness, it would certainly pose a serious challenge to the authority of the GDP as a measure of social progress. So what exactly does the evidence show?

What I call here the 'happiness wars' were kicked off more than four decades ago by the US economist Richard Easterlin. In 1974, he published a paper provocatively entitled 'Does economic growth improve the human lot?' The article explored three types of evidence. First, it looked at how life-satisfaction changed across different income groups in the same country. Next, it examined life-satisfaction across countries. Finally, it explored the average life-satisfaction within a country over time.[27]

What Easterlin found was fascinating. In the first place, it was clear that within a country, happiness is linked to income. Higher income groups systematically report higher levels of happiness than lower income groups. Aside from one or two nuances, this finding has been supported consistently in the intervening years and no one really disagrees with it. Statistically speaking, being richer really does appear to make you happier. Or, at least happier than your neighbour.[28]

Paradoxically, however, across the nation as a whole, average life-satisfaction appears to be remarkably stable over time. Easterlin found that in the US, for example, where data on life-satisfaction had been recorded since 1946, the average reported life-satisfaction score really hadn't changed in almost three decades.

Again, this finding seems more or less to have endured the test of time. Political ups and downs – the revolution in Cuba, the collapse of communism in Russia – can certainly generate short-term changes in reported life-satisfaction. But these short-term effects rarely last, it seems.

Real income per head has tripled in the US since 1950, but the percentage of people reporting themselves very happy has barely increased at all. Since about the 1970s it has even declined slightly. In Japan, there has been little change in life-satisfaction over several decades. In the UK the percentage reporting themselves 'very happy' declined from 52 per cent in 1957 to 36 per cent in 2005, even though real incomes had more than doubled in that period.[29]

The most widely accepted explanation for what came to be known as the 'Easterlin paradox' is called the 'relative income effect'. Even though, on aggregate, having more income doesn't make the nation as a whole any happier, it certainly pays off to be richer than those around you.

At the societal level, though, there is a clear danger that this positional race doesn't contribute much to overall prosperity. 'The stock of status, measured as positive advantages, showed a sustained increase in the post-war years', acknowledges the economic historian Avner Offer. 'Much of the pay-off, however, was absorbed in positional competition'.[30]

It begins to look as though economic growth is a kind of 'zero sum game'. The population as a whole gets richer. Some people are better off than others and positions in society may change. But the process adds little or nothing to overall wellbeing. We might even have to dub this a 'negative sum game'. Because, ultimately, the environmental and social costs of the 'game' can have a profoundly negative impact on all of us.

This is of course a profoundly challenging conclusion for a growth-based economic paradigm. And not surprisingly, it is particularly fiercely contested. Most of the arguments revolve around the third area of Easterlin's data: reported life-satisfaction across nations. Here his findings were more ambiguous. Some high income countries reported higher life satisfaction than some low income countries. But the differences were not absolutely clear-cut.

At the time he was carrying out his research, the evidence on life-satisfaction across poorer countries was much sparser than it is today. In fact, it would be fair to say that Easterlin's article was one of the factors that triggered a massive effort to capture better data across more nations. Occasionally, this effort betrays a kind of urgency to demonstrate that economic growth is a legitimate means to a better life. But the results have certainly been interesting.[31]

The broad consensus emerging from the data is that rich economies do, on the whole, report significantly higher levels of happiness and life-satisfaction than poor economies. But the absolute gains in life-satisfaction associated with an increase in income are much smaller for richer economies than they are for poorer ones. As Figure 3.2 suggests, we seem to be right back to the idea of diminishing marginal utility.[32]

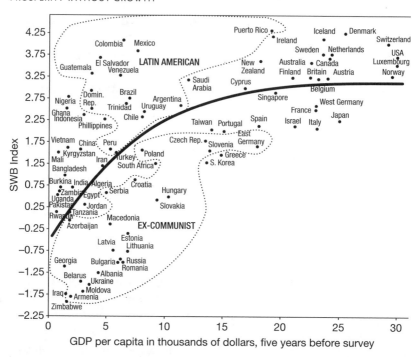

Figure 3.2 Subjective wellbeing (SWB) and income per capita
Source: Inglehart et al. (2008) (see note 33)

To get the measure of subjective wellbeing (SWB) plotted in Figure 3.2, political scientist Ronald Inglehart and his colleagues used two similar measures – one that asked people about their happiness and one that asked them how satisfied they were with their lives – taken from five successive waves of the World Values Survey, between 1981 and 2007.[33]

By using survey results over such a long period of time, Inglehart and his co-authors were able to retest the Easterlin paradox. Did subjective wellbeing move within individual nations over time or not? Inglehart found that for approximately three-quarters of the nations in the survey it did. But for the richest economies the changes were only observed in the happiness component of the measure and not reflected in the life-satisfaction measure.

This rather odd finding led him to hypothesise two separate mechanisms through which economic growth leads to higher subjective wellbeing. In the poorest countries, higher income led directly to increased wellbeing through improvements in the material standard of living, better reflected in the life-satisfaction measure. But in the rich nations, the impacts of growth are indirect and improved wellbeing depends on cultural changes and the expansion of people's sense of freedom, better reflected in the happiness measure.

Using a sophisticated causal 'path analysis', Inglehart managed to show that economic development had no statistically significant direct link to improved wellbeing at all. Its link was at best indirect. It turns out that economic development is one of several factors involved in increasing people's sense of freedom, and this in its turn is highly correlated with wellbeing.

But there are also other, more important, influences on people's sense of freedom. Slightly more important than economic development, statistically speaking, is the level of democratisation in a nation. More important than either is the degree of social tolerance in a particular society. It is the increased sense of freedom that contributes most directly to increased happiness.[34]

Not surprisingly, these findings too have been disputed. Easterlin has claimed that Inglehart's methodology is flawed, while others have claimed that Easterlin's logic is flawed. And so the happiness wars go on.[35]

But there are vital lessons to be learned from them. The first is, quite simply, how much is at stake here. If economic growth doesn't actually 'improve the human lot', then its potentially damaging impacts on the planet become not just unfortunate but tragic. Accepting such a conclusion is deeply unsettling (if not impossible) for a profession which has built its entire intellectual framework around the idea that economic growth makes us better off.

What emerges slowly from the complex data is that throwing away that edifice altogether is not entirely justified either. There are still huge gains to be made by bringing people out of poverty. In Figure 3.2, for instance, SWB rises steeply for countries whose income is below about $15,000 per capita. A small increase in GDP leads to a big rise in wellbeing. It is mainly in the richer economies where the differential gains are small.

This finding underlines one of the key messages of this book. There is a very strong case for the developed nations to 'make room for growth' in poorer countries. It is in these poorer countries that higher incomes really make a difference. In richer countries the returns on additional growth appear to be much more limited.

Another important lesson is that our sense of wellbeing depends intrinsically on what kind of society we live in, and in what happens within that society. Life-satisfaction is higher in more tolerant societies. It can fall dramatically when meaning and identity are threatened. These are important findings and we'll come back to them later in the book.

In the meantime, there are some tougher questions to be asked about the measurement process itself. Happiness-based measures of utility and expenditure-based measures of utility seem to behave in very different ways. And since they both claim to measure utility we can conclude that there is a problem somewhere. One or other – perhaps both – of these measures appears not to be doing its job properly.[36]

The wellbeing protagonists claim it's the GDP that's failing. But the self-report measures also have their critics. One of the most worrying criticisms is that people are known to be inconsistent in assessments of their own happiness.

Nobel Prize-winner Daniel Kahneman has shown that if you 'add up' people's assessment of momentary pleasures, you don't get the same answer as you do when you ask them about their happiness 'taking all things together'. Many people will say that their children are one of their most important sources of happiness. But when you look at people's time-use records, you find that those with children spend far more time engaged in activities which they don't actually find pleasurable.[37]

Some psychologists have suggested that this inconsistency arises because pleasure is, in fact, only one of several components of happiness or life-satisfaction. People also feel happiness from being deeply engaged in something. And they only feel fulfilled when their lives have a sense of meaning.[38]

When it comes to finding a reliable concept of prosperity, we appear to be no further forward. Arguably, there are as many reasons for not equating prosperity with reported life-satisfaction or happiness as there are for not equating it with exchange values. For one thing, the overriding pursuit of immediate pleasure is a very good recipe for things not going well in the future. This point has been highlighted incisively by Avner Offer: 'True prosperity is a good balance between short term arousal and long-term security', he writes.[39]

Neither the GDP – which counts mainly present consumption – nor self-report measures, which count mainly present happiness – provide an accurate reflection of this balance. Just because humans suffer from myopic choice and find it hard to make a sacrifice now, even for the sake of something better later, doesn't justify taking a view of prosperity based on more or less instantaneous gratification.

More fundamentally, to equate prosperity with happiness goes against our experience of what it means to live well. People can be unhappy for all sorts of reasons, some of them genetic, even when things do go well. Equally, they may be undernourished, poorly housed, with no prospect of improvement and yet declare themselves (some might say foolishly) completely content with their lot.

Bounded capabilities for flourishing

Sen uses these distinctions to argue (with a nod to Aristotle) for a third concept of the living standard based on the *capabilities* that people have to *flourish*. The key questions we should be asking, he insists, are to do with how well people are able to function in any given context.

'Are they well nourished? Are they free from avoidable morbidity? Do they live long?' he asks. 'Can they take part in the life of the community? Can they appear in public without shame and without feeling disgraced? Can they find worthwhile jobs? Can they keep themselves warm? Can they use their school education? Can they visit friends and relations if they choose?'[40]

There is a clear resonance between Sen's questions and Townsend's dimensions of poverty. In fact, the aspects of life that Sen cites in this extract – nutritional health, life expectancy, participation in society

– coincide closely with the constituents of prosperity identified from time immemorial in a wide range of writings.

In his later work, Sen stresses not so much the functions themselves – whether people actually live long, have a worthwhile job or participate in the community – as the capabilities or freedoms they have to do so. His point is that, in a liberal society, people should have the right to choose whether or not to participate in society, to work in paid employment, and perhaps even whether to live a healthy life. It is the *capability* to flourish that constitutes progress.[41]

Nonetheless, there are some clear reasons to retain the central importance of the functions themselves. In the first place, abstract capabilities are pretty uninformative. Any attempt to operationalise this idea of development ends up needing to specify what the important functions are.

This point is emphasised in an interesting report to the Netherlands Environmental Assessment Agency on the feasibility of Sen's approach within public policy. Even when it is the freedom to function that people value most, argues the report, this is largely because the functions themselves are valued too. The measures that it proposes are related to outcomes rather than to freedoms.[42]

But there are other reasons not to take the focus on freedom too far. In a world in which there are any kind of limits, certain kinds of freedoms are either impossible or immoral. The freedom to kill indiscriminately is clearly one of them.

The freedom to achieve social recognition at the expense of child labour in the supply chain, or to find meaningful work at the expense of a collapse in biodiversity, or to participate in the life of the community at the expense of future generations, may well be others. The freedom endlessly to accumulate material goods may simply be inaccessible to a world approaching 10 billion people.

This is the most important lesson that sustainability brings to any attempt to conceptualise prosperity. Capabilities for flourishing are a good starting point from which to define what it means to prosper. But this vision needs to be interpreted carefully: not as a set of disembodied freedoms, but as a range of 'bounded capabilities' to live well – within certain inevitable limits.

These limits are established in relation to two critical factors. The first is the finite nature of the ecological resources within which life on earth is possible: the regenerative capacity of our ecosystems, the available resources, the integrity of the atmosphere, the soils and the oceans.

None of these is infinite. Each stands in a complex relationship to the web of life on earth. We may not yet know exactly where all the limits lie. But we know enough to be absolutely sure that, in most cases, even the current level of economic activity is destroying ecological integrity and threatening ecosystem functioning – perhaps irreversibly. To ignore these natural bounds is to condemn our descendants – and our fellow creatures – to an impoverished planet.

The second limiting factor on our capability to live well is the scale of the global population. This is simple arithmetic. With a finite pie and any given level of technology, there is only so much in the way of resources and environmental space to go around. The bigger the global population, the faster we hit the ecological buffers. The smaller the population, the lower the pressure on ecological resources. This basic tenet of systems ecology is the reality of life for every other species on the planet. And for those in the poorest nations.

The point is that a fair and lasting prosperity cannot be isolated from these material conditions. Capabilities are bounded on the one hand by the scale of the global population and on the other by the finite ecology of the planet.

In the presence of these ecological limits, flourishing itself becomes contingent on the entitlements of those who share the planet with us, and on the freedoms of future generations and other species. Prosperity in this sense has both intra-generational and inter-generational dimensions. As the wisdom traditions suggest, there is an irredeemably moral dimension to the good life. A prosperous society can only be conceived as one in which people everywhere have the capability to flourish in certain basic ways.

Deciding on those basic 'entitlements' is not a trivial task. What does it mean for us to flourish? What are the functions that society should value and provide for? How much flourishing is sustainable in a finite world?

Sen has tended to stop short of clear prescriptions in this regard, even though some are implicit in his writing. The philosopher Martha Nussbaum has gone furthest in this direction. Her list of 'central human capabilities' bears some striking resemblances to things we have already discussed in this chapter. It includes the following:

- life (being able to live to the end of a human life of normal length);
- bodily health;
- bodily integrity (to be secure against violent assault; having opportunities for sexual satisfaction and choice in matters of reproduction);
- practical reason (being able to form a conception of the good life);
- affiliation (being able to live with and towards others);
- play; and
- control over one's environment.[43]

Ultimately, any such list needs to be negotiated in open dialogue before it can be taken as the basis of policy. But in practice, there is a surprisingly strong overlap between the components in such a list and the constituents of prosperity identified across numerous domains and by innumerable philosophers, writers and sages.

Physical and mental health matter. Educational and democratic entitlements count. Trust, security and a sense of community are vital to wellbeing. Relationships matter. Meaningful employment and the ability to participate in the life of society appear to be important almost everywhere. People suffer physically and mentally when these things are absent. Society itself is threatened when they decline.

The challenge is to create the conditions in which these basic entitlements are possible. This task is likely to require a closer attention to the social, psychological and material conditions of living – for example, to people's psychological wellbeing and to the resilience of communities – than is familiar in free-market societies.

Crucially, though, it doesn't mean settling for a vision of prosperity based on curtailment and sacrifice. Capabilities are inevitably bounded by material and social conditions. Some ways of functioning may even be foreclosed completely, particularly where they rely heavily on material throughput. But social and psychological wellbeing is not in any case best served by materialism, as we shall see more clearly later. At the end of the day, this new vision of prosperity may serve us better than the narrow materialistic one that has ensnared us.

The possibility that humans can flourish, achieve greater social cohesion, find higher levels of wellbeing and still reduce their material impact on the environment is an intriguing one. It would be foolish to think that it will be easy to achieve — for reasons discussed in more detail in the next chapter. But it should not be given up lightly. It may well offer the best prospect we have for a lasting prosperity.

4

THE DILEMMA OF GROWTH

The alternative to expansion is not, as some occasionally seem to suppose, an England of quiet market towns linked only by steam trains puffing slowly and peacefully through green meadows. The alternative is slums, dangerous roads, old factories, cramped schools, stunted lives.

Ted Heath, 1973[1]

Prosperity isn't just about income. Point made. And rising prosperity is not the same thing as economic growth. That's clear. We can redefine prosperity in coherent, meaningful ways: for instance, in terms of the capabilities that people have to flourish. As we've seen. And these broader conceptions are entirely consistent with our wider understandings of human wellbeing. But this doesn't in itself ensure that prosperity without growth is feasible.

It's good to have a clear philosophical vision. It's vital to have a sense of what we're aiming for, a direction for social progress. But we also need to articulate a path to take us there. And there's still a chance that the architecture of growth might play some role in that. Even though income is not the same as wellbeing, it is clearly in some sense functional in delivering at least some of the components of wellbeing. Economic growth may not be a useful end in itself. It might still be the means to that end.

Could it be that, without growth, our ability to flourish diminishes entirely? Evidence for this would certainly need to be taken seriously. The present chapter explores this question. It examines, in particular, three closely related propositions, each of which might offer a partial defence of economic growth.

The first is that material opulence – though not synonymous with prosperity – is a necessary condition for flourishing. The second is that economic growth is closely correlated with certain basic entitlements – health or education, perhaps – that are in themselves essential for prosperity. The third is that growth is functional in maintaining economic and social stability.

Any of these propositions, if supported, could threaten our prospects for achieving prosperity without growth and would place us instead between the horns of an extremely uncomfortable dilemma. On the one hand, continued growth looks ecologically unsustainable; on the other, it appears essential for lasting prosperity. Making progress against such an 'impossibility theorem' is vital.

Material abundance as a condition of flourishing

At first sight it might seem odd to reopen the relationship between material abundance (opulence) and prosperity. Chapter 3 disposed of any simple linear relationship between material consumption and flourishing. More isn't always better, even in something as basic as food.

Admittedly, our ability to flourish declines rapidly if we don't have the proper nutrition or adequate shelter. And this motivates a strong call to increase incomes in poorer nations. But in the advanced economies, despite some persistent inequalities, we are largely beyond that point. Material needs are broadly met and disposable incomes are increasingly dedicated to different ends: leisure, luxury, social interaction, experience.

Clearly, though, this hasn't diminished our appetite for material consumption. So why is it that commodities continue to be so important to us, long past the point at which material needs are met? Are we really natural-born shoppers? Have we been genetically programmed, as the psychologist William James believed, with an 'instinct for acquisition'? What is it about material goods that continues to entrance us even beyond the point of usefulness? And sometimes even beyond the point of good health.

As it turns out, modern neuroscience does provide some support for James' notion of instinctive acquisition. Our brains evolved in an ancestral environment of relative scarcity. Food was scarce, sex was rare, shelter was hard to come by. Our propensity to overconsume 'is a relic of a time when individual survival depended upon fierce competition for scarce resources', argues neuropsychologist Peter Whybrow.[2]

How did this affect us? A core element in our neural design is that a pulse of dopamine is delivered to key areas of the brain whenever we obtain what in any given moment we desire the most. 'We experience this pulse of chemicals as a pulse of satisfaction', explains neuroscientist Peter Sterling. 'The pulse soon fades, so to obtain another, we repeat the behaviour.'[3]

This relentless repetition is reinforced by a couple of additional design features in the human brain. One of these is the role of habit. Cognitive efficiency demands that our brains relegate as many decisions as possible to the realm of automaticity. It was vital for our evolution and it's critical to the efficiency of everyday life. But habituation makes conscious changes of behaviour notoriously difficult for us. So we sometimes end up totally unaware that we're responding to a dysfunctional (or out-of-date) satisfaction circuit.[4]

The second feature is adaptation. As we come to expect our reward, the satisfaction we receive diminishes, causing us either to accelerate our striving or diversify our desires. Paradoxically perhaps, one of the features of capitalism is the extent to which it has narrowed the scope of legitimate desire to material satisfactions. With the objects of desire so limited, argues Sterling, 'we consume them more intensely as the circuit adapts, and eventually they become addictions'.[5]

It's a perverse reflection on a society which claims to lionise 'free choice'. But the reality is strangely recognisable. Capitalism claims to offer us a diversity of desires. But this expansion of choice has one key characteristic: the objects of desire are primarily materialistic in nature. The freedom not to consume is sometimes harder to come by than the freedom to consume.

Moreover, one kind of freedom tends to obscure another. The freedom always to travel everywhere by car encroaches on the space for those who would rather walk or take the bus. The freedom to shop voraciously encroaches on the sociability of public space. The freedom to live a materialistic life undermines our freedom to empathise with and care for others. It's almost as though, in a capitalist society, the perfect adaptability of our brains to their ancestral environment has become a slave to the possibility of abundance.

And yet, there is clearly a puzzle here. If the analysis in Chapter 3 is correct, our desires were never entirely material in nature. Prosperity was always more than material satisfaction. So how is it that capitalism could have emerged so successfully, when it appears only to deliver to the material side of our desires?

The answer to this puzzle lies in another evolved characteristic of the human psyche: the tendency to imbue material things with social and psychological meanings. Again there are evolutionary, neuro-psychological explanations for this tendency. Amongst the most fascinating, perhaps, is the argument that symbolism evolved in response to our fear of death.

'We build character and culture', claimed the cultural anthropologist Ernest Becker, 'in order to shield ourselves from the devastating awareness of our underlying helplessness and the terror of our inevitable death.' In a fascinating exposition of Becker's ideas, psychologist Sheldon Solomon and his colleagues explore the evolution of language and symbolism as a part of the armoury of 'terror management'.[6]

I want to return to this theme a little later in the book, as it deserves a deeper exploration in our search for solutions. But whether this particular analysis is right or wrong, there is a wealth of evidence from anthropology which supports the basic point: stuff is not just stuff to us. Materials matter in non-material ways. Consumer goods provide a symbolic language in which we communicate continually with each other, not just about raw things, but about what really matters to us: family, friendship, sense of belonging, community, identity, social status, meaning and purpose in life.[7]

And crucially, these social conversations provide, in part, the means to participate in the life of society. Prosperity itself, in other words, depends on them. 'The reality of the social world', argues sociologist Peter Berger, 'hangs on the thin thread of conversation'.[8] And this conversation hangs in its turn on the language of material goods.

There's a lovely illustration of the power of this seductive relationship in a study led by consumer researcher Russ Belk. He and his colleagues explored the role of desire in consumer behaviour across three different cultures. Commenting on what fashion meant to them, one of Belk's respondents remarked: 'No one's gonna spot you across a crowded room and say "Wow! Nice personality!"'[9]

The object of this particular respondent's striving is immediately identifiable as a basic human desire to be noticed, to be included, to be liked, to find friendship – possibly more (as the singles ads put it). All of these things are fundamental components of participating in the life of society, of flourishing.

It's tempting to think that this is a predominantly Western (and relatively modern) phenomenon. Belk's study and numerous others suggest otherwise. The objective of the consumer, quite generally, according to anthropologist Mary Douglas, is 'to help create the social world and find a credible place in it'. The symbolic role of material commodities has been identified, by anthropologists, in every single society for which records exist.[10]

It is of course abundantly true in consumer society. But this is no longer unique to the West. 'One of the defining features of India's middle classes at the turn of the millennium', argues anthropologist Emma Mawdsley, 'is their appetite for "global" culture, and their pursuit of "western" lifestyles, possessions and values'. Very similar values and views are clearly discernible in China, in Asia, in Latin America and across vast swathes of Africa.[11]

The consumer society is now, to all intents and purposes, a global society. One in which, for sure, there are still 'islands of prosperity, oceans of poverty'. But in which the 'evocative power of things' increasingly creates the social world and provides the dominant arbiter of personal and societal progress.[12]

To some extent, this finding confounds the neat distinction between story and stuff that emerged in the previous chapter from the wisdom of

Solon. It turns out that the material and the non-material dimensions of prosperity are inextricably intertwined through the language of goods. Though it is essentially a social rather than a material task, our ability to participate in the life of society depends on this language.

And it's a language we learn at an early age. Anyone who has ever felt – or watched their kids feel – the enormous pressure of the peer group to conform to the latest fashion will understand how access to the life of society is mediated by sheer stuff. Prosperity depends more on opulence, it would seem, than is obvious at first glance.

But there are important nuances within this relationship. And these nuances offer a vital clue as to how we might confront – and get beyond – our dependency on material things. One of these is the importance of relative or positional effects. We saw in the previous chapter how the influence of income on subjective wellbeing is largely a positional one. What matters – more than the absolute level of income – is having more or less than those around us.

This is particularly true in highly unequal societies where income disparities signal significant differences in social status. Income levels speak directly of status; and sometimes of authority, power and class as well. But, in addition, as we now see, income provides access to the 'positional' or status goods that are so important in establishing our social standing.

And there is little doubt that at the individual level social position counts. 'A positive social ranking produces an inner glow that is also matched with a clear advantage in life expectation and health', argues Avner Offer.[13]

But if this process is, as the previous chapter suggested, little more than a zero sum game, then there is little to lose, and perhaps quite a lot to gain, by changing it. A different form of social organisation – a more equal society – in which social positioning is either less important or signalled differently – is a clear possibility.

This suggestion is borne out by the remarkable evidence marshalled by Richard Wilkinson and Kate Pickett in *The Spirit Level*. Looking at a range of health and social issues across OECD nations they conclude that the benefits of equality don't just accrue to the less fortunate members of society. Inequality has damaging impacts across the nation as a whole.[14]

Clearly, we would still need to confront the social logic that conspires to lock people into positional competition (Chapter 6). We would also have to identify less materialistic ways for people to participate in the life of society (Chapter 7). But in principle, these strategies could allow us to distinguish prosperity from opulence and reduce our dependency on material growth. In other words, this particular aspect of the dilemma of growth may just turn out to be avoidable.

But relative effects and symbolic goods don't entirely exhaust the relationship between income and human flourishing. Material conditions still matter. And income is vital to deliver them. What if rising levels of income are required in and of themselves to establish and maintain absolute levels of capability? This is where the second proposition comes in.

Income and basic entitlements

The possibility that certain basic entitlements – such as life expectancy, health and education – rely inherently on a rising GDP would cast a serious doubt on our ability to flourish without growth. There is, after all, very little doubt that huge health inequalities persist both within and across nations. 'Social justice is a matter of life and death', argued the Marmot review of health inequality in the UK. 'It affects the way people live, their consequent chances of illness and their risk of premature death.'[15]

The review found that even within a developed nation like the UK, poorer people have greater infant mortality rates, higher levels of obesity and lower life expectancy. One study for London revealed that life expectancy in Haringey (a poorer area) is 17 years shorter than it is in Chelsea (a richer one). People living in more deprived areas have worse levels of drug abuse, more alcohol-related hospital admissions and higher incidences of postnatal depression. Children brought up in those areas have lower educational attendance and fewer qualifications.[16]

Critically, the review rejected the idea that combatting health inequality was simply a question of restoring economic growth, pointing out that in fact the economic growth of the previous decades had done nothing to narrow health inequalities within the UK. Some of them had even widened. But to what extent is this also true across nations?

We can make some progress on this question by looking at the data: for example, by mapping per capita income across countries against certain key indicators of health. These correlations in themselves don't prove or disprove a causal link of course. But they provide a starting point in understanding the relationship between income and health.

Life expectancy is probably the first place to look. It would not be impossible to argue that a nation was prosperous if the average life expectancy were only 50 or 60 years and the quality of those years was demonstrably better than anything achievable in a longer lifetime. But typically in the twenty-first century, and particularly in more developed nations, a much longer lifespan is achievable and considered perfectly normal. Longevity is a fundamental indicator of prosperity.

Figure 4.1 shows the pattern of life expectancy against income (measured as per capita GDP) in more than 180 different nations. It's an interesting and instantly recognisable pattern. The difference between the poorest and the richest countries is again striking. Life expectancies are less than 50 years in parts of Africa and more than 80 years in many developed nations. And just as with life-satisfaction, the advantage of being richer as a nation appears to show diminishing returns in terms of longer lives, beyond a certain income level. In fact, the overall relationship between life expectancy and income across nations looks rather similar to the relationship between life-satisfaction and income.[17]

As for life-satisfaction, there is some positive correlation with income, even across the richest economies. Each doubling of income is associated with around 2.9 years of additional life expectancy. This would certainly suggest some continuing benefits for economic growth, even for the richest nations. But it's clear that the biggest gains come far faster for the poorest nations. If anything, the contrast between poor nations and rich nations is even more striking than it was for life satisfaction, with a steeper slope for poor countries and a flatter slope past the turning point for the rich countries.[18]

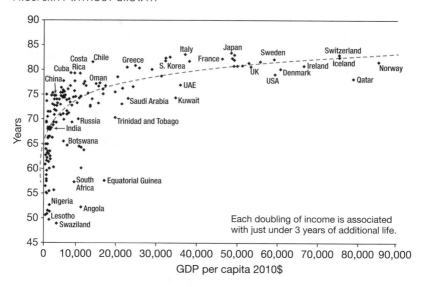

Figure 4.1 Life expectancy at birth and income per capita
Source: Data from Human Development Index (see note 17)

Statistical correlations hide considerable cultural differences, however. A closer inspection of the data reveals some real surprises. There is a kind of health 'sweet spot' on the upper left of the curve where high life expectancy is achieved at relatively low incomes. Life expectancy in Cuba, Costa Rica and Chile, for instance, is higher than life expectancy in the USA. Indeed, in Chile, which has an average per capita income of just $12,000 a year, life expectancy is higher than it is in Norway, which has an average per capita income seven times higher than its Latin American counterpart.

These anomalies underline the fact that culture and social organisation matter. There is no simple magic formula which translates high income into good health. Or low income into bad health. On the other hand, of course, persistent extreme poverty over long periods of time has a devastating effect on health.

This finding is certainly reinforced by the data on child mortality (Figure 4.2). One of the Millennium Development Goals (MDG) agreed in the year 2000 was to reduce under-5 mortality by two-thirds before 2015. Some remarkable progress was made. But the goal

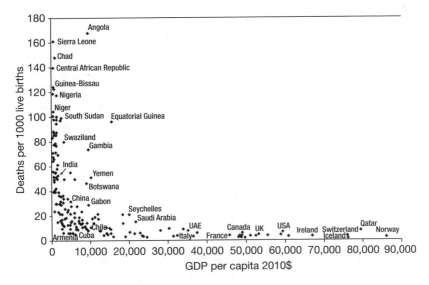

Figure 4.2 Under-5 mortality rate and income per capita
Source: Data from Human Development Index (see note 20)

was missed by quite a wide margin, largely because of the high child mortality rates in the poorest regions.[19]

Figure 4.2 tells a story of absolute health disaster in the poorest countries of the world. Particularly striking is the extremely steep decline in child mortality as per capita income rises from less than $1,000 to around $15,000, and the near flat trend in mortality rates for incomes between $15,000 and $84,000 per capita.[20]

The human story played out behind these statistics is shocking. While the rich get richer, the poorest countries languish in a poverty compounded by family tragedy. For the want of basic health care, almost six million children still die before their fifth birthday across the world. In sub-Saharan Africa the mortality rate is 9 per cent, 15 times higher than it is in developed nations. In some African nations, as Figure 4.2 shows, it is almost twice that level. Angola is a striking example, with an under-5 mortality rate of 167 deaths per 1,000 live births.

Equally striking is the speed with which the gains from growth diminish. Some rather poor countries achieve mortality rates that are as low or even lower than some very rich countries. The under–5 mortality rate in Armenia is lower than it is in the USA, even though Armenians enjoy an average income of barely £2,500 per capita; less than 5 per cent of the income enjoyed by Americans.

Similar lessons emerge from an analysis of the relationship between income and education. Figure 4.3 shows the mean years of schooling achieved across the world for different countries. We see the same disparity between the very poor and the very rich. We find the same familiar pattern of diminishing returns with respect to income. But even so, the impacts of growth don't entirely disappear. Each doubling of income leads to just over a year of additional schooling.[21]

Once again, it is possible to find low-income countries providing educational participation rates that are as high as the most developed nations. Interestingly, it's the East European nations which seem to occupy the educational 'sweet spot' on the upper left of the curve. Estonia, with an average income of just $15,000, scores higher on the index than Japan, Ireland or Norway, countries with income levels four and five times higher.

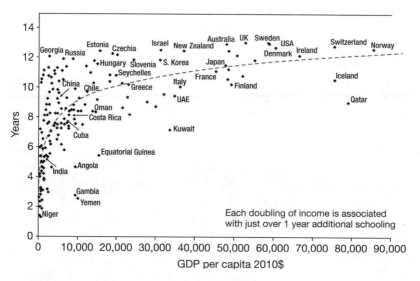

Figure 4.3 Mean years of schooling and income per capita

Source: Data on schooling from the Human Development Index (see note 21)

Understanding the complex relationships between income and human flourishing is a particularly important area for study. And much more exploration of these relationships is warranted. But nothing we have seen so far rules out the possibility that richer economies could achieve prosperity without growth. The same levels of access to good health or to education or even to happiness appear possible on much lower incomes that those associated with Western nations.[22]

These cultural achievements don't necessarily ensure that prosperity can be assured when income starts moving in the opposite direction. The conventional wisdom would certainly suggest exactly the opposite. It's pretty much taken for granted that when economies collapse, bad things happen. Even the hint of stagnation is seen as a recipe for disaster in the political mind. And it isn't just credit ratings and political credibility that suffer.

When people lose their jobs, and even worse their homes, or when they become overwhelmed with debt, all the evidence shows that they are more likely to turn to alcohol, or to junk food, or to drugs. Or to become mentally ill; or sometimes even to take their own lives: the suicide rate in Greece doubled in the aftermath of the financial crisis.[23]

Almost all the former Soviet bloc countries experienced reduced longevity in the immediate post-Soviet era. In Russia itself, life expectancy fell dramatically following the collapse of the Soviet Union, particularly amongst men. Between 1989 and 1994, the average life expectancy fell by almost five years. Perhaps most strikingly, after a brief resurgence, this decline continued, even after the economy had begun to recover. It was to be more than two decades before longevity reached the levels once enjoyed during the Soviet era – still a decade shorter than in Cuba (Figure 4.4).[24]

A similar story of decline in longevity in spite of economic recovery is visible in the case of South Africa. But the context and the contributing factors are rather different here. A striking feature of human development across Africa since 1990 is the collapse in life expectancy irrespective of growth rates. This is largely down to the devastating impact of Aids. Clearly growth is not enough, in itself, to guarantee improved prosperity, even in something as basic as life expectancy.

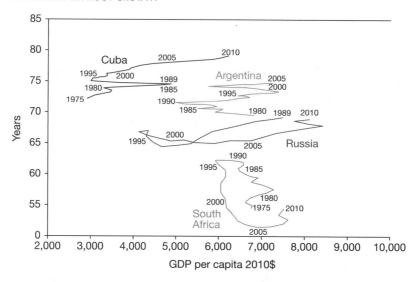

Figure 4.4 Life expectancy through times of economic crisis
Source: Data from the World Development Indicators Database (see note 24)

But Figure 4.4 also shows some rather different responses to adversity, which are equally striking. Following the breakup of the Soviet Union, the formal economy in Cuba more or less collapsed, partly because of the sudden removal of subsidised Soviet oil. GDP per capita fell by over 40 per cent in the space of a few years. Astonishingly, though, life expectancy in Cuba continued to improve at more or less the rate it had done prior to the collapse.

One recent study identified significant health improvements in Cuba in the aftermath of the collapse. Calorific intake was reduced by over a third. But obesity was halved and the percentage of physically active adults more than doubled. Between 1997 and 2002, 'there were declines in deaths attributed to diabetes (51%), coronary heart disease (35%) [and] stroke (20%)'.[25]

The ability to improve life expectancy in the face of a faltering economy is also evident in Latin America, where good health seems much less dependent on income growth. In Argentina, economic output was erratic to say the least over a quarter of century between 1980 and 2005, with two major and sustained economic contractions.

But the gains in life expectancy over the same period were substantial and consistent. In Iceland, perhaps surprisingly, both health and happiness improved in the wake of a banking crisis that hit the country even harder than most.[26]

Finally, the country with the highest life expectancy in the world is Japan (Figure 4.1), where for over two decades now income growth has been more or less stagnant. But during the two 'lost decades' (between 1990 and 2010), life expectancy in Japan grew faster than it had done at any point during the previous three decades.

It's easy to get mired in statistics and carried away by anecdotes. But there's an undeniable urgency to come to terms with some harsh realities. The swiftly diminishing returns on growth beyond a certain income; the huge advantages of income growth below that point; and the remarkable performance of some poorer countries who are able to enjoy levels of human wellbeing on a par with the richest nations on earth on a fraction of the income: all of these lessons are vital in our ability to understand the complex relationship between GDP growth and prosperity.

None of them so far rules out the possibility that good health outcomes, good education outcomes and high levels of human wellbeing could be achieved without relentless growth having to continue indefinitely even in the richest economies. On the contrary, the story is much more about the desperate need for decent incomes in the poorest countries, and the creativity of some development paths in delivering prosperity at surprisingly low income levels.

Income growth and economic stability

The example of Russia (and also of Greece) does, however, return us to the third proposition identified above: that growth is functional in maintaining economic and social stability. It is clear from the evidence in Russia that collapsing economies do present a risk of humanitarian loss. Economic stability or, at the very least, some form of social resilience, is important for prosperity.

There are interesting differences in how countries respond to economic hardship. Some countries – notably Cuba, Iceland, Japan,

Argentina – have been able to ride out quite severe economic turbulence and yet maintain or even enhance national health. Others have watched health deteriorate and life expectancy tumble in the face of economic recession.

Some of the explanation for these differences must lie in social structure. The transition of ex-Soviet states to a market economy was characterised by very profound changes in social structure, not the least of which was a collapse in state provision of health and social care. Little surprise, in these circumstances, that life expectancy faltered. In Cuba, by contrast, continuing State-led social provision was almost certainly a contributing factor in the health improvements that followed the economic collapse.

Humanitarian loss in the face of economic turbulence, in other words, may be more dependent on social structure and political response than on the degree of economic instability that is encountered. There are some interesting policy lessons here for the prospect of prosperity without growth, which we shall return to later in the book (Chapters 7 and 10).

But the risk of humanitarian collapse is enough to place something of a question mark over the possibility that we can simply halt economic growth. If halting growth leads to economic and social collapse, then times look hard indeed. If it can be achieved without collapse, prospects for maintaining prosperity are considerably better.

Critical here is the question of whether a growing economy is essential for economic stability. Is growth functional for stability? Do we need economic growth, after all, simply to keep the economy stable?

The conventional answer is certainly that we do. To see why, we need to explore a little further how such economies work. A detailed discussion of this is deferred to Chapter 6. But the broad idea is simple enough to convey.

Capitalist economies place a high emphasis on the efficiency with which inputs to production (labour, capital, resources) are utilised. Continuous improvements in technology mean that more output can be produced for any given input.[27] Efficiency improvement stimulates demand by driving down costs and contributes to a positive cycle of expansion. But crucially it also means that fewer people are needed to produce the same goods from one year to the next.

As long as 'aggregate demand' grows fast enough to offset this increase in 'labour productivity', there isn't a problem. But if it doesn't, then this dynamic means that less labour is needed and someone somewhere loses their job.[28]

If demand slows for any reason – whether through a decline in consumer confidence, through commodity price shocks or through a managed attempt to reduce consumption – then the systemic trend towards improved labour productivity leads to unemployment. This, in its turn, leads to diminished spending power, a loss of consumer confidence and further reduces demand for consumer goods.

From an environmental point of view this may be desirable because it leads to lower resource use and fewer polluting emissions. But it also means that retail falters and business revenues suffer. Incomes fall. Investment is cut back. Unemployment rises further and the economy begins to fall into a spiral of recession.

Recession has a critical impact on the public finances. Social costs rise with higher unemployment. But tax revenues decline as incomes fall and fewer goods are sold. Lowering spending risks real cuts to public services. Reduced social investment affects people's capabilities for flourishing – a direct hit on prosperity.

Governments must borrow more – not just to maintain public spending but to try and restimulate demand. But in doing so they tend to increase the national debt. Servicing this debt in a declining economy is problematic at best. Just maintaining interest payments takes up a larger proportion of the national income.

The best that can be hoped for here is that demand recovers and it's possible to begin paying off the debt. This could take decades. It took Britain almost half a century to pay off public debts accumulated through the Second World War. The Institute for Fiscal Studies has estimated that the 'debt overhang' from the 2008 financial crisis could last into the 2030s.[29] On the other hand, if the debt accumulates and the economy fails to recover, the country is doomed to bankruptcy.

Crucially, there is little resilience within this system. Once the economy starts to falter, feedback mechanisms that had once contributed to expansion begin to work in the opposite direction, pushing the economy further into recession.[30] With a growing (and ageing) population these dangers are exacerbated. Higher levels of growth are required to protect the same level of average income and to provide sufficient revenues for (increased) health and social costs.

In short, modern economies are driven towards economic growth. For, as long as the economy is growing, positive feedback mechanisms tend to push this system towards further growth. When consumption growth falters the system is driven towards a potentially damaging collapse with a knock-on impact on human flourishing. People's jobs and livelihoods are put at risk.

'I believe that the rising intolerance and incivility and the eroding generosity and openness that have marked important aspects of American society in the recent past have been, in significant part a consequence of the stagnation of American middle-class living standards during much of the last quarter of the twentieth century', writes the US political economist Benjamin Freedman in *The Moral Consequences of Economic Growth*.[31]

Ted Heath made a similar point, in the quotation at the top of this chapter. So did his successor as British Prime Minister, Margaret Thatcher, who in response to those questioning growth once famously declared: 'there is no alternative'.

If the end of growth were really to mean a complete loss of stability and the beginnings of instability, these arguments would certainly carry some weight. But is that really the case? Some, at least, of the examples we've looked at in this chapter seem to confound the received wisdom.

There is, of course, something of an irony here. Because at the end of the day the answer to the question of whether growth is functional for stability is this: in a growth-based economy, growth is functional for stability. The capitalist model appears to have no easy route towards a steady state position. Its natural dynamics seem to push it towards one of two states: expansion or collapse.

Later (Chapters 8 and 9) we explore the possibilities for amending this conclusion. In the meantime, we appear to have returned to the dilemma with which this chapter started. Or at least to a more precise incarnation of it. Put in its simplest form the 'dilemma of growth' consists in two diametrically opposed propositions.

- Growth is unsustainable – at least in its current form. Burgeoning resource consumption and rising environmental costs are compounding profound disparities in social wellbeing.
- 'De-growth' is unstable – at least under present conditions. Declining consumer demand leads to rising unemployment, falling competitiveness and a spiral of recession.[32]

This dilemma looks at first like an impossibility theorem for a lasting prosperity. But it cannot be avoided and has to be taken seriously. The failure to do so is the single biggest threat to sustainability that we face.

5
THE MYTH OF DECOUPLING

The belief that economic growth can be detached from destruction appears to be based on a simple accounting mistake.

George Monbiot, 2015[1]

The conventional response to the dilemma of growth is to appeal to the concept of 'decoupling'. More efficient production processes. More sustainable goods and services. More profit with less stuff. Smart growth; green growth; sustainable growth: this is the promise of decoupling.

It's vital to distinguish between *relative* and *absolute* decoupling. The former refers to any decline in the material intensity (or the emission intensity) of economic output. It signals an improvement in the efficiency of the economy, but it doesn't necessarily mean we're using fewer materials (or emitting fewer pollutants) overall. Absolute decoupling refers to the situation when resource use (or emissions) decline in absolute terms, even as economic output continues to rise.

Needless to say, in most cases, it is an overall decline that we need, if we are to meet ecological limits, avoid resource scarcity and escape from the dilemma of growth.

In the case of climate change for instance, achieving the 1.5°C goal agreed in Paris would require net carbon dioxide emissions from the burning of fossil fuels and from industry to have fallen from their current level – around 36 billion tonnes of carbon dioxide (Gt CO_2) – to very close to zero, before the middle of this century. For this to happen while the economy continues to grow at anything like historical rates implies relative (and absolute) decoupling on a massive scale.[2]

Most economists simply appeal to technology to achieve such a feat. Even quite sophisticated economists have a faith in decoupling that borders on the religious. Paul Krugman, for example, points (rightly) to the fact that physical scientists sometimes misunderstand what economic growth actually is. 'They think of it as a crude, physical thing, a matter simply of producing more stuff', he writes in the *New York Times*. 'And don't take into account the many choices – about what to consume, about which technologies to use – that go into producing a dollar's worth of GDP.'[3]

Yet his conviction that these 'many choices' will allow for even the most stringent ecological goals to be achieved without ever compromising economic growth leads him to denounce growth sceptics as 'prophets of despair'. 'The idea that economic growth and climate action are incompatible may sound hard-headed and realistic', he declares. 'But it's actually a fuzzy-minded misconception.' Very similar claims are made by the many advocates of green growth or smart growth.[4]

George Monbiot, on the other hand, is equally vehement that growth is incompatible with absolute decoupling. 'Consume more [or] conserve more', he writes in the article cited at the top of this chapter. 'Sorry, but we just can't do both.'[5] Is Monbiot a fuzzy-headed prophet of despair or is Krugman a technologically naïve, growth-zealot? On the surface, at least, it would seem obvious that their diverse positions cannot simultaneously be right.

Strangely, the answer is not so simple. Both positions have elements of truth in them. One of the problems lies in how we ask the question.

Are there 'many choices' about the products and services that together contribute to economic output, as Krugman suggests? The answer is clearly yes. Does the evidence suggest that some of these choices are substantially less carbon intensive than others? Again, the answer is unequivocally positive.

How far have these technological possibilities actually taken us in support of either relative or (more importantly) absolute decoupling at a global scale? This is a question we can explore directly by looking at the historical evidence. Part of the aim of this chapter is to do exactly this. The answer, as we shall see, is more on the Monbiot than the Krugman side of the fence. It certainly doesn't suggest much support for untamed optimism.[6]

But this answer doesn't exhaust our concerns. The question is not whether some efficiency measures are possible. (They clearly are.) Nor whether, in the past, we have managed to harness these efficiencies to eliminate threats from environmental change or resource scarcity. (We clearly haven't.) The question is whether we can achieve enough efficiency gains in the future to continue to pursue economic growth, indefinitely, while still remaining within the 'safe operating space' of a finite planet.

This question depends on so many imponderables that it is difficult, at first, to get a clear handle on it. Easy answers betray a slippery logic. Firm conclusions dissolve into a fog of counterfactuals. But we can reduce some of this confusion by appealing to arithmetic. If the rate of increase in efficiency is greater than the rate of economic growth, then typically speaking the overall material throughput will decline. If not, then it won't.

If the carbon efficiency of the economy increases at 2 per cent per year and economic output rises at 3 per cent per year, then the overall level of carbon emissions will rise. We will have relative but not absolute decoupling. If the carbon efficiency rises at 3 per cent per year and the economy grows at 2 per cent per year, then the overall level of carbon emissions will decline and we'll have achieved absolute decoupling.

Such an outcome still won't necessarily be enough to meet a given target, such as the 1.5°C climate goal. But for any such goal, and for any given rate of economic growth, we can at least identify the average rate at which technological efficiency must improve if we are to meet the target. Figuring this out will give us a more realistic idea of the challenge ahead.

As the title of this chapter suggests, the evidence that decoupling offers a coherent escape from the dilemma of growth is, ultimately, far from convincing. The speed at which resource and emission efficiencies have to improve if we are to meet carbon targets are at best heroic, if the economy is growing relentlessly. And, as we shall see in more detail below, they're far beyond anything we've achieved historically.

This is not to suggest that decoupling itself is either unnecessary or impossible. On the contrary it's vital – with or without growth. But it does suggest considerable caution in accepting the 'myth' that economic growth will, if left to proceed along anything like its usual course, lead to higher efficiencies and lower emissions. A much more nuanced approach to decoupling is needed. The aim of this chapter is to respond to that need.

Relative decoupling in historical perspective

Put very simply, relative decoupling is about doing more with less: more economic activity with less environmental damage; more goods and services with fewer resource inputs and fewer emissions. At heart, it's about doing things more efficiently. And since efficiency is one of the things that modern economies are supposed to be good at, decoupling has a familiar logic and a clear appeal as a solution to the dilemma of growth.

Resource inputs represent a cost to producers. So the profit motive should stimulate a continuing search for efficiency improvement in industry to reduce input costs. This seems clear enough at the level of the individual enterprise, particularly in a capitalist economy. But from a global perspective the critical question is whether or not this profit motive translates into an overall decline in resource intensity.

There is some evidence that it might do. The amount of primary energy needed to produce each unit of the world's economic output has fallen more or less continuously over most of the last half-century.

The global 'energy intensity' is now almost 25 per cent lower than it was in 1980. In other words, global energy efficiency has increased on average by around a third.[7]

These gains have not been uniform across different countries and regions. High income nations have significantly improved their energy efficiency since the oil price shocks of the 1970s. The energy intensity of the US economy is about half what it was in 1980, signalling that the energy efficiency of the economy has pretty much doubled. From a much higher base, China has also made some dramatic reductions in energy intensity. The energy efficiency of the Chinese economy has more than tripled in the same period.[8]

Outside these examples, the pattern is much less clear. Energy intensity has actually increased in some places in recent decades, even in certain European countries (Greece, Turkey, Portugal). And in emerging economies and developing nations, achievements have been very mixed. In Brazil, the energy intensity of the economy increased by almost a third, signalling a significant decline in the efficiency of the Brazilian economy with respect to primary energy supplies. Across the Middle East, energy intensity more than doubled between 1980 and 2011.[9]

Not surprisingly, though, where improved energy efficiency does happen, it tends to lead to declining emission intensities. For example, the carbon dioxide intensity of the global economy (Figure 5.1) fell from about 760 grams of carbon dioxide per dollar ($gCO_2/\$$) in 1965 to just under 500 $gCO_2/\$$ in 2015. This represents a decline of almost 35 per cent in half a century, a fall in carbon intensity of a little under 1 per cent, year on year.[10]

Worryingly, over the last decade, the fall in the global carbon intensity has been much less marked, as more of the world's growth has shifted to countries with higher carbon intensities. In fact, the rate at which the carbon efficiency of the economy is improving has itself fallen consistently over each of the last four decades. Between 2004 and 2015, the decline in global carbon intensity was less than 0.2 per cent per year. Clearly, there is little room for complacency here.[11]

To make matters worse, relative decoupling is barely half the story. It measures only the resource use (or emissions) per unit of economic output. For relative decoupling to offer any way at all out

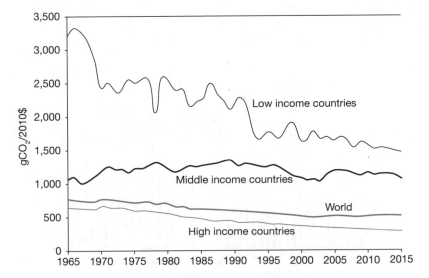

Figure 5.1 Annual carbon dioxide emission intensities, 1965–2015
Source: Data from the World DataBank (see note 10 and Jackson 2016)

of the dilemma of growth, the resource intensity of the economy must decline at least as fast as economic output rises. And efficiency must continue to improve as the economy grows, if overall burdens aren't to increase. Ultimately, we need to demonstrate not relative but absolute decoupling of resource use from economic growth. Historical evidence of this is much harder to find.

Absolute decoupling in historical perspective

Carbon dioxide emissions are a case in point. Compare Figure 5.1, which illustrates progress in relative decoupling, with Figure 5.2, which shows the absolute level of carbon dioxide emissions across the world. The declining trends in the earlier figure are translated into clearly rising trends in the later one. The fall in carbon intensity has simply been swamped by rising economic output. Absolute decoupling is nowhere to be seen.

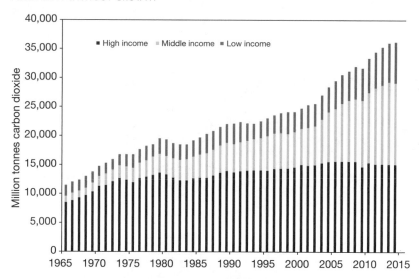

Figure 5.2 Annual carbon dioxide emissions by world region, 1965–2015
Source: Data from the World DataBank (see note 10 and Jackson 2016)

Annual carbon dioxide emissions from the burning of fossil fuels (and from industry) have more than tripled since 1965. Over 60 per cent more carbon dioxide is going into the atmosphere today than was the case in 1990 – the year adopted by the Kyoto Protocol as its base year, the year against which policy makers hoped to measure a decline. Even within the last decade, emissions have been growing at more than 2 per cent per year on average.[12]

There are some suggestions of limited progress. In the years since the financial crisis, the rate of growth in carbon dioxide emissions has slowed down significantly. Most of this is due to falling economic growth rates. But some of it has been due to a continued decline in the carbon intensity of output. Across the high income countries, this has even led to a very slight decline in the absolute level of emissions for the first time in decades.[13]

Unfortunately, even this result cannot entirely be trusted. The problem is that carbon emissions are usually measured on a territorial basis. Emissions attributed to the United States (for example) are those from households and enterprises within the United States.

Emissions attributed to China are assumed to be from Chinese homes and factories.

But one of the features of the modern economy is its global interconnectedness. Many of the goods consumed in America and Europe are manufactured in China and other emerging economies. Many of the materials used to produce these manufactured goods are mined or extracted in even poorer countries.

As a result, a significant proportion of the energy that's needed to maintain consumer lifestyles in affluent nations never appears on the energy accounts of those countries at all. It appears instead on the accounts of poorer countries. A significant proportion of the carbon emissions for which rich consumers are ultimately responsible ends up being attributed to citizens in poorer countries. This is the 'accounting error' that George Monbiot was referring to in the article quoted at the top of this chapter.

The potential impact of this accounting error becomes clearer when we place the carbon emissions of high income countries side by side with carbon emissions from the rest of the world. Figure 5.3 illustrates that, even as emissions from rich countries began to stabilise in the early years of the twenty-first century, so emissions from the rest of the world began to accelerate, and these 'poor country emissions' had surpassed 'rich country emissions' by the time of the financial crisis.

Some of this steep increase is due to a massive growth in infrastructure investment in poorer countries. But some of it is associated with exports to richer countries. The reality is we can't quite unpack what's going on here, without slightly more sophisticated accounting models than have traditionally been used in policy.

Fortunately, in recent years, these sophisticated models have become more available. Instead of just measuring territorial emissions, newer 'footprint' accounts add up all the emissions attributable to the consumption of goods and services within a given country or region, even if the emissions themselves take place elsewhere in the world.[14]

These studies confirm that national emission accounts systematically fail to provide an accurate picture of carbon responsibilities. The carbon 'embedded' in imports just doesn't make it to the balance sheet. There are typically more carbon emissions associated with

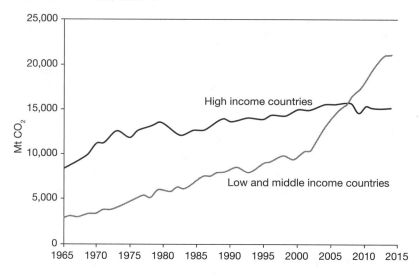

Figure 5.3 Carbon dioxide emissions in richer and poorer nations, 1965–2015
Source: Data from the World DataBank (see note 10 and Jackson 2016)

affluent lifestyles than ever appear in the numbers reported by the richer nations to the UN under the Framework Convention on Climate Change (FCCC).

This difference can sometimes be large enough to undermine the apparent progress towards climate change targets completely. A reduction in UK greenhouse gas emissions of almost 18 per cent between 1990 and 2007, as reported under UN FCCC guidelines, turned into a 9 per cent increase in emissions, when measured using a footprint methodology. The carbon footprint of the UK fell significantly through the financial crisis, but by 2012 it had begun to creep upwards again as the economy started to recover. Similar stories are to be found in other high-income countries.[15]

What's true for carbon is also true for material footprints. Apparent declines in resource consumption in advanced economies, as measured by their 'domestic material consumption', have tempted optimistic observers to speak of rich countries soon reaching a state of 'peak stuff', a maximum level of resource throughput soon to be followed by a convenient decline.[16]

According to the OECD, there was both relative and absolute decoupling of material consumption from GDP in its member countries between 1980 and 2008. Material intensity fell by 42 per cent and per capita consumption fell by 1.5 per cent over the same period. Some countries – notably the UK and Japan – have seen rather large absolute declines in domestic material consumption, suggesting that 'peak stuff' may already have arrived.[17]

But a couple of groundbreaking studies have cast serious doubt on this hypothesis. These studies pointed out that domestic material consumption omits any account of the raw material extraction associated with the import of finished and semi-finished goods, and in doing so underrepresents the material dependency of the economy.

The new studies use a methodology which adds up all the resource inputs attributable to the consumption patterns of an economy, in much the same way as the carbon footprint adds up all carbon emissions, wherever they may occur. The recent studies compared this 'material footprint' with the domestic material consumption measure over two decades for almost 200 nations.[18]

The results are striking. The studies confirm that there was some relative decoupling of domestic material consumption from GDP in many developed economies. But the 'material footprint' of the OECD nations as a whole still rose by almost 50 per cent between 1990 and 2008 (Figure 5.4). There was no absolute decoupling of GDP from resource use over this period.

Since the GDP of the OECD nations rose by only 53 per cent over the same period, there was barely any relative decoupling either. Once again, patterns of global trade and incomplete accounting practices had obscured an uncomfortable truth. The myth of 'peak stuff' has little basis in reality.[19]

Figure 5.4 shows a dip in both domestic material consumption and the material footprint towards the end of the period. This is an early indication of the impending financial crisis. During 2007 and 2008, material commodity prices were rising fast (Figure 1.1) and it's interesting to speculate on the extent to which these price rises caused the decline in material footprint and perhaps even precipitated the subsequent recession (see Chapter 2).

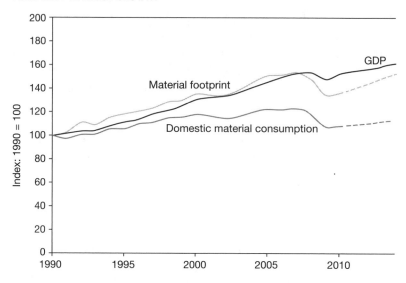

Figure 5.4 The material footprint of OECD nations, 1990–2014
Source: Data from WorldData and UNEPlive (see note 19)

But there should be no doubt here: this dip is not in any sense a decoupling of material throughput from the GDP. On the contrary, it shows that material consumption and economic output are still very strongly coupled. Material indicators decline as GDP declines and rise when it does. That is the nature of coupled systems. By 2010, both material indicators are once again rising.

Ultimately, at the global level, what counts of course is the rate at which resources are extracted from the ground. So the final arbiter on material decoupling – and the possibilities for escaping the dilemma of growth – are worldwide trends on primary resource extraction. Here there is little disagreement. Global resource extraction continues to rise for many key resources (Figure 5.5).[20]

Particularly notable is the increased consumption of structural materials. Production of iron ore, bauxite, copper and cement have all risen faster than world GDP in the last two decades. Production of iron ore and cement have more than tripled.

Reasons for this are not particularly hard to find. China's hunger for iron ore is well documented. As the emerging economies build

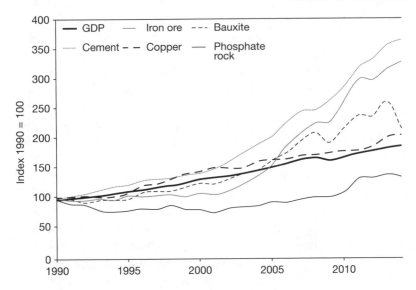

Figure 5.5 Global trends in resource production, 1990–2014
Source: Data from US Geological Survey and World Bank (see note 20)

up their infrastructures, the rising demand for structural materials is one of the factors that put an upward pressure on commodity prices in the pre-crisis years.[21]

Once again, what's striking about Figure 5.5 is not just the absence of absolute decoupling, but the scarcity of any evidence of relative decoupling either. Global resource intensities have increased significantly across a range of key materials. Resource efficiency is going in the wrong direction. Even relative decoupling just isn't happening.

Too often, the mainstream position gets lost in general declarations of principle: growing economies tend to become more resource-efficient; efficiency allows us to decouple emissions from growth; so the best way to achieve targets is to keep growing the economy. This argument is not at all uncommon in the tangled debates about environmental quality and economic growth.[22]

It contains some partial truths – for example, that efficiency improvements have occurred, particularly in advanced economies (Figure 5.1). It also draws support from some limited evidence on air pollutants such as sulphur dioxide. These emissions sometimes show an inverted-U-shaped relationship with economic growth: emissions grow in the early stage of growth but then peak and decline.[23]

But on closer inspection it turns out that this relationship mainly holds for local, visible environmental effects such as smoke, river water quality and acid pollutants. It isn't uniformly true even for these pollutants. And it simply doesn't exist at all for key indicators of environmental quality such as carbon emissions, resource extraction, municipal waste generation and species loss.[24]

It's clear that history provides little support for the plausibility of decoupling as a sufficient solution to the dilemma of growth. But neither does it rule out the possibility entirely.

A massive technological shift; a significant policy effort; wholesale changes in patterns of consumer demand; a huge international drive for technology transfer to bring about substantial reductions in resource intensity right across the world: these are the least that will be needed to have a chance of remaining within ecological limits.

The message here is not that decoupling is unnecessary. On the contrary, it's essential. The question is, how much is achievable? How much decoupling is technologically and economically viable? With the right political will, could relative decoupling really proceed fast enough to achieve real reductions in emissions and throughput, and allow for continued economic growth?

The arithmetic of growth[25]

Arithmetic is key here. A simple mathematical identity governs the relationship between relative and absolute decoupling. It was put forward almost 40 years ago by Paul Ehrlich and John Holdren.

The so-called IPAT equation tells us quite simply that the impact of human activity is the product of three factors: the size of the population; its level of affluence expressed as income per person; and a technology intensity factor, which measures the impact associated with each dollar we spend.[26]

This equation provides a convenient 'rule of thumb' to figure out when relative decoupling will lead to absolute decoupling. The rate of growth of overall impact (carbon emissions, say) is approximately equal to the sum of the growth rates of population, per capita income and carbon intensity.

If the carbon intensity declines faster than the sum of the growth rates of population and income, then relative decoupling will lead to absolute decoupling. If it declines more slowly, we'll still have relative decoupling, but not absolute. At the global level, emissions will continue to rise.[27]

For as long as the intensity factor is declining, then we are safe in the knowledge that we have relative decoupling. But for absolute decoupling we need overall impact to go down as well. And that can only happen if the intensity goes down fast enough to outrun the pace at which population and income per capita go up.

A simple example illustrates this. Carbon intensities have declined on average by 0.6 per cent per year since 1990. That's good; but not good enough. Global population has increased at a rate of 1.3 per cent. And average per capita income has increased by 1.3 per cent each year (in real terms) over the same period. So the rate of growth of carbon emissions is approximately $1.3 + 1.3 - 0.6 = 2$ per cent per year, leading over time to a 62 per cent increase in emissions, which is exactly what is reflected in the data.[28]

The same identity allows us a quick check on the feasibility of decoupling carbon dioxide emissions from growth in the future. Suppose for the sake of argument that we wanted to get global emissions down to a tenth of their current level by the middle of this century. This would be equivalent to reducing annual emissions at an average rate of just over 6 per cent per year by 2050.[29]

According to the UN's median estimate, the world's population will reach 9.7 billion people by 2050 – an average growth of 0.8 per cent each year. So if global per capita income were to grow and global carbon intensity were to decline at the rates they have done since 1990 (around 1.3 per cent and –0.6 per cent respectively), then carbon emissions would end up growing at around 1.5 per cent a year. To get global emissions to fall to a tenth of its current level, the emission intensity would need to decline at an average rate of just over 8 per cent year on year.[30]

Though useful to get a sense of the orders of magnitude, this global approach fails to pick up some of the complexities associated with different stages of global development. In middle income countries, for instance, income is growing faster than in the other regions. In low income countries population is growing faster than elsewhere. In both regions, the carbon intensity of output is typically higher and has historically fallen more slowly. Such differences can have a big impact on the global picture.

In fact, a regionalised approach reveals a somewhat harder task. Using the UN's population estimates and assuming that regional incomes grow and regional carbon intensities decline at rates typical of the last quarter of a century, it turns out that emissions would increase by more than 2 per cent each year. By 2050, carbon dioxide emissions would be well over double what they were in 2015.[31]

Achieving a ten-fold reduction in carbon emissions, on the other hand, would require the average carbon content of economic output to be less than 20 gCO_2/\$ in 2050, a 26-fold improvement on the current global average (Figure 5.6, Scenario 1). This would mean reducing the global emission intensity on average by 8.6 per cent each year, almost 10 times as fast as it has actually declined over the last 50 years, and well over 50 times faster than it declined over the last decade.[32]

Challenging though this task already appears, there would still be serious doubts as to its potential to meet the 1.5°C target. What matters for climate change is the cumulative burden of carbon dioxide in the atmosphere. So everything depends on how quickly emissions can be brought down.

Assuming we started straight away and achieved a more or less linear reduction in emissions towards 3.6 $GtCO_2$ by 2050, the carbon budget associated with the target (Chapter 1) would be used up by 2025, and beyond that point we would need technologies and strategies that could take carbon out of the atmosphere faster than we added carbon to it, in order to have a decent chance of restricting global temperature rise to less than 1.5°C.

On a closer examination, the rate of 'negative emissions' required to stay within the carbon budget is daunting. Through the late 2020s and early 2030s we would need to be taking carbon out of the atmosphere at a rate of around 25 $GtCO_2$ a year. The potential to achieve this level of negative emissions on that timescale is highly speculative at the very least.[33]

One option would be to go for an even deeper reduction target. Let's suppose we went for 95 per cent reduction in carbon emissions rather than 90 per cent by 2050. This would mean getting the carbon intensity down to around 10 $gCO_2/\$$ (Figure 5.6, Scenario 2). Not surprisingly, the speed of technological change needed to achieve this is faster: around 10.4 per cent reduction in carbon intensity year on year.

A deeper cut definitely makes life easier in the long run, with a lower requirement for negative emissions in the second half of the century. But it doesn't do much to contain the need for negative emissions in the short term, which still peak at around 25 $GtCO_2$ in the late 2020s. A far better option, it turns out, would be to choose an earlier year for the target reduction.

Let's say we aimed to hit our reduction target in 2035 rather than in 2050. This would about halve the peak demand for negative emissions. But it would clearly also involve us in a frantic rush to introduce low carbon technologies at an even faster pace. In fact the carbon dioxide intensity of the economy would have to fall on average by almost 13 per cent each and every year to achieve 90 per cent reduction and over 15 per cent to achieve 95 per cent reduction in annual carbon emissions.

If that weren't already heroic enough, we should be under no illusions about the divided nature of the world described by this scenario. Business-as-usual economic growth has usually been taken to mean a steady 2 per cent growth in incomes in the most developed countries while the rest of the world does its best to catch up – China and India leaping ahead at 5–10 per cent per annum at least for a while, with Africa, South America and parts of Asia languishing in the doldrums for several decades to come.

But if we're really serious about fairness we should look at scenarios in which the poorer countries could match the income levels of the richer ones. If rich country incomes grow at 2 per cent each year, we need quite phenomenal growth rates in poorer countries – around 7.6 per cent each year in middle income countries and almost 12 per cent per year in low income countries – in order for incomes to converge.[34]

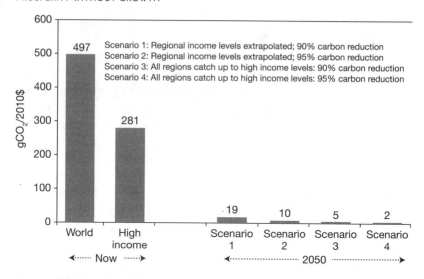

Figure 5.6 Carbon dioxide intensities: now and required to meet carbon targets
Source: Calculations carried out by the author (see also Jackson 2016)

Hugely ambitious, but this is what it would take for us to be living in a more equal world by 2050. These levels of growth would place an even greater demand on technological progress, if we were to have a decent chance of restricting global temperature rise to 1.5°C. Once again, arithmetic is key.

The global economy in this hypothetical world would be almost 11 times bigger in 2050 than it is today. And in this scenario, the carbon intensity would have to be less than 5 $gCO_2/\$$ to achieve the 90 per cent (Figure 5.6, Scenario 3). To reach 95 per cent reduction, the carbon content of each dollar of output would have to be around 2 $gCO_2/\$$ by 2050, more than 200 times lower than the average carbon intensity of the global economy today (Figure 5.6, Scenario 4).

Meeting these targets before 2035, instead of 2050, would mean reducing carbon intensity of the economy by anything up to 18 per cent year on year, at least one hundred times faster than we are doing at the moment.

Beyond 2050, with incomes still growing at 2 per cent a year, the challenge is only exacerbated. The economy in 2100 would have to be 30 times the size of today's economy. And to all intents and purposes, nothing less than a complete decarbonisation of every single dollar would do. Even before the middle of the century, we will need to be taking carbon out of the atmosphere. The long-run net carbon intensity of each dollar of economic output will have to be less than zero.

What kind of economy is that? What are its consumption activities? What are its investment activities? What does it run on? What keeps it going? How is economic value created by removing carbon from the atmosphere?

One thing is clear. This is a completely different kind of economy than the one we have at the moment, which drives itself forward by using up more and more materials and emitting more and more carbon into the atmosphere.

Stark choices

Playing with numbers may seem like dancing angels on the head of a pin. But simple arithmetic reveals stark choices. Are we really committed to eradicating poverty? Are we serious about reducing carbon emissions? Do we genuinely care about resource scarcity, deforestation, biodiversity loss? Or are we so blinded by economic growth that we daren't do the sums for fear of revealing the truth?

The Paris Agreement was an extraordinary moment of unprecedented commitment to combat climate change. But our current direction of travel is entirely wrong. Emissions and resource use are rising not falling. The pace of decoupling is painfully slow by comparison with what is needed. And it's become slower not faster over recent decades.

We can never entirely discount the possibility that some massive technological breakthrough is just round the corner. But it's clear that early progress towards carbon reduction will have to rely on options that are already on the table: enhanced energy efficiency, renewable energy and perhaps carbon capture and storage. A massive uplift in investment in these low carbon technologies is absolutely vital.

In fact, it is this need for what we might broadly call 'ecological investment' which begins to transform the economics of the twenty-first century. Protecting, maintaining and enhancing the ecological assets on which our economy and our own wellbeing both depend turns out to be vital to the economics of a finite world (Chapters 8 and 9).

There is no dispute at all that technological innovation is essential to change. And few would disagree that the technological opportunities are legion. We can look at Figure 5.6 as a stirring call to action rather than as a relentless impossibility theorem. Krugman's 'many choices' are a reality. The potential for change is massive.

But none of this will happen automatically. None of it flows easily from the logic of conventional economics. There is no simple formula that leads from the efficiency of the market to the meeting of ecological targets. Simplistic assumptions that capitalism's propensity for efficiency will allow us to stabilise the climate or protect against resource scarcity are nothing short of delusional.

The truth is that there is as yet no credible, socially just, ecologically sustainable scenario of continually growing incomes for upwards of nine billion people. And the critical question is not whether the complete decarbonisation of our energy systems or the dematerialisation of our consumption patterns is technically feasible, but whether it is possible in our kind of society.

The analysis in this chapter suggests that it is entirely fanciful to suppose that 'deep' emission and resource cuts can be achieved without confronting the structure of market economies. It is to this question that we now turn.

6

THE 'IRON CAGE' OF
CONSUMERISM

As every hunted animal knows, it is not how fast you run that counts, but whether you are slower than everyone else.

The Economist, November 2008[1]

A sense of anxiety pervades modern society. At times it tips over into visceral fear. The financial crisis of 2008 was such a time. Financial institutions became almost paralysed by fear. Banks refused to lend, even to each other; consumers stopped spending because of it. Governments displayed signs of being totally bewildered, both by the speed of change and by the implications of failure.

Fear may not be all bad. The threat of imminent collapse may have been the only force strong enough to bring so many countries together in late 2008, with a pledge to 'achieve needed reforms in the world's financial systems'. Decisiveness in the face of fear is what the G20 leaders called for during the early phase of financial recovery.

And yet the sense of a more fundamental, a more pervasive anxiety underlying the modern economy is an enduring one.[2] Could it really be the case, as *The Economist* suggests, that we are still behaving like hunted animals, even in the twenty-first century, driven by the fine distinction between predator and prey? If we are, it would be good to recognise it. And to understand why. For, without that understanding, solutions to the dilemmas we face will inevitably prove elusive.

Admittedly, the dilemma of growth isn't helping much, looking as it does like an impossibility theorem for lasting prosperity. Perhaps at some instinctive level, we have always understood this. Maybe we're haunted by subconscious fear that the 'good life' we aspire to is already deeply unfair and can't last forever. That realisation – even repressed – might easily be enough to taint casual joy with existential concern.

And of course the analysis in Chapter 5 doesn't allay those fears. It doesn't entirely close down the idea of decoupling as an escape from the dilemma of growth. But it certainly tempers blind optimism. Efficiency is a grand idea. And capitalism sometimes delivers it. But even as the engine of growth delivers productivity improvement, so it also drives forward the scale of throughput. Nowhere is there any evidence that efficiency can outrun – and continue to outrun – scale in the way it must do if growth is to be compatible with sustainability.

There is still a possibility that we just haven't tried hard enough. With a massive policy effort and huge technological advances, perhaps we could reduce resource intensities the two orders of magnitude or so necessary to allow growth to continue – at least for a while. And yet, the idea of running faster and faster to escape the damage we're already causing is itself a strategy that smacks of panic. So, before we settle for it, a little reflection may be in order.

Accordingly, this chapter confronts the structure of modern capitalist economies head on. In particular, it explores two interrelated features of economic life that are central to the growth dynamic. On the one hand, the profit motive stimulates newer, better or cheaper products and services through a continual process of innovation and 'creative destruction'. At the same time, the market for these goods relies on an expanding consumer demand, driven by a complex social logic.

These two factors combine to drive 'the engine of growth' on which modern economies depend and lock us in to an 'iron cage' of consumerism.[3] It's essential to get a better handle on this twin dynamic, not least so that we can identify the potential to escape from it. The starting point is to unravel some of the workings of modern capitalism.

Varieties of capitalism

Capitalism is an elusive concept. It isn't a simple, homogeneous entity. And it certainly thrives or survives in numerous varieties. The most widely used formulation defines capitalism in terms of the private ownership of the 'means of production'. Common definitions also stress the importance of a 'profit motive' as a defining motive within the economic system.[4]

What does this mean in practice? Broadly, it means that private individuals (capitalists) invest their money (their 'capital') in the factories, the farms, the mines, the supply chains and the distribution networks (also the 'capital') that allow society to produce goods and services. Typically, ownership is motivated by the desire to make a profit or to 'earn a return' on the money invested. Often, it is assumed that a part of this profit is then reinvested in further expansion.

One of the difficulties is that the term 'capital' itself evades a clear definition. In simple terms, capital simply means a stock of something. But in economics it is taken to refer both to money and monetary assets (financial capital) and also to the physical assets such as buildings, factories and production facilities (physical capital) that money can buy. It's this transformational quality that leads Marxian economists to define capital (and capitalism) not so much as a thing but as a set of processes of circulation and accumulation.[5]

These various definitions might seem a bit arbitrary. Strangely, though, they become quite important when it gets to deciding whether or not capitalism can do without growth. If we define capitalism in terms of a process of accumulation of capital, for instance, then it becomes pretty clear that doing without growth means doing without capitalism. And an anti-growth position would then have to be an anti-capitalist position as well.

But if we define capitalism in terms of the ownership of productive facilities, then everything depends on the behaviour of those who own this capital. The question of whether there's an inevitable link between ownership and expansion tends to get lost in the furious arguments that rage over the virtues and vices of capitalism – and those of its rival forms of organisation.

I want to come back to this question at the end of the book (Chapter 11), as it has some interesting repercussions for debates about prosperity and growth. But what's immediately clear from empirical experience is that the forms of ownership of capital can vary enormously from context to context.

In oligarchic capitalism, the means of production are owned by a few powerful firms or individuals. In shareholder capitalism, the ownership is spread much more widely across society. Today, for instance, anyone with a pension participates in the ownership of any number of companies. In most advanced economies, we are all to some extent capitalists.

The existence of something called 'state capitalism', in which companies are owned by the government but run for profit, is an indication of just how malleable the basic definition of capitalism can be. And even the most capitalistic states are prepared to take ownership in some sectors. The financial crisis has blurred this boundary even more, of course, with national governments taking substantial equity stakes in financial institutions.[6]

The organisational forms of capitalism also vary. Political economists Peter Hall and David Soskice distinguish between 'liberal market economies' and 'coordinated market economies'. The former place more faith in the power of liberalised, deregulated markets. The latter argue for stronger social institutions and more strategic relationships (rather than competition) between firms.[7]

In reality, almost every economy in the world is to some extent a 'mixed economy'. Some private ownership is combined with some state ownership or state guidance of the economy. And though much is made of the virtues of the 'free' or 'open' markets, very few markets are entirely free. Some are captured by monopoly interests. Others rely more on state regulation.

As Adam Smith himself understood very clearly, some state intervention is needed to prevent or break up monopoly power. In fact, the bigger corporations become, the greater this need for the state. The efficient, free market which Smith proposed relied inherently on the fact that enterprises were relatively small, open to competition and responsive both to supplier pressure and to consumer demand. But there is a risk that big firm capitalists in particular are an 'order of men, whose interest is never exactly the same with that of the public', argued Smith, 'Who have generally an interest to deceive and even oppress the public and who accordingly have, upon many occasions, both deceived and oppressed it'.[8]

It's continually surprising to find economists who still espouse a vision of capitalism that combines a high degree of market liberalism with a unhealthy dose of oligarchic 'big-firm' behaviour thrown in and argue vociferously against any role for the state. The rationale for this vision is often that it offers the best possibilities for unbounded long-term expansion. And recommendations abound as to how best to nurture and protect this rare and beautiful creature, so that we can get as much growth from it as possible.[9]

But this vision faces some rather severe criticisms, and the evidence of its own somewhat dubious success in practice. Besides, there are other much more humane, much more responsible and ultimately much richer visions of capitalism out there that offer considerable potential for a better economy and a more sustainable prosperity.[10]

We'll come back later to the question of whether any of these forms of capitalism are possible without growth. But for now it's sufficient to recognise, first, that capitalism exists in multiple varieties; and, second, that all of these varieties have some important structural components in common.

Structures of capitalism

At its heart, the mechanism of capital is strikingly simple. Firms employ labour (people) and capital (buildings and machinery) to produce the goods and services that households want and need. Households (people) offer up their labour and capital (savings) to firms in exchange for incomes. Revenue from the sale of goods and services is what allows firms to provide people with incomes. People spend some of this income on more consumer goods. But some of it they save. These savings are invested (directly or indirectly) back into firms. This, in a nutshell, is the 'circular flow' of the economy (Figure 6.1).[11]

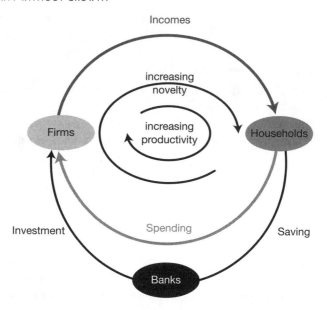

Figure 6.1 The 'engine of growth' in market economies
Source: Drawn by the author based on standard economic texts (see note 11)

Missing from this over-simplified picture of the economy are what's called the public sector (government) and the foreign sector (overseas firms, households and governments). The representation of the financial sector is also massively simplified.

This missing complexity is crucial. Partly because it introduces a whole new set of actors and a whole new set of possibilities: different ways of spending and producing, saving and investing. These possibilities offer some potential (as we shall see in Chapter 8) for reconfiguring the economy. But they also complicate the basic simplicity of Figure 6.1 enormously.

In one sense, the financial crisis emerged precisely out of the complexity generated by the evolution of a globalised financial sector. And as we saw in Chapter 2, that complexity was in part the result of trying to keep the system going. Global credit markets facilitate one of the most fundamental features of capitalism: the dual role of saving and investment.

The basic functioning of this feature is simple enough. Households give over part of their income to savings. These savings are invested – either directly or through an intermediary (for example, a bank, building society or investment house) in businesses to generate profits.

Profit is key to this system. Why would households give their savings to firms rather than simply hanging on to them or spending the money on consumer goods? Only because they expect to receive a healthy 'return' on their capital at some point in the future. This return is created out of the stream of profits from the firms they invest in.

Firms themselves seek profit for several reasons. In the first place, it provides them with working capital (cash) to invest in maintenance and improvements themselves. Second, it's needed to pay off the company's creditors – people who've lent the firm money in expectation of a return. Third, it's used to pay dividends to shareholders – people who've bought a share in the company.

A company that shows good returns attracts more investment. The value of the company will rise because people are prepared to pay more for shares in it. When share values are rising, more people will be keen to buy them. Creditors know they will get their money back with interest. Shareholders know that the value of their shares will rise. The company knows that it has sufficient resources to maintain its capital stock and invest in new processes and technologies.

This ability to reinvest is vital. At a basic level, it's needed to maintain quality. Without it, buildings and equipment inevitably get run down. Product quality is lost. Sales decline. The company loses its competitive position and risks going out of business.[12]

Investment is also needed continually to improve efficiency or productivity – in particular labour productivity. The role of efficiency in capitalism has already been noted (Chapter 5). The driver for efficiency is essentially the profit motive: the need to increase the difference between revenues from sales and the costs associated with the so-called factor inputs: capital, labour and material resources.

Cost minimisation becomes a core task for any firm. But it involves some inherent trade-offs. Amongst these is that capital investment is needed (in addition to its role in maintenance) to achieve cost reduction in the other two factors: labour and materials. Switching to more energy efficient appliances or less labour-intensive processes requires capital. And this continuing capital need both motivates the search for low-cost credit and highlights the dangers of credit drying up. It also explains why reducing capital costs indefinitely isn't an option.[13]

When it comes to choosing which of the other two factors to target, a lot depends on the relative price of labour and materials. In a growing economy with full employment, wages tend to rise in real terms. Until very recently at least (Figure 1.1), material costs have tended to fall in real terms. So in practice, companies have invested preferentially in technologies that reduce labour costs even if this increases material costs: an obvious counter to the trend of resource productivity discussed in Chapter 5.[14]

For a company, then, higher labour productivity lowers the cost of its products and services. Forgoing that possibility runs the risk that the company finds itself at a disadvantage compared with national and international competitors. In this case, it would sell fewer goods, report lower profits to its shareholders, and risk capital flight from the company.

At the national level, this dynamic plays out in several ways. Over the long run, productivity can lead to rising wages, low interest rates and higher standards of living. If workers produce more, then they can command higher wages without putting pressure on corporate profits or inflation. Central banks can thus keep interest rates lower than would otherwise be the case, feeding a virtuous cycle of consumer and business and consumer spending and low inflation. A country with rising labour productivity has improved chances in international markets.

This dynamic explains some of the recent concern over declining labour productivity growth across the world and in advanced economies in particular. Labour productivity across the OECD nations has declined more or less consistently over the last four decades, from around 4 or 5 per cent each year in the mid-1960s to less than 0.5 per cent in 2015 (see Figure 2.2).

For a while at least, the US had seemed to buck this declining trend. Labour productivity growth was rising in the last two decades of the twentieth century. But since the turn of the millennium the output per hour has declined in the US too. There's even evidence to suggest that the growth rate in the productivity of labour has peaked within developing and emerging economies. Globally, productivity growth seems to have been declining since the financial crisis.[15]

Understanding the dynamic between labour productivity, working hours and economic growth is important for all sorts of reasons. Not least is the insight it provides into the minds of economists. For instance, the disparity between productivity in the EU and the US prompted the authors of one recent study to describe the US as 'forging ahead' and to condemn the performance of certain EU countries as 'dismal' because of their low labour productivity.[16]

We'll have occasion later (Chapters 8 and 9) to question this judgement. But for now the key point is that the general trend (and indeed the desired direction of travel) in capitalist economies is still quite clearly towards increasing labour productivity. Since this means producing the same quantity of goods and services with fewer people, the cycle creates a downward pressure on employment that's only relieved if output increases.

Efficiency quite literally drives growth forwards. By reducing labour (and resource) inputs, efficiency brings down the cost of goods over time. This has the effect of stimulating demand and promoting growth. Far from acting to reduce the throughput of goods, technological progress serves to increase production output by reducing factor costs.[17]

The phenomenon of 'rebound' attests to this. Money saved through energy efficiency, for example, gets spent on other goods and services. These goods themselves have energy costs that offset the savings made through efficiency, and sometimes wipe them out entirely (a situation described as 'backfire'). Spending the savings from energy-efficient lighting (say) on a cheap short-haul flight (as one UK supermarket recently recommended) is one sure-fire recipe for achieving this.[18]

This somewhat counterintuitive dynamic helps explain why simplistic appeals to efficiency will never be sufficient to achieve the levels of decoupling required for sustainability. In short, *relative* decoupling sometimes has the perverse potential to *decrease* the chances of *absolute* decoupling.

But efficiency alone doesn't guarantee success in business, either. Making the same thing more and more efficiently doesn't work for a couple of reasons. The first is that there are physical limits to efficiency improvement in specific processes. At the basic level, these constraints are laid down by the laws of thermodynamics.[19]

The second is that failing to diversify and innovate risks losing out to competitors producing newer and more exciting products. The economist Joseph Schumpeter was the first to suggest that it is in fact novelty, the process of innovation, that is vital in driving economic growth. Capitalism proceeds, he said, through a process of 'creative destruction'. New technologies and products continually emerge and overthrow existing technologies and products. Ultimately, this means that even successful companies cannot survive simply through cost minimisation.[20]

The Venezuelan economist Carlota Perez describes how creative destruction has given rise to successive 'epochs of capitalism'. Each technological revolution 'brings with it, not only a full revamping of the productive structure, but eventually a transformation of the institutions of governance, of society, and even of ideology and culture'.[21]

In this climate, the ability to adapt and to innovate – to design, produce and market not just cheaper products but newer and more exciting ones – is vital. Firms who fail in this process risk their own survival. 'Competition among business firms evolved such that the principal weapon used to combat rivals became innovation', writes the US economist William Baumol. 'In such an environment, no firm dares to fall behind in the innovation race, in which the penalty for the laggards is often the death of the company.'[22]

Clearly, the economy as a whole doesn't care if individual companies go to the wall. Indeed that must inevitably be the destruction part of the process of creative destruction. It's a different matter, though, if the process of creative destruction stops, because without it economic expansion eventually stops as well.

The role of the entrepreneur – as visionary – is critical here. But so is the role of the investor. It is only through the continuing cycle of investment that creative destruction is possible. When credit dries up, so does innovation. And when innovation stalls, according to Schumpeter, so does the long-term potential for growth itself.

At this point, it's tempting to wonder what the connection is between this self-perpetuating but somewhat abstract vision of creative capitalism, and the needs and desires of ordinary human beings. The circular flow of production and consumption may once have been a useful way of organising human society to ensure that people's material needs are catered for. But what does this continual cycle of creative destruction have to do with human flourishing?

Does this self-perpetuating system really contribute to prosperity in any meaningful sense? Isn't there a point at which enough is enough and we should simply stop producing and consuming so much?

One of the things that prevents this happening, clearly, is the structural reliance of the system itself on continued growth. The imperative to sell more goods, to innovate continually, to stimulate higher and higher levels of consumer demand is driven forwards by the pursuit of growth. But this imperative is now so strong that it seems to undermine the interests of those it's supposed to serve.

The cycles of creative destruction become ever more frequent. Product lifetimes plummet as durability is designed out of consumer goods and obsolescence is designed in. Quality is sacrificed relentlessly to volume throughput. The throwaway society is not so much a consequence of consumer greed as a structural prerequisite for survival. Novelty has become a conscript to and an agent for economic expansion.

This doesn't mean that innovation is always destructive. Or that creativity is intrinsically bad. On the contrary, the creative spirit can and does enrich our lives. It's potential to do so is already demonstrated. Proponents point quite rightly to the human benefits that creative entrepreneurship can bring: advances in medical science, for example, which have contributed to increased longevity; or the sheer variety of experience which now contributes to the quality of modern life.[23]

But neither can we see novelty as entirely neutral in the structural dynamic played out through capitalism. In fact, there is something even more deep-rooted at play here, conspiring to lock us firmly into the cycle of growth. The continual production of novelty would be of little value to firms if there were no market for the consumption of novelty in households. Recognising the existence, and understanding the nature, of this demand is essential.

Social logic

It is perhaps not surprising to discover that the desire for novelty is linked intimately to the symbolic role that consumer goods play in our lives. We saw already (Chapter 4) that material artefacts constitute a powerful 'language of goods' that we use to communicate with each other – not just about status, but also about identity, social affiliation, and even – through giving and receiving gifts for example – about our feelings for each other, our hopes for our family, and our dreams of the good life.[24]

This is not to deny that material goods are essential for our basic material needs: food, shelter, protection. On the contrary, this role is critical to our physiological flourishing: health, life expectancy, vitality.

But stuff is not just stuff. Consumer artefacts play a role in our lives that goes way beyond their material functionality. Material processes and social needs are intimately linked together through commodities. Material things offer the ability to facilitate our participation in the life of society. And, in so far as they achieve this, they contribute to our prosperity (Chapter 3).

One of the vital psychological processes here is what consumer researcher Russ Belk called *cathexis*: a process of attachment that leads us to think of (and even feel) material possessions as part of the 'extended self'.[25] This process is evident everywhere. Our relationships to our homes, our cars, our bicycles, our favourite clothes, our books, our CD or DVD collection, our photographs all have this character of being or appearing to be a 'part of us'.

Our attachments to material things can sometimes be so strong that we even feel a sense of bereavement and loss when they are taken from us. 'Hollow hands clasp ludicrous possessions because they are links in the chain of life. Without them, we are truly lost', claimed the marketing guru Ernest Dichter in *The Science of Desire*.[26]

Some of these attachments are fleeting. They burn with novelty momentarily and are extinguished as suddenly when something else attracts our attention. Others last a lifetime. Possessions sometimes offer a sanctuary for our most treasured memories and feelings. They allow us to identify what is sacred in our lives and distinguish it from the mundane.

This kind of materialism, flawed though it may be, even offers some kind of substitute for religious consolation. In a secular world, having something to hope for is particularly important when things are going badly. Retail therapy works for a reason.[27]

Novelty plays an absolutely central role in all this. In the first place, of course, novelty has always carried information about social status. As Thorstein Veblen pointed out over a century ago, 'conspicuous consumption' proceeds through novelty. Many of the latest consumer appliances and fashions are accessible at first only to the rich. New products are inherently expensive, because they are produced on a small scale. They may even be launched at premium prices deliberately to attract those who can afford to pay for social distinction.[28]

After distinction comes emulation. Social comparison – keeping up with the Joneses – rapidly expands the demand for successful products and facilitates mass production, making once luxury goods accessible to the many. And the sheer wealth and enormous variety of material goods has a democratising element to it. It allows more and more people to go about inventing and reinventing their social identities in the search for a credible place in society.

Arguably it is precisely this cornucopia of material goods and its role in the continual reinvention of the self that distinguishes consumer society from its predecessors. Material artefacts were always capable of carrying symbolic meaning. They were often used to establish social position. Only in modernity has this wealth of material artefacts been so deeply implicated in so many social and psychological processes.

The symbolic role of goods is even appropriated in modern society to explore deep existential questions about who we are and what our lives are about. Novelty is seductive in its own right here. It offers variety and excitement; it allows us to dream and hope. It helps us explore our dreams and aspirations for the ideal life and escape the sometimes harsh reality of our lives.[29]

And it is precisely because material goods are flawed but somehow plausible proxies for our dreams and aspirations that consumer culture seems on the surface to work so well. Consumer goods, suggests anthropologist Grant McCracken, provide us with a tangible bridge to our highest ideals. They fail, of course, to provide a genuine access to those ideals, but in failing they leave open the need for future bridges, and so stimulate our appetite for more goods. Consumer culture perpetuates itself precisely because it succeeds so well at failure!

Again, it is important to remember that this dynamic doesn't by any means exhaust our relationship to material goods. Consumption is also vital to us in simple material ways. It is as much about ordinary everyday survival as it is about the social and psychological processes of identity, affiliation, aspiration and self-expression. But it is this social dynamic, rather than physiological flourishing, which serves to explain why our desire for material goods appears so insatiable. And why novelty matters to us.

Novelty and anxiety

It's tempting to dismiss such a system as pathological. And in some senses it clearly is. Psychologist Philip Cushman has argued that the extended self is ultimately an 'empty self' which stands in continual need of 'being "filled up" with food, consumer products, and celebrities'. At its most extreme, this need leads towards compulsive shopping, unsustainable debt and psychological despair.[30]

But it is also vital to recognise that this pathology is not simply the result of some inherent quality in the human psyche. We are not by nature helpless dupes, too lazy or weak to resist the power of manipulative advertisers. On the contrary, human creativity, emotional intelligence and resilience in the face of adversity are visible everywhere, even in the face of an apparently pathological consumerism.

Rather, what emerges from this analysis is that the empty self is a product of powerful social forces and the specific institutions of modern society. Individuals are at the mercy of social comparison. Institutions are given over to the pursuit of consumerism. The economy is dependent on consumption for its very survival.

Perhaps the most telling point of all is the rather too perfect fit between the continual consumption of novelty by households and the continuous production of novelty in firms. The restless desire of the 'empty self' is the perfect complement for the restless innovation of the entrepreneur. The production of novelty through creative destruction drives (and is driven by) the appetite for novelty in consumers.

Taken together these two self-reinforcing processes are exactly what is needed to drive growth forwards. As the ecological economist Douglas Booth remarks: 'The novelty and status-seeking consumer and the monopoly-seeking entrepreneur blend together to form the underpinning of long-run economic growth.'[31]

It's perhaps not surprising that this restlessness doesn't necessarily deliver genuine social progress. Sometimes it even undermines wellbeing and contributes to social recession. And there are some pretty clear reasons for that. Amongst them is that this is a system driven by anxiety.

The extended self is motivated in part by the anxiety of the empty self. Social comparison is driven by the desire to be situated favourably in society. Creative destruction is haunted by the fear of being left behind in the competition for consumer markets. Thrive or die is the maxim of the jungle. It's equally true in the consumer society.

It's an anxious and ultimately a pathological system. But at one level it works. The relentless pursuit of novelty may undermine wellbeing. But the system remains economically viable as long as liquidity is preserved and demand keeps rising. It collapses when either of these stalls.

On the other hand, it looks less and less like a place where decoupling can offer us a viable escape route from the impasse of a destructive materialism. Nature and structure conspire together to lock us firmly into the iron cage of consumerism. And the consequences for people and planet seem bleak at best.

And yet there is something unsettling here. Is the consumer economy really so perfect a fit for human nature? Are we really living, as Voltaire's Candide might have said, in the 'best of all possible worlds'? Or is it rather that certain well-documented aspects of human nature – our selfishness, our pursuit of status, our desire for novelty, even our spiritual hunger – are just what is needed to keep the economic system going? Is the system still serving us, or is it rather that we are now serving the system? Escaping the iron cage of consumerism demands that we address this crucial question.

7
FLOURISHING – WITHIN LIMITS

Frugality is one of the most beautiful and joyful words in the English language, and yet one that we are culturally cut off from understanding and enjoying. The consumption society has made us feel that happiness lies in having things, and has failed to teach us the happiness of not having things.

Elise Boulding[1]

In mid–2008, shortly before the collapse of Lehman Brothers, the savings ratio of the UK household sector reached an unprecedented low point. It had been falling more or less continually since the early 1990s, as the level of personal debt rose alarmingly. By the first quarter of 2008, household debt had almost surpassed the GDP of the entire nation and consumption exceeded real disposable income by almost 7 per cent.[2]

Households in the UK – and in several other advanced economies – were 'maxing out their credit cards' and running down their savings just to stay in the game. The story seemed to underline every harsh conclusion from the previous chapter: a story of ordinary people spending money they don't have, on things they don't need, to create impressions that won't last on people they don't care about.

And then, at the point of the crisis, a strange thing happened (Figure 7.1). The savings ratio suddenly reversed its reckless fall and turned sharply in the opposite direction. Within the space of a year it had more than regained the ground lost since the 1990s.

This rediscovered thrift was perilously short-lived, as Figure 7.1 reveals. Aside from one or two reversals during the rocky post-crisis years, the cash savings ratio has resumed its precipitous descent, and by 2015 savings were once again languishing in negative territory, leading to renewed fears for the health of the economy (see Chapter 2).

But my point here is not to herald the next crisis. Rather, it is to highlight the curious pro-cyclical behaviour of the high street. When recession beckons, it seems, and with confidence in the economy at an all-time low, the instinct of ordinary people is no longer to spend, spend, spend, but instead to hunker down, to put money aside, to focus on longer-term needs rather than short-term pleasures, and to pay just a little more attention to their own and their family's financial security.

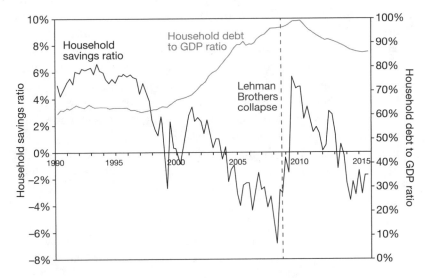

Figure 7.1 UK household debt and savings ratios, 1990–2016
Source: Data from the UK National Accounts (see note 2)

There are two things that make this economic behaviour interesting. The first is that it happens at all. If human beings really were the voracious novelty-seeking hedonists who serve so well in boom times to keep the economy growing, how would they ever find it in themselves to exercise restraint in times of crisis? At the very least, here is 'hard' economic evidence, if any were needed, that people are not just short-term pleasure seekers. The human psyche sometimes finds a way to be considerably more circumspect than emerges from the picture in the previous chapter.

The second interesting feature is that this unexpected reluctance to consume turns out to be a poor fit with the dynamics of growth. The economist John Maynard Keynes called this the 'paradox of thrift'. These are circumstances where the normal rules of prudence are turned on their head. It's entirely rational for each individual (or firm) to want to try and save a bit more in a crisis. But it turns out to be bad for growth – and ultimately bad for savings, too. Increased saving depresses high-street spending still further, deepening and lengthening the recession.

'Our enormously productive economy demands that we make consumption our way of life', wrote the US marketing consultant Victor Lebow in 1955, 'that we convert the buying and use of goods into rituals, that we seek our spiritual satisfactions, our ego satisfactions, in consumption'. The reliance of the economic system itself on continued expansion means that we 'need things consumed, burned up, worn out, replaced, and discarded at an ever increasing pace', he concluded.[3]

Here is a tantalising indication that the snug fit between nature and structure might not be so perfect after all. What looks like a system in which the needs of the human psyche are cleverly aligned with the demands of the economy now begins to look like a system in which precisely the opposite pertains. Economic success relies on persuading people back out onto the high street to spend. But this demand no longer resonates so easily with ordinary people. Politicians and policy-makers and bankers and financiers and advertisers now find they have to work much harder to encourage the kind of spending that will 'put the economy back on track'.

Opening a huge new shopping centre at the height of the financial crisis in October 2008, London Mayor Boris Johnson waved a credit card in front of the TV cameras, as though over-extended credit had nothing to do with the mess we were already in. Londoners had made a 'prudent decision to give Thursday morning a miss and come out shopping', he said of the huge crowds who attended the opening.[4]

In the wake of the 9/11 attacks in 2001, George Bush famously appeared in front of the cameras with a similar exhortation: 'Mrs Bush and I would like to encourage Americans everywhere to go out shopping.' There are all sorts of things that might be said about this extraordinary statement, under extraordinary conditions. But as an exemplar of the persuasive extremes that politicians will go to keep people spending money it probably stands supreme.[5]

The point is not whether people listen to these exhortations. Or whether growth does or doesn't 'recover'. But rather that this degree of exhortation should be necessary at all, if the economy were so perfectly aligned with the needs of human beings. And once we concede that this might not be the case, that there may be moments and circumstances in which the demands of the economy and the needs of people are in opposition to each other, it's remarkable how much evidence of this disjuncture we begin to find.

The paradox of materialism

The task of the economy is to deliver and to enable prosperity. But prosperity is not synonymous with material wealth and its requirements go beyond material sustenance. Rather, prosperity has to do with our ability to flourish: physically, psychologically and socially. Beyond sheer subsistence or survival, prosperity hangs on our ability to participate meaningfully in the life of society.

This task is as much social and psychological as it is material. And it gives rise to the intriguing possibility, first encountered in Chapter 3, that human beings might flourish and thrive with considerably lower levels of material consumption; that we might even achieve better outcomes – greater social cohesion and higher personal fulfilment – with less stuff.

But the appealing idea that after our material needs are satisfied we could do away with material things altogether flounders on a simple and powerful fact: material goods provide a vital language through which we communicate with each other about the things that really matter: family, identity, friendship, community, purpose in life. Stuff and story turn out to be intimately entangled with each other.

There is clearly a paradox here. If participation is really what matters, and material goods provide a language to facilitate that, then richer societies ought to show more evidence of it. But the very opposite appears to be the case, and has been for some time.

Writing over 40 years ago, the ecologist Murray Bookchin suggested that modern society had already reached 'a degree of anonymity, social atomization and spiritual alienation that is virtually unprecedented in human history'. And at the turn of this millennium, the sociologist Robert Putnam documented the extent of this collapse of community in his provocative book *Bowling Alone*.[6]

For years before the financial crisis, modern Western society was already in the grip of a social recession. Commentators from the political left point to rising rates of anxiety and clinical depression, increased alcoholism and binge drinking, and a decline in morale at work. Those from the right highlight the breakdown of community, a loss of trust across society and rising political apathy. Prescriptions for change vary according to the political hue of the commentator. But there is a remarkable agreement on the phenomenon itself.[7]

The extent of this paradox differs across nations. Surveys tend to show that Scandinavian countries retain higher levels of trust and belonging. Latin American economies tend to outperform other countries on subjective wellbeing. And almost a quarter of a century after the collapse of the Soviet Union, social wellbeing is still lower across Eastern European nations.[8]

Not surprisingly, trust in political institutions and in financial institutions in particular fell significantly in the wake of the financial crisis. But it's also acknowledged that some at least of the reasons for the breakdown in trust lie in the erosion of geographical community.

A study for the BBC in the UK confirms this trend. Using an index to measure geographical community in different BBC regions, the study revealed a remarkable change in British society since the early 1970s. Incomes doubled on average over a 30-year period. But the BBC's 'loneliness index' increased in every single region measured.

In fact, according to one of the report's authors 'even the weakest communities in 1971 were stronger than any community now'.[9]

The increasing number of people living in isolation has a number of different causes. The authors of the study link the changes largely to enhanced mobility. 'Increased wealth and improved access to transport has made it easier for people to move for work, for retirement, for schools, for a new life', reports the BBC. They might also have mentioned that the mobility of labour is one of the requirements for higher productivity in the growth economy.

In other words, this kind of evidence provides for a sneaking suspicion that some degree of responsibility for the negative aspects of modern society is attributable to the pursuit of growth itself. As evidence of our ability to flourish, it doesn't look good. And it becomes even more puzzling why exactly rich societies continue to pursue material growth.

A life without shame

Amartya Sen came close to addressing this puzzle in his early work on the 'living standard'. Sen argued that the material requirements for physiological flourishing tend to be fairly similar in all societies. After all, the basic human metabolism doesn't change so much across the species. Crucially, however, the material requirements associated with social and psychological capabilities can vary widely between different societies.

Sen's argument harks back to Adam Smith's insight on the importance of shame in social life. 'A linen shirt, for example, is, strictly speaking, not a necessary of life', wrote Smith in *The Wealth of Nations*. 'But in the present times, through the greater part of Europe, a creditable day labourer would be ashamed to appear in public without a linen shirt, the want of which would be supposed to denote that disgraceful degree of poverty which, it is presumed, nobody can well fall into without extreme bad conduct.'[10]

Sen broadens this argument to a wider range of goods, and a deeper sense of flourishing. To lead a 'life without shame', he claimed in 'The Living Standard', 'to be able to visit and entertain one's friends, to keep track of what is going on and what others are talking about, and so on, requires a more expensive bundle of goods and services in a society that is generally richer and in which most people already have, say, means of transport, affluent clothing, radios or television sets, and so on'. In short, he suggested, 'the same absolute level of capabilities may thus have a greater relative need for incomes (and commodities)'.[11]

Putting aside for a moment the fact that higher incomes have – in the same token – been partly responsible for diminished flourishing, there is an even more striking point to be noted here. If we take for granted the indispensability of material commodities for social functioning, we would have to accept that there is never *any* point at which we will be able to claim that enough is enough.

This is the logic of Sen's argument. The baseline for proper social functioning is always the current level of commodities. And the avoidance of shame – a key motivation for human behaviour – will drive material demand relentlessly forward in anything other than an entirely equal society.

This is in effect a different reframing of the social logic explored in the last chapter. But the social trap is now even clearer. At the individual level it makes perfect sense to avoid shame. It is essential to social (and psychological) flourishing. But the mechanism for doing so in the consumer society is inherently flawed. At the societal level it can only lead to fragmentation and anomie. And in doing so it undermines the best intentions of the individual as well.

It looks suspiciously like the language of goods just isn't doing its job properly. All that's left is an undignified scrap to try and ensure that we're somewhere near the top of the pile. Most worrying of all is that there is no escape from this social trap within the existing paradigm.

While social progress depends on the self-reinforcing cycle of novelty and anxiety, the problem can only get worse. Material throughput will inevitably grow. And the prospects for flourishing within ecological limits evaporate. Prosperity itself – in any meaningful sense of the word – is under threat. Not just from the financial crisis. Nor even from the continuing economic fragilities. But from the relentless surge of materialism, and from the economic model that perpetuates it.

An alternative hedonism

This vision of society as a process of relentlessly chasing material advantage stands only, if it stands at all, in the face of a fierce resistance from a surprising range of sources. Even John Stuart Mill railed against it. 'I am not charmed with the ideal of life held out by those who think that the normal state of human beings is that of struggling to get on', he wrote in 1848; 'that the trampling, crushing, elbowing and treading on each other's heels, which form the existing type of social life, are the most desirable lot of human kind'.[12]

Mill proposed an alternative vision. 'The best state for human nature', he declared, 'is that which, while no one is poor, no one desires to be richer, nor has any reason to fear being thrust back, by the efforts of others to push themselves forward.'

It would be easy to dismiss this as naïve utopianism, were it not for the fact that it came from one of the founders of classical economics. And that Mill made no claim that his more humanitarian vision was the most likely state of human nature. Only that it was the best. That it represented the best in human beings, rather than the worst. It was a recognition, if any were needed, that human nature has within it the wherewithal to behave in more and in less civilised ways. And that the possibilities for organising society in ways better than those witnessed in the mill towns and workhouses of the mid-nineteenth century was something worth aspiring to.

The relentless role of selfish competition and the excessive commoditisation of everyday life have been a recurrent theme in critiques of capitalism, particular over the last couple of decades. The philosopher Kate Soper has pointed to a growing appetite for an 'alternative hedonism' – sources of satisfaction that lie outside the conventional market. She describes a widespread disenchantment with modern life – a sense that consumer society has passed some kind of critical point, where materialism is now actively detracting from human wellbeing.[13]

Anxious to escape the work and spend cycle, we are suffering from a 'fatigue with the clutter and waste of modern life' and yearn for certain forms of human interaction that have been eroded. We would welcome interventions to correct the balance, according to

Soper. A shift towards an alternative hedonism would lead to a more ecologically sustainable life that is also more satisfying and would leave us happier.[14]

Some remarkable statistical evidence tends to support this view. Psychologist Tim Kasser has highlighted what he calls the high price of materialism. Materialistic values such as popularity, image and financial success are psychologically opposed to 'intrinsic' values like self-acceptance, affiliation, a sense of belonging in the community. Yet these latter are the things that represent our deepest source of wellbeing. They are the constituents of prosperity. Kasser's findings are striking. People with higher intrinsic values are both happier and have higher levels of environmental responsibility than those with materialistic values.[15]

A recent meta-study, led by social psychologist Helga Dittmar, supports this view. 'Every day, thousands of advertisements tell us that people are happy, worthwhile, and successful to the extent that they have money, possessions, and the right image', writes Dittmar. 'Yet numerous philosophic and religious perspectives across both time and culture have suggested that focusing one's life around the acquisition of money, possessions, and status saps one's spirit and undermines one's quality of life.'[16]

The study set out to draw together the statistical evidence from 175 individual studies on the relationship between materialism and wellbeing from across the world. Dittmar and her colleagues found 'a clear, consistent negative association between a broad array of types of personal well-being and people's belief in, and prioritization of, materialistic pursuits in life'.

This finding is extraordinary not just because it highlights the dangers of an increasingly materialistic society, but also because it suggests there really is a kind of double or triple dividend in a less materialistic life: people are both happier and live more sustainably when they favour intrinsic goals that embed them in family and community. Flourishing within limits is a real possibility, according to this evidence.

A quiet revolution

This possibility is being explored in practice, in numerous 'social experiments' from all around the world. Against the surge of consumerism, there are already those who have resisted the exhortation to 'go out shopping', preferring instead to devote time to less materialistic pursuits (gardening, walking, enjoying music or reading, for example) or to the care of others. Some people (up to a quarter of the sample in a recent study) report that they have accepted a lower income precisely so that they could achieve such goals.[17]

Beyond this quiet revolution of intrinsic values lies a series of more radical initiatives aimed at living a simpler, more ethical and more sustainable life. 'Voluntary simplicity' is at one level an entire philosophy for life. It draws extensively on the teachings of the Indian cultural leader Mahatma Gandhi, who encouraged people to 'live simply, that others might simply live'. In 1936, a student of Gandhi's defined voluntary simplicity in terms of an 'avoidance of exterior clutter' and the 'deliberate organisation of life for a purpose'. Former Stanford scientist Duane Elgin picked up this theme of a way of life that is 'outwardly simple, yet inwardly rich' as the basis for revisioning human progress.[18]

Psychologist Mihalyi Csikszentmihalyi has offered a scientific basis for the hypothesis that our lives can be more satisfying when engaged in activities which are both purposive and materially light. These conditions are more likely, he says, to provide a good balance between the skill needed and the challenge associated with achieving a desired task. This balance between skill and challenge leads to specific psychological state, which Csikszentmihalyi describes as 'flow' – a state of heightened focus and immersion in activities such as art, play and work.[19]

Individual efforts to live more simply are more likely to succeed in a supportive community. And this realisation has led to the emergence of so-called 'intentional communities' where people come together under the declared aim of living simpler, more sustainable lives. Some of these initiatives began, interestingly, as spiritual or religious communities, attempting to create a space where people could reclaim the contemplative dimension of their lives that used to be offered by religious institutions.

The Findhorn community in northern Scotland is an example of this. Findhorn's roots lie in the desire for spiritual transformation. Its character as an eco-village developed more recently, building on principles of justice and respect for nature. Another modern example is Plum Village, the 'mindfulness' community established by the exiled Vietnamese monk Thich Nhat Hanh in the Dordogne area of France, which now provides a retreat for over 2,000 people.[20]

These initiatives are modern equivalents of more traditional religious communities like those of the Amish in North America; or the network of Buddhist monasteries in Thailand where every young male is expected to spend some time before going out into professional life.

Not all networks have this explicit spiritual character. The early years of the twenty-first century saw a host of secular initiatives aimed at simplifying society and helping people live more sustainability. The Simplicity Forum, for example, launched in North America in 2001, is a loose secular network of 'simplicity leaders' who are committed to 'achieving and honoring simple, just and sustainable ways of life'.[21]

These kinds of initiatives achieved a surprising allegiance across a number of developed economies. One study on downshifting in Australia found that 23 per cent of respondents had engaged in some form of downshifting in the five years prior to the study. A staggering 83 per cent felt that Australians are too materialistic. An earlier study in the US found that 28 per cent had taken some steps to simplify and 62 per cent expressed a willingness to do so. Very similar results have been found in Europe.[22]

Motivating many of these initiatives is the idea that some of these changes have real benefits to the quality of our lives. The 'slow movement' arose from a protest by the Italian journalist Carlo Petrini against the opening of a fast food restaurant in the Piazza di Spagna in Rome. From this emerged first the 'slow food' movement and later a 'cultural revolution against the notion that faster is always better'.[23]

By the end of the first decade of the twenty-first century, the qualitative benefits of a less materialistic lifestyle were a core element in community-based initiatives for environmental change. The Transition movement was born from a single Transition Town called Totnes in the UK, where a small group of activists established a local community-based campaign to engage people in changing their lifestyles and reforming local infrastructures. The initiative was motivated by the need to respond to the twin threats of scarce resources and climate change.[24]

The example swiftly spread to other towns and neighbourhoods and its founders established a set of guidelines aimed at replicating the idea across the world. These guidelines outlined the practical process of forming local community groups and informing them of the ways they could address global problems with local solutions. But they also highlighted the processes of social and personal transformation that must go along with this, emphasising the collective advantages of a less materialistic, less energy-intensive way of life.[25]

Research on the success of these initiatives is quite limited. But the findings from studies that do exist are interesting. In the first place, the evidence confirms that 'simplifiers' appear to be happier. It is sometimes possible to have more fun with less stuff. Consuming less, voluntarily, can improve subjective wellbeing – completely contrary to the conventional model.[26]

At the same time, intentional communities remain marginal. The spiritual basis for them doesn't appeal to everyone, and the secular versions seem less resistant to the incursions of consumerism. Some of these initiatives depend heavily on having sufficient personal assets to provide the economic security needed to pursue a simpler lifestyle.

More importantly, even those in the vanguard of social change turn out to be haunted by conflict – internal and external. These conflicts arise because people find themselves at odds within their social world. Participation in the life of society – a key ingredient in a meaningful prosperity – becomes a challenge in its own right. People are trying to live, quite literally, in opposition to the physical, institutional and social structures that dominate society.[27]

Examples of the perverse effect of dominant structures are legion: private transport is incentivised over public transport; motorists are prioritised over pedestrians; energy supply is subsidised and protected, while demand management is often chaotic and expensive; waste disposal is cheap, economically and behaviourally; recycling demands time and effort: 'amenity centres' are few and far between and often already overflowing with waste.

Equally important are the subtle but damaging signals sent by government, regulatory frameworks, financial institutions, the media, and our education systems: business salaries are higher than those in the public sector, particularly at the top; nurses and those in the caring professions are consistently lower paid; private investment is written down at high discount rates, making long-term costs invisible; success is counted in terms of material status (salary, house size, etc.); children are brought up as a 'shopping generation' – hooked on brand, celebrity and status.[28]

Little wonder that people trying to live more sustainably find themselves in conflict with the social world around them. These kinds of asymmetry represent a culture of consumption that sends all the wrong signals, penalising pro-environmental behaviour, and making it all but impossible even for highly motivated people to act sustainably without personal sacrifice.

I will come back to this point when we begin to explore questions of governance (Chapter 10). It's clearly important to take this evidence seriously. As laboratories for social change, intentional households and communities are vital in pointing to the possibilities for flourishing within ecological limits. But they are also critical in highlighting the limits of voluntarism.

Simplistic exhortations for people to resist consumerism are destined to failure. Particularly when the messages flowing from government are so painfully inconsistent. People readily identify this inconsistency and perceive it as hypocrisy. Or something worse. Under current conditions, it's tantamount to asking people to give up key capabilities and freedoms as social beings. Far from being irrational to resist these demands, it would be irrational not to, in our society.

In the normal course of events, social conditions determine the rules by which ordinary people seek to live. Culture shapes and constrains our lives. When things are working well, social structures are properly aligned with collective values and provide a cultural framework within which people can flourish, allowing us to live meaningful, purposive lives. When things go badly, institutional structures wage war on human values, undermining prosperity and damaging society.

This, I would argue, is precisely where we find ourselves. It explains the restless dissatisfactions of consumerism. It makes sense of the paradoxes of thrift and materialism. It motivates the rise of a value-led anti-consumerism. And it draws support from a long succession of insights into the human condition from religion, from philosophers, from wisdom traditions, from poetry, from literature and from art: we are not and never were entirely the selfish hedonists that conventional economics expects and needs us to be. A simple and yet ferociously destructive misconception of human nature lies at the heart of modern capitalism.

The evolution of selfishness

The idea that human beings are primarily selfish and ultimately insatiable has a long and convoluted history. Some of its roots are to be found in the Christian doctrine of original sin, against which Rousseau once railed (Chapter 1). But it has achieved a particularly powerful incarnation in the model of human nature which informs and sustains modern economics. Not only are people inherently selfish, according to this economic conception, but it is precisely this self-interest which leads society towards the greater good.[29]

One of the earliest articulations of this idea was a satirical poem, first published in 1705, called the *Fable of the Bees*. Its author, Bernard de Mandeville, was a Dutch physician living in London at the time. His poem told the story of a thriving and successful beehive, in which the bees suddenly become honest and virtuous. The effect, in de Mandeville's poem, is disastrous. The bees lose all motivation to succeed, the hive collapses and the remaining bees go off to live empty lives in a hollow tree.[30]

De Mandeville's intention is to satirise those complaining of corruption in the politics of the day. Self-interest, claims de Mandeville, is the principal driver of economic vitality and consequently serves the best interests of society. It should not be railed against or reined in because it's the source of our wealth and our wellbeing, argues the *Fable of the Bees*.

The poem was particularly influential on the Scottish moral philosopher Adam Smith, the man widely regarded as the father of economics. 'It is not from the benevolence of the butcher, the brewer and the baker that we expect our dinner, but from their regard to their own self-interest', Smith famously wrote in *An Inquiry into the Nature and Causes of the Wealth of Nations*. Everyone is continually exerting himself in his own self-interest, said Smith. 'It is his own advantage, indeed and not that of the society, which he has in view', but 'he is in this, as in many other cases, led by an invisible hand to promote an end which was no part of his intention'.[31]

The metaphor of the invisible hand turned out to be an extraordinarily powerful one and it has been central to modern economics. Even though Smith himself wrote passionately about the dangers of corporate interests and the indispensable role for government in curbing these, this one single metaphor has motivated a ferocious defence of the virtues of an unbridled 'free market' in which self-interest is given full rein. 'The great merit of the capitalist system', wrote the economist Edward Robinson, 'is that it succeeds in using the nastiest motives of nasty people for the ultimate benefit of society'.[32]

It still isn't easy to see why exactly economics conflated self-interest with human nature almost entirely. Partly perhaps because this elision conferred simplicity on the mathematical models which economics was busy developing to explore the dynamics of the market. And partly because, over more or less the same period, the supposed centrality of self-interest to the human psyche was gaining support from one of the most powerful intellectual developments of the nineteenth century, the theory of evolution.

In its simplest terms, Darwin's theory of natural selection has two key components: the idea of spontaneous variation in the characteristics of plants and animals, and the process through which these variations are selected. This selection process was, broadly speaking, one of competitive struggle, in which the fittest survive and the weakest perish.

Darwin's drew this process quite explicitly from Malthus's *Essay on Population*, which (as we saw in Chapter 1) had a huge influence on early nineteenth-century thought and, of course, still resonates with environmental concerns today. In an autobiographical essay published after his death, Darwin once described the process through which he transplanted Malthus's concept of struggle into his own work.

'In October 1838, that is fifteen months after I had begun my systematic enquiry', he wrote, 'I happened to read for amusement "Malthus on Population", and being well prepared to appreciate the struggle for existence which everywhere goes on from long-continued observation of the habits of animals and plants, it at once struck me that under these circumstances favorable variations would tend to be preserved, and unfavorable ones to be destroyed. The result of this would be the formation of new species'. 'Here then', he wrote, 'I had at last got a theory by which to work.'[33]

The fierce intellectual battles that raged between the followers of Darwin and the nineteenth-century church were as much about the implications of the theory in terms of the character of human beings as they were about the story of creation. Natural selection appeared to give selfishness an unassailable importance in the evolution of the human species. If selection takes place at the level of the individual, it should, in the long run, favour the evolution of individuals who exhibit only selfish (i.e., self-preserving) behaviour. Selfishness attained not just a legendary but an evolutionary status.

It is interesting to note the parallels between early economics and nineteenth-century evolutionary thought. Just as the self-interest of economic agents is supposed to lead 'as if by an invisible hand' to the most favourable outcome for society, so the self-interest of individuals is supposed to lead through 'the survival of the fittest' to the most favourable outcome for species. Economics has continued to 'borrow' credibility for the centrality of self-interest from the theory of evolution ever since. But this credibility is critically, perhaps fatally, flawed.[34]

Beyond the selfish gene

Evolutionary explanations of behaviour are by no means confined to the idea that human beings are inherently selfish. The existence of genuinely altruistic behaviour is a fact of biology. Darwin himself at first believed this fact was 'insuperable, and actually fatal to my whole theory'. His own attempt to solve the problem was to suggest that selection operates not only on individuals but also on families or groups, a proposal that has never been definitively settled.[35]

It was to be almost another century before the 'problem of altruism' achieved a more satisfactory solution. In 1963, the British biologist William Hamilton published a landmark paper in which he proposed that selection operated not at the level of the individual but at the level of the gene. This proposal (now widely accepted) provided a mechanism for the evolution of altruism, without recourse to the idea of group selection. Though the individual may perish, the genes that he or she shares with other members of the species have a better chance of survival as a result of the sacrifice.[36]

Hamilton's work laid the foundation for a long-awaited continuation of Darwin's project to provide an evolutionary basis for human psychology. During the following decades, this foundation was strengthened and broadened, first through the work of evolutionary biologists and later through the emergence of a sophisticated neuroscience of human behaviour.[37]

These ideas might have remained within the confines of biology, had it not been for the publication in the mid-1970s of two groundbreaking popular books. In 1975, the biologist Edward Wilson published a landmark volume on *Sociobiology*, a new science of human behaviour. It was grounded solidly in the emerging evolutionary insights into human behaviour.

A year later, a young Oxford scientist named Richard Dawkins published a book called *The Selfish Gene* in which he pursued the implications of Hamilton's insight that the fundamental unit of evolutionary selection is the gene. Together these two books brought the new evolutionary theories about human behaviour to a wide and diverse audience. They caused a furore of interest, and not a little controversy.[38]

Some of the controversy arose from Dawkins' clever and provocative but potentially misleading title. What many people took from the title (and Dawkins himself sometimes inferred) is that the selfishness of the human species is indelibly written in our genes and there is nothing much to do about it. But even on a strict biological reading of the evidence this doesn't quite stack up. It is only true to the extent that another completely different sentence is also true: namely, that our altruism is also indelibly written in our genes and there is not much we can do about it.

What Hamilton and others had shown was that the 'selfishness' of the gene is entirely consistent with the unselfishness of human beings. Even if the primary 'aim' of the gene is its own genetic continuance – which, by the way, is a highly anthropomorphic interpretation of gene selecton – it is entirely mistaken to assume that human motivations are all selfish. Evolution doesn't preclude moral, social and altruistic behaviours. On the contrary, social behaviours evolved in humans precisely because they offer selective advantages to the species.

This simple insight leads to a much more nuanced view of what it means to be human. Selfishness clearly exists. But so, undeniably, does altruism. Both kinds of behaviours are genetically possible in us. Both had evolutionary advantages to our species over long periods of time. Selfishness served us well under conditions of fight or flight. But altruism was fundamental to our evolution as social beings.

All of us are to a greater or lesser extent torn between the two. Neither has absolute reign over the other. Evolutionary psychology describes a tension in the human psyche between self-regarding and other-regarding values. Equally interesting, from the perspective of understanding consumerism, it also recognises another tension: between novelty-seeking values and conservative or traditional values. The first is adaptive in fast-changing conditions. But the second is absolutely vital in providing the stability needed to raise families and form cohesive social groups.

The psychologist Shalom Schwartz and his colleagues have formalised these insights into a theory of underlying human values. Using a scale that has now been tested in over 50 countries, Schwartz suggests that our values are structured around these two distinct tensions (Figure 7.2) in our psychological make-up: between selfishness (self-enhancement, in Schwartz's scheme) and altruism (self-transcendence) on the one hand, and between novelty (or openness to change) and tradition (or conservation) on the other.[39]

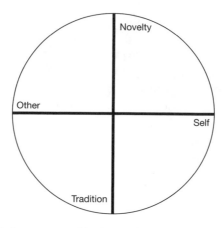

Figure 7.2 An evolutionary map of the human heart
Source: Author's depiction of the Schwartz circumplex (see note 39)

An evolutionary explanation for these tensions makes absolute sense. As society evolved in groups, people were caught between the needs of the individual and the needs of the group. And as they struggled for survival in sometimes hostile environments, people were caught between the need to adapt and to innovate and the need for stability. In other words, both individualism and the pursuit of novelty have played an adaptive role in our common survival. But so have altruism and conservation or tradition.

As a result, we certainly have it in us, at one extreme, to behave as voracious novelty seekers. But at the other end of the spectrum, we are absolutely prepared (as the example at the top of this chapter clearly shows) to hunker down and conserve our resources. Sometimes we can be persuaded to borrow to the hilt in pursuit of the latest fad or fashion. At other times, it's hard to stop us stuffing spare cash under the mattress as fast as we can, just to keep it safe for a rainier day.

This evolutionary map of the human heart reveals the crux of the matter. What we've created in consumer capitalism is an economy which privileges, and systematically encourages, one specific segment of the human soul – the upper right quadrant in Figure 7.2. We've done this, in part, because the economy that we've created is best served by selfish, novelty-seeking behaviour. Without the self-serving hedonist lurking within us, the economy itself is in danger of collapsing.

This combination of intellectual conceit and structural weakness has created a self-fulfilling prophecy. As the game theorist Robert Axelrod once demonstrated, the balance of behaviours in a society depends on how that society is structured. When technologies, infrastructures, institutions and social norms all reward self-enhancement and novelty, then selfish sensation-seeking behaviours prevail over more conservative, altruistic ones.[40]

But where social structures favour altruism, self-transcending behaviours are rewarded and selfish ones are penalised. When long-term vision is integrated into our institutions, then novelty seeking has a chance at least of being tempered by more cautionary behaviours.

Each society strikes this balance between altruism and selfishness (and between novelty and tradition) in different places. And where this balance is struck depends crucially on social structure. Social structures can change and can be changed. They are amenable to policy. And all the evidence suggests that the time is ripe for such changes, because the existing structures are poorly aligned with human interests and values.

In summary, we are faced with an unavoidable challenge. A limited form of flourishing through material success has kept our economies going for half a century or more. But it is completely unsustainable and now threatens to undermine the conditions for a shared prosperity. This materialistic vision of prosperity has to be dismantled.

The idea of an economy whose task is to provide capabilities for flourishing within ecological limits offers the most credible vision to put in its place. But this can only happen through changes that support social behaviours and reduce the structural incentives to unproductive status competition.

The rewards from these changes are likely to be significant. A less materialistic society will be a happier one. A more equal society will be a less anxious one. Greater attention to community and to participation in the life of society will reduce the loneliness and anomie that has undermined wellbeing in the consumer economy.

What exactly does this all mean for economics? What would economics look like if we stretched its vision of human nature along these two axes of the human psyche? How might the economy be transformed if it were governed by institutions that protect and nurture what matters most in us? The next couple of chapters explore these questions in more detail.

Above all, it's vital to understand that this vision of a different society, a different economics, is categorically not some kind of heroic demand to 'change human nature'. Neither is it about curtailing human possibilities. Rather it's about allowing ourselves the freedom to become fully human. It's about recognising the depth and breadth of the human soul. And it's about building an economics to reflect that vision.

8

FOUNDATIONS FOR THE ECONOMY OF TOMORROW

Economy is the art of making the most of life.

George Bernard Shaw, 1910[1]

We are living in a material world. We must eat and drink to survive; find shelter and clothing to protect ourselves; build schools for our children and hospitals for those who are sick. The everyday reality of our lives is an inherently material one. One of the most essential aims of the economy is provide for these material needs.

But our lives are never entirely material. Our social world is as important as, sometimes more important than, the material world. Identity, love, joy, meaning: these are all a vital part of what it means to be human.

These immaterial goods are not in themselves producible, tradable commodities. But each of them carries a material footprint. We express our love through gifts. We define our identities through possessions. We shop to allay our anxieties. Material goods are a language through which we communicate. Desire, affiliation, longing, affection, importance: these are some of the conversations that we are capable of having because of the intimate, ethereal relationship to material stuff.

There is nothing inherently pathological here. Materialism is not synonymous with greed. Saints have appetites too. The language of goods whispers unequivocally in everyone's ear. We need not even be fully cognizant of these subterranean vocabularies. They are almost instinctive in their expression, virtually subconscious in their manifestation, and present in every single society for which we have anthropological evidence.

But there are pathologies in consumer society. One of these is the hyper-materialisation of our social world. Consumerism entails handing over vast swathes of social life to material expression: a process driven, as we've seen, as much by the structural needs of the economy as it is by our own desires and needs, accelerated massively by advertising, marketing and the demand for economic expansion.

The tragedy of consumerism is not just that it is damaging the planet. But that it is doing so in pursuit of false gods and elusive dreams. On the other hand, this tragedy presents an opportunity: to build a better vision of progress with a more robust view of human nature at its core. This is our chance to create an economics fit for purpose – an economy capable of delivering a lasting prosperity.

The task is not straightforward, as we shall see. But it is definable. It is specifiable. It offers surprisingly clear avenues for development. We can articulate clear conceptual foundations for it. And we can begin to build on those foundations through concrete empirical examples and identifiable tasks: a systematic re-construction of economics that offers both meaning and hope to the idea of social progress. The aim of this chapter is to frame that process.

I want to focus in particular on four distinct foundations for the economy of tomorrow: the nature of enterprise, the quality of work, the structure of investment and the role of money. Taken together, I shall argue, these four elements hold the potential for a radical transformation of the economy with the potential to deliver a lasting prosperity.

Enterprise as service

Starting from first principles, it is surprisingly easy to characterise the nature of economic activities from which the economy needs to be built. There are several key characteristics.

In the first place, the goal of enterprise must be to provide the capabilities for people to flourish. Second, this must happen without destroying the ecological assets on which our future prosperity depends. So enterprise needs to be low in carbon, efficient in resource use and non-extractive in nature. In short, economic activities must 'tread lightly' on the earth. Finally, enterprise should also afford decent, satisfying livelihoods for people. Employment matters in any economy. Work is not just the means to a livelihood but a key avenue for participation in society.

Former Oxfam researcher Kate Raworth has usefully visualised these criteria by combining the concept of planetary boundaries (see Chapter 1) with the concept of social boundaries: a set of minimum standards for decent living, including food, water, health, energy, education and jobs. Raworth pointed out that, even as some planetary boundaries are already exceeded, some social conditions are still not achieved for vast numbers of the world's population.

'Between a social foundation that protects against critical human deprivations, and an environmental ceiling that avoids critical natural thresholds, lies a safe and just space for humanity – shaped like a doughnut', she wrote. 'This is the space where both human well-being and planetary well-being are assured, and their interdependence is respected.' There is a remarkable resonance between the social conditions laid out in the Oxfam paper and the capabilities identified in this book.[2]

The critical question addressed in this chapter concerns the nature of the economic activities that will deliver these capabilities. What kinds of enterprise could offer us meaningful work as 'producers' and valuable goods as 'consumers' without destroying the quality of our environment and undermining our future prosperity? It might seem like too tall an order. But there is one simple idea that has a surprising potential to help us here: the concept of service.

If prosperity is as much about social and psychological functioning – identity, affiliation, participation, creativity – as it is about material stuff, then it is mistaken to think of economic activity in terms of the throughput of material stuff. Rather we should construe the goal of enterprise as delivering the 'human services' that improve the quality our lives: nutrition, shelter, health, social care, education, leisure, recreation, and the maintenance and protection of physical and natural assets.

These services almost always depend on materials to some degree. Sometimes, indeed, materiality is an inherent part of the service provided. Food, clothing, shelter are undeniably material commodities. But, even in these cases, it's possible to redefine economic activity in terms of service.

Food is fundamentally material. But the service of nutrition is no simple function of the material quantity of food. In fact it's a highly non-linear function of food intake, as we've already noted (Chapter 3). Less (food) can sometimes be more or better (nutrition). Some foods could even be called disservices (at least in the quantities we tend to consume them). Some 'goods', paradoxically, may turn out to be 'bads'. To focus on service rather than on product is to recognise these subtleties.[3]

Another good example is the concept of 'energy services'. No one wants oil or coal or gas in and of themselves. When people purchase fuel, it is with the explicit intention of achieving certain energy services from them: warmth, light, mobility, for instance. This might seem like an arbitrary redefinition, but it has some profound ramifications.

The same level of warmth (or thermal comfort), for instance, can be achieved in many different ways. In a well-insulated house, you can have comparable warmth with much lower consumption of oil or gas. And the critical point here is that lower consumption of oil or gas means fewer greenhouse gas emissions.

Thinking in terms of services reveals new ways to decarbonise or dematerialise human activities. When the value proposition of enterprise revolves around the delivery of dematerialised services rather than the manufacture of material products, there is a huge potential to rethink the relationship between economic output and material throughput. 'Servicization', this strategy has sometimes been called.[4]

It's vital to note that this is not simply another framing of the transformation to 'service-based economies' that has characterised development in the rich world over recent decades. For the most part that's been achieved, as we've seen, by reducing heavy manufacturing, continuing to import consumption goods from abroad and expanding financial services to pay for them.[5]

In fact, we have to be a little careful about any of the sectors for which, in principle, we see some potential for 'servicization'. Leisure and recreation, for example, is one of the fastest-growing sectors in modern economies and ought in principle to be a prime candidate for dematerialisation. In practice, the way we spend our leisure time can be responsible for as much as 25 per cent of our carbon footprint.[6]

Yet there is clearly some mileage in the idea. Focusing on service rather than on material throughput offers the potential for a fundamental transformation of enterprise. It is ultimately services rather than stuff that matters to us, whether this is in nutrition or housing or transport or health care, or education, or leisure. Almost all of our needs can be cast in terms of services.[7]

Perhaps surprisingly, the seeds for such a transformation already exist, often in local, community-based initiatives or in social enterprise: community energy projects, local farmers' markets, slow food cooperatives, sports clubs, libraries, community health and fitness centres, local repair and maintenance services, craft workshops, writing centres, outdoor pursuits, music and drama, yoga, martial arts, meditation, gardening, the restoration of parks and open spaces.[8]

In formal terms, many of these activities tend not to feature too highly on the conventional radar. They represent a kind of 'Cinderella economy' sitting neglected on the margins of consumer society. Some of them scarcely register as mainstream economic activities at all.[9]

So it's odd to find suggestions that services could provide the basis for a 'new' engine of growth. Pointing out that ever greater consumption of resources is (in itself) a 'driver of growth' in the current paradigm, US ecological economist Robert Ayres argues that, 'in effect, a new growth engine is needed, based on non-polluting energy sources and selling non-material services, not polluting products'.[10]

The same idea is implicit in the concept of the 'circular economy', popularised in recent years by the Ellen MacArthur Foundation. The circular economy is characterised by strategies of reuse, refurbishment, remanufacturing and recycling. The overall aim is reduce the linear throughput associated without compromising the quality of the services that material goods can provide.[11]

We'll come back in the following chapter to the question of whether or not this strategy provides a new engine of growth. The suggestion is still essentially an appeal to decoupling. Growth continues, while resource intensity (and hopefully throughput) declines. But here at least is something in the way of a blueprint for what such an economy might look like. It gives us more of a sense of what people are buying and what businesses are selling in this new economy.

It also gives us an insight into the kinds of jobs that characterise the new service-based economy. They will differ in some precise ways from jobs in the prevailing consumer economy. And, perhaps more importantly, as we see in the next section, there are likely to be more of them.

Work as participation

Work matters. It's more than just the means to a livelihood. It is also a vital ingredient in our connection to each other – part of the 'glue' of society. Good work offers respect, motivation, fulfilment, involvement in community and, in the best cases, a sense of meaning and purpose in life.

Sadly, the reality is somewhat different. Too many people are trapped in low-quality jobs with insecure wages, while others are threatened with long-term unemployment from rapid technological transitions. These processes undermine the creativity of the workforce and threaten social stability. The long-term implications for the economy are nothing short of disastrous.

Youth unemployment rose dramatically through the financial crisis, particularly in developed economies. Two-thirds of European countries now have youth unemployment rates higher than 20 per cent. In Greece and Spain, youth unemployment is over 50 per cent.

This is not only an enormous waste of human energy and talent but a recipe for civil and social unrest. So there is a huge premium on any strategy that might increase the availability and the quality of employment.[12]

At the heart of the problem lies an issue we have already identified as a key dynamic in capitalism – the pursuit of increasing labour productivity; the desire continually to increase the output delivered by each hour of working time. Though it's often viewed as the engine of progress, the relentless pursuit of increased labour productivity also presents society with a profound dilemma (Chapter 6).

As each hour of working time becomes more productive, fewer and fewer hours of labour are needed to deliver any given level of economic output. In fact, with labour productivity continually rising, aggregate demand must rise at the same rate if the total number of employed hours is to stay the same. As soon as demand falls – or even stagnates – then unemployment rises.

With labour productivity continually rising, there is only one escape from this 'productivity trap', namely to reap the rewards in terms of reduced hours worked per employee – or in other words to share the available work amongst the workforce.

So it's perhaps not surprising to find that proposals to shorten the working week are enjoying something of a revival in recent years. In fact, the idea has a strong pedigree. In an essay entitled 'Economic possibilities for our grandchildren', published in the 1930s, John Maynard Keynes foresaw a time when productivity gains would allow us all to work less and spend more time with our family, our friends and our community.[13]

Since the time Keynes was writing, societies have indeed taken some of the labour productivity gains achieved through technology in the form of increased leisure time. Working hours across the OECD have declined by 12 per cent since 1970. In France the decline is over 25 per cent. In the absence of these overall declines in working hours, unemployment across advanced economies would have been much higher than it currently is.[14]

Sharing the available working time by reducing working hours is thus an important strategy for ensuring that everyone has access to a livelihood, particularly when demand growth is hard to come by.

This is the option pursued, for example, by ecological economist Peter Victor, in a study designed to test a low or no-growth scenario for the Canadian economy. The key policy intervention used to prevent wide-scale unemployment is a reduction in working hours. In fact, unemployment is halved in Victor's model, even as GDP output stabilises.[15]

A telling example of the practical success of work-share in maintaining employment is the case of Trumpf, a machine-tool maker in the south German city of Ditzingen. The company managed to get through the financial crisis without laying off any of its 4,000 German workers, while in the US, the same company laid off almost 15 per cent of its workforce. The difference was that, in Germany, Trumpf took advantage of government incentives to reduce working hours rather than firing people.[16]

Work-share is a natural companion to any proposals involving a slowing down of economic growth. But it turns out that there is another rather interesting way of addressing the same problem. Namely, to challenge the assumption of ever-increasing labour productivity.[17]

If the idea of resisting productivity growth sounds perverse at first, it is probably because we've become conditioned by the language of efficiency. Time is money. Productivity is everything. The drive for increased labour productivity occupies reams of academic literature and haunts the waking hours of CEOs and finance ministers across the world.

It isn't just ideology, of course. Our ability to generate more output with fewer people has been at least partly responsible for lifting our lives out of drudgery. How many people nowadays would prefer to keep their accounts in longhand, wash hotel sheets by hand or mix concrete with a spade? A few may still – with good reason – prefer the humble broom to the diabolical (and wholly unsustainable) 'leaf-blower'. But between the back-breaking, the demeaning and the downright boring, increased labour productivity has a lot to commend itself.

On the other hand, this logic doesn't mean we should eliminate labour altogether. Work remains one of the ways in which humans participate meaningfully in society. Reducing our opportunities to work – or reducing the quality of our experience in doing so – represents a direct hit on our prosperity. And there are clearly situations in which the pursuit of labour productivity growth makes much less sense. Certain kinds of tasks rely inherently on the input of people's time.

The care and concern of one human being for another, for instance, is a peculiar 'commodity'. It cannot be stockpiled. It is not deliverable by machines. Its quality rests primarily on the attention paid by one person to another. This is not to say that technological advances offer nothing to the caring professions. They clearly do. But these advances cannot ultimately substitute for the time spent by caregivers. Pressurising nurses, doctors, teachers and care workers turns out to be counterproductive in all sorts of ways. Compassion fatigue is a rising scourge in a health sector hounded by meaningless productivity targets.[18]

Something similar happens in handicraft. It's the accuracy and detail inherent in crafted goods that endows them with lasting value. It's the attention paid by the carpenter, the potter, the seamstress or the tailor which makes this detail possible. Chasing time out of the production process reduces costs. But when time is what endows the product with quality, there's a danger that value itself is eroded.

A parallel phenomenon occurs in the creative industries. As the US economists William Baumol and William Bowen pointed out half a century ago, it's the time spent in rehearsal that makes for a good musical performance. It's hours in the studio that lead to an enduring piece of art. Indeed, artistic endeavours generally tend to resist the logic of labour productivity because their vital ingredient is the time and skill of the artist. Nothing much is to be gained – and much would be lost – by asking the New York Philharmonic to play Beethoven's 9th Symphony faster and faster each year.[19]

For a whole range of professions, it seems, time spent by people in the exercise of care, craft and creativity is the core value proposition. Nothing quite substitutes for the hours spent in work. Time is quality: it's a different take on things, but which offers an instantly recognisable and distinctively more human social logic than the one which sees work as a chore and labour as a cost.

Strikingly, these sectors of the economy – care, craft, culture – are exactly the ones identified in this chapter as the basis for a renewed vision of enterprise. Service-based activities – of the kind described in the previous section – are inherently labour-intensive as well as being potentially lighter in environmental terms.

Figure 8.1 illustrates both of these characteristics. On the vertical axis, it maps the carbon footprints associated with different economic sectors. And it clearly confirms the potential for carbon savings from a transition to services. The carbon footprint of the social and personal services sector (where many of the activities discussed above reside) is between three and five times smaller than the footprint of the manufacturing or extractive sectors.[20]

The horizontal axis of Figure 8.1 maps the employment or labour intensity of each sector. The labour intensity of the 'social and personal services' sector is almost double that of the manufacturing sector and three times that of the financial services sector. In short, the Cinderella economy is carbon light and employment rich.

There's good reason for both of these characteristics. On the one hand, services don't rely inherently require a given level of material throughput. And on the other, they tend to resist the pursuit of labour productivity: the desire continually to increase the output delivered by each hour of working time.

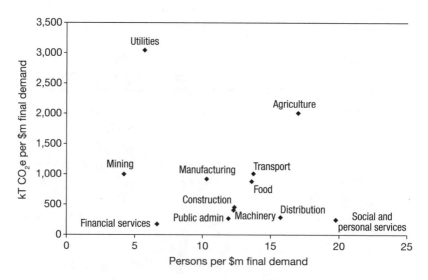

Figure 8.1 Greenhouse gas intensity v. employment intensity across sectors
Source: Jackson et al. (2016) (see note 19)

In summary, Figure 8.1 reveals a compelling alternative to reduced working hours as a means of combating the productivity trap. Namely, it suggests a shift to more employment-rich sectors. Or, put differently, a transition to sectors with lower labour productivity – and lower productivity growth. If labour productivity across the economy as a whole is no longer continually rising, and possibly even declining, then the pressure on jobs is considerably lower.

Perhaps the most telling point of all is that people often achieve a greater sense of wellbeing and fulfilment, both as producers and as consumers of these material-light, employment-rich activities, than they do in the time-poor, materialistic, supermarket economy in which much of our lives is spent.[21]

In short, achieving full employment may have less to do with chasing endlessly after labour productivity in the hope of boosting growth and more to do with building local economies based around care, craft and culture. In doing so, we have the potential to restore the value of decent work to its rightful place at the heart of society.

Investment as commitment

Achieving such a transition demands investment. But this is not very surprising. Investment is the foundation for any economy. Investment embodies one of the most vital relationships in economics – namely, the relationship between the present and the future. The fact that people set aside a proportion of their income at all reflects a fundamentally prudential aspect of human nature. Engaging in projects that last over time embodies our commitment to the future and is the basis for prosperity of any kind.

The success and sustainability of this commitment strategy depends inherently on the destination for our savings and the focus of our investments. When large proportions of investment are dedicated towards nothing more than asset price speculation (Chapter 2), the productive relationship between the present and the future is fundamentally perverted, destabilising the economy and undermining prosperity.

Even taking speculative behaviour aside, the investment portfolio of the conventional economy still fails any robust test of sustainability. Too much of it is directed at the extraction of rents from finite material resources. Much of the rest is dedicated either to chasing labour productivity or to the relentless production of novelty: the creation and re-creation of ever newer markets for ever newer consumer products (Chapter 6).

The result of these strategies is a portfolio of capital investments dominated by the production and reproduction of consumerism. The vital relationship between the present and the future is distorted through lenses of speculation and short-term profiteering. And the prospects for transforming enterprise and employment in the ways described above remain heroic at best.

It's worth stepping back for a second, just to see if we can reframe investment in ways that support rather than undermine the vision of prosperity outlined in this book. The starting point is simple enough: prosperity today means little if it undermines prosperity tomorrow. Investment is the vehicle through which we build, protect and maintain the assets on which tomorrow's prosperity depends.

This vision allows us to identify the kinds of assets towards which we need investment funds to flow. The provision of basic material capabilities is still in some sense a baseline for prosperity, particularly in the poorest countries. Most obviously, people will always need nutrition, shelter and mobility. Investment in these areas clearly still matters. But if it were made in enterprises focused on the services these goods provide, these investments would already make a difference.

Investment in health, education and social care is also absolutely vital. 'The ultimate source of any society's wealth is its people', write Stuckler and Basu. 'Investing in their health is a wise choice at the best of times, and an urgent necessity in the worst of times.'[22]

Beyond these basic capabilities, we could certainly turn our attention to the wellbeing of our communities and the strength of our social life. An investment strategy directed to these ends would build and maintain the physical assets through which individuals can flourish and communities can thrive – what US philosopher Michael Sandel has called 'the infrastructure of civic life': schools and hospitals, public transportation systems, community halls, quiet centres, theatres, concert halls, museums and libraries, green spaces, parks and gardens.[23]

Needless to say, not a single one of these services can do away with material and energy inputs completely. Health care requires medicines and life-saving equipment. Education needs books and computers. Musicians need instruments. Gardeners need tools. Even the lightest recreation activities – dance, yoga, tai chi, martial arts – have to take place somewhere. There is an irreducibly material element to even the lightest economy and the most ethereal vision of enterprise.

But this doesn't mean that our revised investment strategy collapses into the old, familiar one. The critical distinction is to invest in assets that maximise our potential to flourish with the minimum level of material consumption, rather than in assets that maximise the throughput of material commodities – irrespective of their contribution to long-term prosperity.

Ultimately, it's abundantly clear that we must also invest massively in material efficiency. This is obvious from Figure 8.1. Some sectors that are absolutely vital for the economy currently have very high carbon intensities. Most notably, the carbon footprint of the utilities sector (which includes the production and distribution of electricity and heating fuels) is the most carbon-intensive of all. This is hardly surprising, of course. Fossil fuels still provide the lion's share of the world's energy supply. Divesting from the damaging fossil fuel sector and investing in the transition to low carbon energy systems are both essential components of a revised investment strategy.

In fact, one of the most striking developments in the years since this book was first published is the rise of the so-called 'divest–invest' movement: a concerted effort, often student-led and supported by progressive funders, to shift investment markets away from fossil fuels and towards renewable energy, energy efficiency, resource productivity and clean technologies.[24]

The movement has gathered an impressive momentum in recent years, spurred on in particular by some high-profile divestments from major investors. In June 2015, the Norwegian parliament agreed to sell off all the coal-based assets in Norway's $900 billion sovereign wealth fund. Divestment is vital not only to avoid locking in the damaging impacts of fossil fuel technologies for another half a century, but also to free up much-needed funds to invest in alternatives.[25]

Recapitalising the world's energy systems for a low carbon world is a formidable challenge. In the run-up to the Paris conference in December 2015, the IEA estimated that just meeting the climate pledges made by participating nations would entail investments of $13.5 trillion in renewable energy and energy efficiency before the year 2030. Yet it's no longer possible to pretend that this will be enough to meet the 2°C target which had been on the table since Copenhagen, let alone the 1.5°C target adopted in Paris. The likely investment costs for these more stringent targets could be at least an order of magnitude higher.[26]

The sheer size of the investment needed to transform the world's energy system was one of the motivations for the international consensus around a 'green stimulus' in the wake of the financial crisis (Chapter 2). As early as 2008, the UK-based Green New Deal group put forward proposals for a low carbon energy system that would make 'every building a power station' and the creation and training of 'a "carbon army" of workers to provide the human resources for a vast environmental reconstruction programme'.[27]

In the intervening years numerous others have echoed this call. UNEP's global Green New Deal widened the remit of spending to include investment in natural infrastructure: sustainable agriculture and ecosystem protection. Forests, grasslands, arable land, wetlands, lakes, oceans, soils and the atmosphere itself are all essential in providing the services on which life itself depends.

Certainly, the economic rationale for investing in natural assets is unassailable. Ecosystems provide many trillions of dollars' worth of services to the world economy. Many of these ecosystems lie outside the formal realm of the market. But protecting and enhancing them is vital to our economic productivity in the future, as UNEP pointed out.[28]

Less clear are the impacts this vast new portfolio of investment might have on economic performance. There are again those who have argued that it could deliver a new 'engine of growth'. In a paper entitled *Towards a Green Economy* published in 2011, UNEP even argued that 'green growth' based around 'green investment' would be faster than 'brown [or conventional] growth'.[29]

I want to return to this somewhat contentious argument in the following chapter. For now it is clear that this new investment portfolio is essential, irrespective of its impacts on conventionally measured growth. Its key aims must be to protect natural assets, improve resource efficiencies, implement clean, renewable technologies and build the infrastructures needed for a less materialistic and more satisfying life.

Some of these investments – for instance, those in natural assets and public goods – may have to be judged against criteria other than financial market success. This might mean rethinking the way that investment works; the structure of ownership of assets and the distribution of surpluses from them. But the indispensability of the strategy outlined here is blindingly obvious.

Money as a social good

The biggest challenge for such an investment strategy is the question of financing. So far in this chapter, we've been concerned mainly with what is sometimes called the 'real economy'. It's a term often used to describe the patterns of employment, production, consumption and investment in the economy. But it is useful to distinguish this real economy from the financial or 'money economy'.

The money economy describes the wider set of financial flows on which the real economy depends. It includes the flow of money into and out of different economic sectors, the processes of borrowing, lending, creating money (the money supply), and the changes in the financial assets and liabilities of different economic actors. These stocks and flows of money are essential to the financing of investments in the real economy.

This is a complex terrain even to politicians and mainstream economists. Sometimes this complexity seems almost wilful; designed to obscure the profound implications of an economy that benefits the rich and massively inhibits government's powers of social investment. If so, it's been broadly successful. 'It is well enough that the people of this nation do not understand our banking and monetary system', said the US car manufacturer Henry Ford in the 1930s. 'For if they did, I believe there would be a revolution before tomorrow morning.'[30]

To many non–economists, the existence of a debt-based money system itself comes as a complete surprise. We tend to think of money as something printed (or brought into existence electronically) by the Central Bank more or less under the control of the government. The reality is that less than 5 per cent of the money supply is created in this way. Most money circulating in advanced economies is created by commercial banks, almost literally 'out of nothing'.[31]

When a bank agrees to create a loan to a business or a household, it simply enters the amount as a loan on the asset side of its balance sheet and the same amount as a deposit on the liability side of its balance sheet. This deposit is then available to spend on goods and services in the economy. Banks create money by making loans.[32]

There are a number of important implications of this debt-based money system. One of them is the degree of instability that ensues when things go wrong. Another is that government itself can only finance social investment through commercial (interest-bearing) debt. Another still is that the investment portfolio outlined in this chapter ends up having to compete for credit-worthiness against all sorts of other sometimes unsavoury commercial investments.

Sustainable investment must vie for funds, for example, with financial speculation in commodities, property or financial assets. It must prove its worth against entirely unsustainable consumer lending – in which repayment (and punishment for non-payment) is reinforced by legal institutions. It must compete with investments in dirty, extractive industries that degrade the environment, and in supply chains which are profitable only because they involve various forms of modern slavery.

Many of these massively unethical investments will offer highly attractive rates of return in the short term. But in the long term they are entirely unsustainable. The social costs of conventional investment (including the huge cost of unrestrained speculative trading) are rarely factored into financial decisions. Worse still, these costs are borne ultimately by the taxpayer. By contrast, the social benefits of more sustainable investments are almost invisible to mainstream funders who tend to look at unfamiliar portfolios and see only higher risk.

The ethical basis of sustainable investment only rarely attracts a premium. But where it does, it is clearly an important source of financing for the kind of investment proposed here. Impact investing – the channelling of investment funds towards ethical, social and sustainable companies, technologies and processes – is an increasingly important element in the financial architecture.

This kind of investment was in the past seen more as a form of philanthropy. But as the US-based Capital Institute has recently pointed out, it should be seen as a vital complement both to philanthropy proper and to government funding: 'a way to leverage secure philanthropic and public sector dollars, while harnessing the power of social entrepreneurs and market-based solutions to solve some of the world's most intractable problems'.[33]

At the very local level, impact investing meets another profoundly useful social innovation. Community banking is a way of mobilising the savings of ordinary people at community level to provide investment funds for social or environmental finance. Community banks allow people to invest in their own community – for example, in low carbon energy, or in community amenities, and at the same time ensure that the returns from those investments remain within the community.

A fascinating example of small-scale peer to peer lending for social and ecological projects is provided by SPEAR – a French savings intermediary that aims to facilitate transparent, responsible investment. Savers are able to choose the projects in which they want to invest and receive information from the projects themselves as they progress. The average return to savers during 2012 was 2 per cent.[34]

A similar example from North America is the Unified Field Corporation – a California-based community banking initiative. Its Regenerative Communities Initiative develops financial plans for sustainability projects in nine different areas, including organic local food systems, water quality, renewable energy, mobility, affordable green housing, education and the arts.[35]

One of the most popular models for community investment is the credit union: cooperative financial institutions in which individual members pool their savings to provide loans to other members. There are over 6,000 credit unions in the United States alone, holding

$1 trillion in assets and serving 100 million people – more than 40 per cent of the economically active population. Though subject to many of the same regulations as banks, credit unions are typically smaller, more local and designed specifically to be non-profit-making institutions.[36]

Some smaller banks have also pioneered a portfolio of lending which looks remarkably similar to the investment strategy outlined in the previous section. One such example is Triodos Bank, whose entire ethos is built around positively screening its portfolio to invest only in sustainable and ethical projects. Founded in 1980, the bank now finances over 300 sustainable energy projects in Europe generating some 740 megawatts of electricity.[37]

There's considerable potential here to make money work better – to have it support rather than undermine the long-term prosperity of local communities. But it's also very clear that, by comparison with mainstream financial flows, the scale of this funding is simply insufficient to make the transformation happen. What's needed is either a massive scaling-up of these small-scale initiatives, a radical transformation of mainstream finance itself, or a massive public investment programme of a scale not seen in Western economies since at least the Second World War.

A key element in any of those strategies is going to be the nature of the money supply itself. Triodos Bank bears one striking difference to many ordinary banks: it only lends out money deposited in the bank by savers and investors. In other words, it doesn't engage in the kind of debt-based, credit creation that lay at the heart of the financial crisis.

There are some rather strong arguments in favour of changing the existing debt-based money system and returning a greater degree of control over the money supply to government. The so-called Chicago plan – which calls for 100 per cent backing of bank deposits with government-issued money – was first put forward in the 1930s by the US economist Irving Fisher and supported most notably by the Chicago School economist Milton Friedman.[38]

There have been a number of recent calls to revive this idea – perhaps most surprisingly from the International Monetary Fund. A recent IMF working paper identifies several clear advantages to the plan, including: its ability to better control credit cycles, the potential to eliminate bank runs, and the effect of dramatically reducing both government debt and private debt. The plan would essentially return control of the money supply directly to the government.[39]

Similar proposals call for an end to banks' power to create money and the implementation of a so-called 'sovereign money' system. In such a system, governments would no longer have to raise money for public spending and investment on commercial bond markets. Instead they could spend directly into the economy, as and when financing was needed, subject only to the caveat that such spending was non-inflationary. Proposals for such systems are currently under consideration in Iceland and in Switzerland.[40]

'When economists of the calibre of Simons, Fisher, Friedman, Keynes and Bernanke have all explicitly argued for a potential role for [sovereign money], and done so while believing that the effective control of inflation is central to a well-run market economy', argues Adair Turner in a characteristically guarded tone, 'we would be unwise to dismiss this policy option out of hand'.[41]

What's at stake here is the nature of money itself as a vital social good. Money facilitates commercial exchange; it provides the basis for social investment; it has the power to stabilise or destabilise the economy. Handing the power of money creation over to commercial interests is a recipe for financial instability, social inequality and political impotence. Reclaiming that right in the national interest is a powerful tool in the struggle for a lasting and inclusive prosperity.

The economy of tomorrow

The boom and bust economy of the last century has created financial instability, increased social inequality and led to environmental degradation and resource depletion. Austerity has exacerbated these dangers. Chasing prosperity through over-financialised hyper-consumerism has sown the seeds of its own collapse.

None of this is inevitable. The dimensions of a post-crisis economy can be derived from simple first principles. Enterprise as service, work as participation, investment as a commitment to the future and money as a social good: these four principles provide the foundations for transformation. Ultimately, all of them flow from an understanding that the economy is not an end in itself but a means towards prosperity.

The concept of service provides for a new vision of enterprise: not as a speculative, profit-maximising, resource-intensive division of labour, but as a form of social organisation embedded in the community, working in harmony with nature to deliver the capabilities that allow us to prosper.

Work is vital to those capabilities. What we've identified here is the existence of a 'sweet spot' of good work, with multiple benefits for society, in the economies of care, craft and creativity. We can't live entirely from these sectors. But they hold the key to expanding the quality of our lives. And we can usefully import the principles we find there into other economic sectors.

Investment embodies our hopes for the future. What we invest here and now determines how our lives (and our children's lives) will go in the future. A clear and definable investment portfolio emerges from the analysis in this chapter. Its aim is to build, nurture and sustain the assets on which tomorrow's prosperity depends.

Making all this work depends on having a financial system that is fit for purpose. Improving the ability of ordinary people to invest their savings responsibly, in ways that benefit both their own community and a wider environment, is paramount. But deeper and more decisive changes are also needed. Reforming the money system is not just the most obvious response to the financial crisis. It is an essential foundation for the economy of tomorrow.

9
TOWARDS A 'POST-GROWTH' MACROECONOMICS

The purpose of studying economics is not to acquire a set of ready-made answers to economic questions, but to learn how to avoid being deceived by economists.

Joan Robinson, 1955[1]

There's something distinctly odd about our contemporary refusal to question economic growth. As early as 1848, John Stuart Mill, one of the founders of classical economics, reflected on the advantages of a 'stationary state of population and capital'. He insisted that there would be 'as much scope as ever for all kinds of mental culture, and moral and social progress' within such a state.[2]

Keynes' essay 'Economic possibilities for our grandchildren' also foresaw a time when the 'economic problem' would be solved and we would 'prefer to devote our further energies to non–economic purposes'. Like Mill, Keynes saw this change as broadly positive in the sense that we would 'once more value ends above means and prefer the good to the useful'.[3]

In the language of this book, Keynes and Mill were both essentially saying that prosperity without growth is not just possible but desirable. These two were both mainstream economists in their day. They are cited often enough by mainstream economists today. But few mention these passages. Even fewer seem prepared to think in concrete terms about the implications of a 'post-growth' economy.

One of those who has thought in such terms is the former World Bank economist Herman Daly, who made a pioneering case for a 'steady state economy' almost four decades ago now. Daly defined the ecological conditions for this economy rather precisely. If we're to remain within ecological scale, he said, there must be a constant physical stock of capital assets, capable of being maintained by a rate of material throughput that always lies within the regenerative capacities of the ecosystem. Anything other than this, argued Daly, will ultimately erode the basis for economic activity in the future.[4]

In one sense, these conditions motivated the vision outlined in the previous chapter – with very specific implications for enterprise, work, investment and money. What's still missing from that vision is a coherent overview, a sense of how these things all fit together and make sense in economic terms.

In short, we need a convincing macroeconomics for a 'post-growth' society. One in which neither economic stability nor decent employment rely inherently on relentless consumption growth. One in which economic activity remains within ecological scale. One in which our ability to flourish within ecological limits becomes both a guiding principle for design and a key criterion for success.[5]

The aim of this chapter is to elaborate on that task. In particular, I want to make the case that the foundations identified in the previous chapter can in fact be integrated into a coherent macroeconomic whole. The full extent of that task lies beyond the scope of this (and probably of any single) book. Nonetheless, I hope to show that the task itself is definable, meaningful and achievable.

In order to frame the task, let's first take a step back and revisit one of the core arguments in this book. What can we now say about the dilemma of growth? Where do the foundations laid down in the previous chapter leave us in relation to the two horns of that dilemma?

'Our degrowth is not their recession'

The dilemma of growth has us caught between the desire to maintain economic stability and the need to remain within ecological limits. On the one hand, endless growth looks environmentally unsustainable; on the other hand, degrowth appears to be socially and economically unstable.

Logically speaking, there are two distinct escape routes from this dilemma. One is to make growth more sustainable; the other is to make degrowth more stable. There's a particularly striking (and sometimes acrimonious) division between those who choose differently between these two options. Some continue to argue, with increasing vehemence, for growth at all costs. Others have begun, sometimes vociferously, to campaign against it.

Into this latter category falls the *degrowth movement*: an intellectual challenge to the mainstream paradigm that was in its infancy when the first edition of this book was published. In the intervening years, that challenge has definitely become both more visible and more relevant. Not least because, growth itself has shown itself to be haunted by instability.[6]

When inherent instability can only be held at bay by ratcheting up the core dynamics that caused the instability in the first place (Chapter 2), we know we're in trouble. When the very mechanism for maintaining stability ends up undermining its own resource base, it's time to start looking elsewhere for inspiration. Sticking with the status quo just leaves us staring into the face of impending disaster. Growth itself is an accident waiting to happen.

But acknowledging this reality does little to reduce the force of the underlying dilemma. Once consumption begins to falter the economy starts running into trouble. Investment falls, jobs are lost, businesses go bust, government deficits rise and the economy risks falling into a deflationary spiral.

The degrowth response to this challenge is an interesting but not entirely satisfactory one. One of the catchphrases of the movement insists that 'our degrowth is not their recession'. Degrowth is not the opposite of growth or even the absence of growth. Rather it is, in the words of its proponents, a 'missile concept' designed to 'open up a debate silenced by the "sustainable development" consensus'. It is about 'imagining and enacting alternative visions to modern growth-based development'.[7]

So far so good. Imagining and enacting alternative visions is absolutely the task in hand. It's the task that motivates this book as a whole and the last few chapters in particular.

But what does this mean for the economy as a whole? Is production expanding or is it contracting? Is demand rising or is it falling? The word 'degrowth' suggests that one or other of these things is falling. In which case, the challenge is to show how the consequences associated with the second horn of the dilemma are to be avoided. How are jobs protected? How are debts managed? How is stability ensured?

Oddly, the questions themselves have not always met with approval from the degrowth movement, many of whom call for an 'exit from the economy' and regard degrowth as 'an invitation to abandon economistic thinking'.[8]

From a philosophical point of view, it's easy to have some sympathy with this position. When you've discovered near-fatal flaws at the heart of the most influential scientific discipline of our times, it's tempting to reject that discipline in its entirety. Many people do reject economics. Some of my own students come to me with absolutely no wish at all to have anything to do with a subject that they feel has failed so many, so spectacularly. Some of their reasons are good.

Economics has let us down on all sorts of counts. Economists have often been more arrogant than they should have been, swept away by their own secular importance, rather than being persuaded, as Keynes once exhorted them, to become a bit more like dentists, providing a vital service in terms of our economic health, but otherwise maintaining a relatively low profile.[9] But the extent to which a rejection of economics per se has become an acceptable intellectual position never ceases to surprise me. At a conference recently, where I presented some of the economic modelling I will describe later in this chapter, a prominent degrowth advocate challenged me directly afterwards. 'The idea of post-growth economics is an oxymoron', he told me.

There is clearly a question mark over how much of the existing economic architecture it might be possible to keep in a post-growth world. But the idea that we can do without economics altogether must surely be wrong. This is not the moment to abandon the aim of making economic sense of the world; but rather an opportunity to build a new economics, fit for purpose in addressing the enormous challenges we are already facing.

In a sense, the degrowth advocates have no problem at all accepting the first horn of the growth dilemma: that growth is unsustainable. But they tend to deny the validity, or at least diminish the importance, of the second. Degrowth is not necessarily the same thing as negative growth, argue its advocates. And so it doesn't have to lead to instability. But this isn't an entirely satisfactory answer – in part, because it gives us too little to go on in building a post-growth macroeconomics.

'Angelising' growth

Ironically, there is a far bigger, equally passionate and often much more powerful lobby who take almost exactly the opposite position. That is, they have no problem accepting the proposition that degrowth is unstable but they insist absolutely that economic growth is (or at least can become) sustainable. They refuse, almost out of principle, to countenance a post-growth society.

Green growth, smart growth, inclusive growth, sustainable growth: these terms characterise this pro-growth position. They all lay claim to the sunny uplands, a place where it is possible to reduce poverty, meet our environmental targets and overcome our resource constraints while never sacrificing the ability to go on expanding the economy – indefinitely.[10]

The means to achieve this heroic end is decoupling. Endless improvements in the material efficiency of the economy so as to reduce the overall material throughput even as the economy continues to expand (Chapter 5). In this way, claim the green growth protagonists, it will always be possible for the economy to get bigger while the impacts on the planet diminish.

There must of course be some limits to this process. Herman Daly makes the point colourfully. 'The idea of economic growth overcoming physical limits by angelizing GDP is equivalent to overcoming physical limits to population growth by reducing the throughput intensity or metabolism of human beings', he wrote, over 30 years ago. 'First pygmies, then Tom Thumbs, then big molecules, then pure spirits. Indeed, it would be necessary for us to become angels in order to subsist on angelized GDP.'[11]

Even before we reach such 'thermodynamic' limits, we might encounter social limits. An angelised GDP would need us to place more and more economic value on immaterial angels. And, even if this were possible, we may well want to resist the valuation of angels for moral reasons. As Michael Sandel has pointed out, there are some things that money can't (or shouldn't) buy.[12]

But we are almost certainly still some way from those limits. So a more relevant question is whether (for the foreseeable future) the rate of decoupling can outpace and continue to outpace the rate of growth. If it can, then the economy can afford to grow indefinitely, while its impacts on the planet diminish. If it can't, then decoupling cannot ultimately do the work required of it by the proponents of green growth. It can't solve the dilemma.

Here we can certainly make some progress by paying careful attention to arithmetic. It quickly transpires that the technological demands are huge (Figure 5.6), particularly in a fast-growing economy. But it's also the case that enormous technical potential for change exists. Renewable energy technologies, material efficiency improvements, a low-carbon world: all of this is theoretically possible, even with today's technology.[13]

So it all comes down to whether or not it's possible to implement this potential for decoupling. The most crucial question of all turns out to be about society rather than about technology. Is this massive technological transformation possible in our kind of society?

To summarise massively, the answer suggested in this book (Chapter 6) is: no. In our kind of society, in this kind of economy, it is highly unlikely that we will be able to decouple fast enough to remain within environmental limits or (ultimately) to avoid resource constraints.

This is not to reject the technological potential claimed by the green growth advocates. On the contrary, it's clear that it's huge. But that isn't quite the end of the matter. Social logic and the structure of enterprise conspire against us. Simply recognising the power of technology doesn't justify the faith that the eco-modernists want to place in it in their attempt to defend the status quo: precisely because the answer to what's possible depends inherently on the nature of the status quo.

This is the chain of logic that led us first to explore the potential for an alternative social vision (Chapter 7) and then to lay down the foundations for a different kind of economy (Chapter 8). It is clear enough that this vision and these foundations represent a significant departure from conventional economics. It is not yet clear where they leave us in terms of the dilemma of growth.

Beyond the rhetorical divide that separates growth from degrowth lie two serious questions still worth asking. Is the economy of tomorrow a growth-based economy or is it not? Is the economy of tomorrow stable or is it not? These questions still count. A response to the dilemma of growth still matters. Let's turn our attention first to the question of growth.

Is the economy of tomorrow a growth-based economy?

First, it's abundantly clear that tomorrow's economy should not be growing in material terms. Daly's conditions (and Rockström's planetary boundaries) are precise on this point. Continual material growth would compromise our ability to remain with the 'safe operating space' of the planet and undermine our future prosperity. The point about the interventions in the previous chapter is to reduce in absolute terms the material throughput of the economy.

Second, we should underline that some things within this economy will still be growing. Who could argue against an increase in social wellbeing? Or an increase in jobs? Or in the integrity of our natural assets, the resilience of our communities, the quality of our environment, our sense of meaning and purpose? All of these things and many more could still be growing. As a campaign for Triodos Bank puts it: 'growth is about more than just numbers'.[14]

But neither the absence of material growth nor the presence of immaterial growth resolves the dilemma of growth. The critical question is whether the economy itself is still expanding in economic terms. This is one of those points where, for all its faults, the GDP still matters. Not because it's a good proxy for prosperity – it clearly isn't. But because it's a measure of economic activity. And it's the scale of economic activity which is pertinent to the dilemma of growth. So the question we're really asking is whether the interventions identified in Chapter 8 lead to more growth or to less growth. Let's look first at investment.

Does sustainable investment increase or diminish growth?

In the conventional model, investment has two main targets. The first is to increase labour productivity. The second is to stimulate innovation. The latter is critical to the former in creating an expansion of demand, without which the pursuit of labour productivity could simply lead to a rise in unemployment. These two primary roles for investment provide for a virtuous circle when things are going well and a vicious cycle when they're not.

The portfolio of investment outlined in Chapter 8 has a very different character. It consists in building and maintaining the assets from which economic services flow. In particular, it targets the capabilities needed for people to flourish: nutrition, health, education, enjoyment, ecological resilience. The traditional function of investment, framed around increasing labour productivity, is likely to diminish in importance. Innovation will still be vital, but it will be targeted more carefully towards a lasting prosperity: better services with fewer environmental impacts.

Does this new portfolio increase or diminish the growth potential of the economy as a whole? There are certainly those who argue that green investment makes the economy grow faster. What should we make of this claim?[15]

It's worth noting that investment goods are part of the aggregate demand that firms have to supply. Expanding investment directly expands the demand for goods in the economy. These goods still have to be paid for somehow from the national income, so if nothing else changes we would either have to forgo some consumption in order to be able to afford the additional level of investment or increase public or private sector debt. In itself, this would not necessarily lead to a sustainable expansion of output.

The argument that investment can increase output stems from the productive potential that conventional investment claims for itself. By increasing productivity, we would expect both output and income to rise alongside demand. The expansion of investment would therefore 'pay for itself' without compromising the level of consumption.

Everything depends, then, on the productive power of the additional investment. If investment increases without increasing the potential of the economy to supply more goods, then the increase is purely inflationary, pushing up the price of goods across the economy, rather than increasing real economic output. On the other hand, if the investment raises the productivity of the economy as a whole, both demand and supply potential increase and the economy can grow.

So what happens to productivity under this new portfolio? Oddly, there are two or three different answers to this question. The most conventional response would suggest that its growth potential is lower than the conventional portfolio. The reasoning here is very simple: by placing any constraint on the universe of investment you necessarily reduce the available returns. It seems logical that an unconstrained portfolio is more profitable than a constrained portfolio, so the argument goes, because investors are free to choose those investments with the highest returns.

Elegant in principle, this simple formula turns out to be wrong in practice. The reasons are interesting. One suggestion is that unconstrained investment is insufficiently responsive to risk, so that future revenues are undermined by unforeseen environmental or social factors. In this case, constraints on investment can stimulate positive impacts in terms of return, against the conventional logic.[16]

This argument has drawn support from the debate over 'stranded assets'. The policy and economic risks associated with certain fossil fuel companies – particularly coal – are so high, argue proponents, that assets held in such companies are at risk of becoming worthless (or 'stranded') within the foreseeable future. Divesting such assets makes economic as well as ethical sense.[17]

Whatever the reason, it is clear that there are some distinct advantages to a more active 'stewardship' approach to investment. Some sustainable investment funds clearly outperform conventional funds. By taking a better account of environmental and social risk, it appears to be entirely possible to improve the returns on investment capital – at least at the margin, under current conditions.[18]

But this still doesn't entirely settle the matter. The share of sustainable investment in the market as a whole is still very small: of the order of only a few per cent. And the performance of this investment is measured more by the value of shares in the funds than it is by the contribution of the funds to the productive potential of the economy. The crucial question is whether investment of this kind can be brought to scale without affecting overall productivity.

Like so many of the questions we come up against, this one is also haunted by counterfactuality: if the economy were different as a whole, would its productivity be higher or lower than it is right now? We cannot know for sure. But we can hazard some guesses on the factors that would increase (or at least maintain) productivity and those that might decrease it.

Perhaps most obviously, in shifting away from the pursuit of labour productivity and consumer innovation, we have removed the most obvious source of expansion both of supply and of demand in the economic structure. Overall productivity growth may well decline if labour productivity is no longer a primary focus for investment. And the continual expansion of demand associated with product innovation is also likely to be more subdued in an economy focused on the quality of services rather than the relentless novelty of consumer products.

On the other hand, there are some countervailing forces. Investments in resource productivity are likely to have a positive impact on overall productivity. Some investments in renewable energy are likely to bring competitive returns in some market conditions, particularly where these are supported by policy. But in other conditions considerably lower returns might be expected over much longer time frames than traditional financial markets expect. If this were not the case, of course, we would expect to see a lot more renewable energy investment – on the open market – than we currently do.

Critical to this point is the 'energy return on investment' (EROI) – the ratio of the useful energy provided by a particular technology to the energy needed to extract it (Chapter 1). Renewables typically have lower EROI than conventional fossil fuels, meaning that we have to allocate more productive resources in order to capture the same useful energy return from them.

Over time, this balance will inevitably change, as the quality of conventional fuels also declines. Eventually renewables will be essential to prevent a terminal decline in the overall EROI. But the point is that, in a low EROI world, we must expect the productive capacity of the economy as a whole to fall, as financial and energetic resources are diverted away from other productive processes in order to extract and convert useful energy.[19]

In the short term, however, we might be justified in expecting both resource productivity and renewable energy investments to show some positive contributions to productivity growth. Investments in ecosystem protection or in adaptation to environmental change, on the other hand, might not bring conventional financial returns at all, even though they are vital to the protection of ecosystem services.

Such ecological investments (like all investments) still contribute to aggregate demand. But they make no direct contribution to aggregate supply. They are absolutely vital in protecting environmental integrity. And this in its turn is vital for sustaining production at all over the long term. But in the short term, they appear to 'soak up' income without increasing economic output.

Interestingly, this problem has the same basic structure as the problem of funding public sector spending in a welfare economy. Investment in social goods may be less productive in the short term and make a less direct contribution to productivity than investments in manufacturing. Nonetheless, social investment is clearly essential for long-term prosperity.[20]

One other category of investment is worth commenting on. A service-based economy requires a specific shift in investment from manufacturing plant to the infrastructures and facilities required to produce services. The returns of service-based investments are likely to be lower than those of manufacturing investments for a very specific reason: namely, the resistance of services to labour productivity improvements. We'll return to this point in the following section.

In summary, this new portfolio of 'slow capital' is likely to have lower rates of return and longer periods of return than the extractive and speculative investments that characterised investment markets over the last few decades. These new characteristics are useful in some respects. They fit better the needs of long-term savings vehicles such as pension funds, for instance. But they don't immediately suggest that green investment will give us more productivity and faster growth than conventional investment. Some of these new investments, essential though they are, for long-term output, may well slow economic growth down.

Do services provide a 'new engine of growth'?

If the growth potential of sustainable investment is difficult to ascertain in the abstract, the question of the impact of a wholescale shift towards services is somewhat easier to answer. We can bring both a clear conceptual model and a good deal of empirical evidence to bear on it. Both of these suggest that a service-based economy will grow considerably more slowly than a product-based economy.

We've touched already on the reasons for this. Certain kinds of services – particularly in care, craft and culture – resist labour productivity growth. Empirical data support this finding. Between 1995 and 2005, for instance, labour productivity in the personal and social services sector declined by 3 per cent across the EU 15 nations. It was the only sector to show negative productivity growth.[21]

This is no accident, of course. The value of a service is inherently linked to the time spent by people delivering it. Reducing the labour input to these services is both difficult and counterproductive.

This issue has long been recognised in economics. Somewhat pejoratively, it's often referred to as 'Baumol's cost disease' after the US economist William Baumol, who has devoted a substantial portion of a distinguished career to studying the differential performance of service sector activities.

Baumol's 1966 study with Bowen (cited in the previous chapter) highlighted a curious oddity of a somewhat peripheral sector, namely the performing arts. But over the decades, Baumol has developed those early arguments and studied the evidence across sectors that now include craft, health, education, as well as creativity – exactly those sectors we have also identified as the focus for a shift in economic activity. His most recent book *The Cost Disease: Why Computers get Cheaper and Health Care Doesn't* is a fundamental rethink of the value of economic activity which resonates profoundly with the concerns in this book.[22]

The core of Baumol's argument is simple enough to convey. Wherever there is a differential in the productivity growth in different sectors of the economy, there is a tendency for the costs of the less productive sector (Baumol calls this the 'stagnant' sector) to rise in real terms relative to those of the more productive sector (which he calls the 'progressive' sector).

The reason for this relative increase is that wages across the economy will tend to follow the wages in the highest paid sector. Since wages typically rise with labour productivity, the wage level will be set by the progressive sector. Higher wages won't increase costs in the progressive sector because labour productivity will rise as well. But in the 'stagnant' sector, there is no way for firms to protect against wage rises by increasing labour productivity. So the cost of these activities will inevitably rise.

Evidence supports this hypothesis. Empirical data from the US confirm that real prices in service-based sectors have risen continually relative to those in the manufacturing and extractive sectors. 'Industries with relatively low productivity growth (the 'stagnant' industries) show a percentage-point for percentage-point higher growth in relative prices', writes economist William Nordhaus, reporting on a study to test Baumol's hypotheses across 58 industry sectors in the US.[23]

There are a couple of possibilities for the fate of these 'stagnant' sectors. If the demand for their services is price elastic (i.e., demand for them falls when prices rise), then they will progressively lose demand, as prices rise higher and higher. Ultimately, we might expect such services simply to disappear from the economy. Local repertory theatres might be a case in point here. Faced with competition from 'merchandise'–dominated online entertainment (for instance), professional local theatre is at best heavily subsidised and sometimes declining fast in 'rich' economies.[24]

A similar fate could beset certain repair or renovation services. Particularly where newly manufactured goods are ever cheaper to acquire, there is less and less incentive to engage in costly repairs or renovations. Baumol's cost disease explains some of the structural dimensions of the 'throwaway' society with remarkable clarity.

If, on the other hand, the demand for services is price inelastic (i.e., it doesn't change much whatever the price), then Baumol's cost disease predicts that this sector will represent an increasing proportion of the real expenditure across the economy. This would be the case for health services, for instance, and perhaps also for education.

There are real dangers in either case. First, it's likely that useful services, which could contribute positively to human wellbeing and reduce our impact on the planet, will simply disappear. Second, those essential services which are typically provided by government (at local or national level) will be under constant pressure to make 'efficiency savings' or perhaps be cut altogether, because they will inevitably represent a higher and higher proportion of the GDP as time goes by. Hasty responses from policy makers concerned with cutting deficits or reducing budgets will progressively damage the quality of essential services.[25]

'A disturbing moral of this story', writes Baumol, 'is that the products most vulnerable to the cost disease include some of the most vital attributes of civilised communities: health care, education, the arts … [a]ll of these services suffer from cost increases that are both rapid and persistent'.[26]

Ultimately, Baumol and Nordhaus are abundantly clear: an economy which insists on maintaining (let alone expanding) its service sector is heading for zero growth. 'An attempt to achieve balanced growth in a world of unbalanced productivity must lead to a declining rate of growth relative to the growth of the labour force,' writes Baumol. 'In particular, if productivity in one sector and the total labour force remains constant the growth rate of the economy will asymptotically approach zero.'[27]

Nordhaus confirms this hypothesis empirically across the US economy. 'Perhaps the most important macroeconomic result is the operation of Baumol's growth disease over the last half of the twentieth century', he writes. 'The growth disease has lowered annual aggregate productivity growth by slightly more than one-half percentage point over the last half century.' To be clear, what Nordhaus is saying here is that Baumol's disease is at least partly responsible for the secular stagnation that we have already seen across the advanced economies.[28]

The picture for the UK is particularly striking (Figure 9.1). A phenomenal slowdown in productivity growth has occurred in just half a century. The trend growth rate rose from less than 1 per cent per year in 1900 to reach 4 per cent per year in 1966. It declined sharply past that point. Digital and information technology slowed (but did not reverse) the decline through the 1980s and 1990s.[29]

Soon after the bursting of the 'dot-com' bubble at the turn of the millennium, and long before the financial crisis, the decline began to accelerate. By 2013, trend labour productivity growth was negative. The value of the output produced in each hour of work is currently declining in the UK. The implications for economic growth are

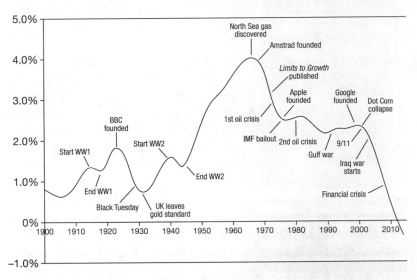

Figure 9.1 The rise and fall of UK labour productivity growth
Source: Jackson and Webster (2016)

profound. In these circumstances, per capita growth is only possible by increasing the labour force or by having everyone work longer hours.

In short, the idea of a structural shift towards services makes a lot of sense. But the argument that it constitutes a new 'engine of growth' does not. For this reason alone, the chances are that the economy of tomorrow has a considerably slower rate of economic growth and may already be heading towards a stationary or quasi-stationary state.

Confronting instability

If the economy of tomorrow is a 'post-growth' economy not just in concept but also in measure, then what can we say about the second horn of the dilemma of growth. Are we inevitably heading towards macroeconomic instability? Or are there ways in which the structural foundations of this new economy might mitigate instability and in doing so allow us to escape the dilemma?

These are amongst the most profound and the most important questions raised by the inquiry in this book. And it's extraordinary to find, more than 80 years after Keynes' essay and twice that since Mill's defence of the stationary state, that we have virtually nothing to go on to help us answer them. There is as yet no fully fledged macroeconomics for a post-growth economy. Yet that is precisely what is needed, not just for environmental but also for secular reasons.

What happens to employment when material consumption is no longer expanding? What happens to inequality as conventional growth rates decline? What can we say about financial stability when capital no longer accumulates? What happens to the public sector in the face of declining aggregate demand?

These are the kinds of questions that we need to ask about this new economy. Conventional wisdom tends to suggest some unsavoury answers. When demand stalls, for instance, unemployment typically rises, tax revenues typically fall and debts rise. These impacts tend to create a 'growth imperative' which in its turn becomes the foundations for the dilemma of growth.

As I indicated at the top of this chapter, a fully articulated post-growth macroeconomics lies beyond the scope of this book. But research undertaken since the financial crisis does allow us to make more progress towards this task than was possible when the first edition of this book was published.

Take, for example, the relationship between demand, employment and labour productivity. This relationship is fundamental to the growth dilemma. It suggests that, as demand stagnates, unemployment inevitably rises, causing inherent social instability.

The most often-cited remedy for this problem is to 'share the available work' by reducing the average working week. This solution is proposed for example in Peter Victor's *LowGrow* model for the Canadian economy, cited in the previous chapter. It has also been explored in some detail in recent work from organisations such as the New Economics Foundation.[30]

But the prescriptions of the previous chapter offer another, more integrated solution to the 'productivity trap'. A structural shift towards service-based enterprise entails a reduction in labour productivity growth. Put otherwise, this shift increases the employment intensity of the economy and facilitates full employment.

In a series of economic simulations, calibrated loosely for the Canadian and UK economies, Peter Victor and I have shown how this kind of structural shift, in combination with work-time policies, can indeed maintain high levels of employment, even as growth rates decline to (and below) zero.[31]

The transition to services offers a more 'holistic' solution to the employment challenge of a low-growth economy. The apparent 'growth imperative' arising from the pursuit of productivity is less decisive than the dilemma of growth suggests. There are routes to full employment that are entirely consistent both with stagnating demand and with improved prosperity.

Of course, a shift of this kind raises deeper questions about the structure of the capitalist economy. One such question concerns the balance between the return to labour (i.e., wages) and the return to capital (profits). This balance betrays an uncomfortable tension at the very heart of capitalism. Wages and profits compete with one another continually for a share of the national income.

To the extent that the share of wages rises in the economy, the share of profits will fall and vice versa. Since wages are, in the conventional model, assumed to follow labour productivity, a decline in labour productivity growth might be expected to lead to a decline in the share of wages in the national income and a rise in the share of capital.

In a world where capital were equally distributed this would simply mean that most of our incomes would come from profits rather than wages. But in a world where capital is very unequally distributed – and ours is clearly such a world – things look very different. Any slight disparity in the ownership of capital, or even in the rate of savings, will lead to escalating inequality.[32]

The algebra of inequality

This tension has been highlighted most notably by the French economist Thomas Piketty in his bestselling book *Capital in the 21st Century*, published to enormous and widespread acclaim six years after the financial crisis.[33]

The astonishing popularity of the 'rock-star economist' is itself a resounding testament to our abiding concern for inequality. But his painstaking analysis reveals an uncomfortable story for capitalism. Late capitalist societies are busy reversing the gains in equality achieved through the twentieth century. Capital's share of income is rising and, as a result, relative inequality is getting worse not better.[34]

Piketty places the responsibility for this trend unequivocally on declining growth rates. Like Benjamin Friedman in *The Moral Consequences of Economic Growth*, he implies that only growth can bring civility, in part because an expanding economy allows for a degree of 'catching up' by the poorest in society without much sacrifice or compromise by the rich.[35]

The French economist goes even further, however. At the heart of his epic treatise is a fundamental 'law of capitalism', which asserts that, in the long run, capital's share of income tends towards a certain algebraic 'product' given by the rate of return on capital times the savings rate divided by the growth rate. It's the division by the growth rate that proves problematic here. As every high-school student knows, any finite number divided by something vanishingly small rapidly approaches infinity. Simple algebra seems to dictate that capital's share of income is set to rise explosively in a post-growth economy.[36]

Piketty's answer is a clarion call for a tax on capital in order to redistribute the benefits of capital to the poorest in society. It's a relatively simple 'auxiliary hypothesis' to correct the dysfunctional heart of capitalism. His proposals for a tax on capital have elicited a noisy backlash; and these squabbles in their turn undoubtedly contributed to the book's success. But in the noise and the hype, something else happened. The egalitarian dreams of post-growth advocates took a massive hit from the world's most famous economist.

For those of us working towards those dreams, Piketty's intervention was a double-edged sword. Its clarity of focus on inequality was very welcome. But the idea that only growth can save us from disastrous inequality poses some pretty serious challenges to our endeavour and represents what appears at first to be yet another 'growth imperative'.

The challenge was serious enough that Peter Victor and I decided to spend some time exploring the algebra of inequality. What we found was fascinating. Piketty's 'fundamental law' regarding capital's share of income only holds when the growth rate, savings rate and rate of return on capital remain unchanged over long periods of time.

When they move about, as they usually do, the economy is always chasing equilibrium but never quite arrives. And in the gap between algebra and reality, almost anything can happen. In some circumstances, Piketty is right: declining growth can lead to rising inequality. In others, the exact reverse can happen: even degrowth can be compatible with improved equality.[37]

This was certainly good news of a kind. Even more striking were the circumstances under which this reverse situation actually happens. The most critical factor in the analysis is something called the 'elasticity of substitution between labour and capital'. This parameter indicates the ease with which it is possible to substitute capital for labour as the relative prices of capital and labour change.

At higher levels of substitutability between capital and labour, inequality does indeed escalate out of control as growth rates decline, just as Piketty predicted. But in an economy with a lower elasticity of substitution, the dangers are much less acute. In fact, when the elasticity of substitution between capital and labour is less than one, it's possible to reduce income inequality, even as the growth rate declines to zero.

The most striking thing about this finding is that low elasticities of substitution between capital and labour are associated precisely with the essential 'service-based' sectors on which we have already focussed so much attention. The Cinderella sectors of the previous chapter are less amenable to the substitution of capital for labour, because of the key role of people's time and skill in delivering them.

In summary, the endless mining of working life in pursuit of productivity gains for the owners of capital is not just detrimental to prosperity but also inimicable to social justice. But conversely, when we protect, nurture and properly value the time spent by people working in the service of each other, a post-growth economy has the potential to become more equal rather than less.

Could it be that the impossibility theorems guarding the path towards a post-growth economics are in fact less robust than they appear to be? Just how much of what appears to propel us relentlessly towards growth − under pain of collapse − is an artefact of happenstance? Or the result of misunderstanding? These questions are certainly worth asking, even of our most cherished beliefs. Charting the course towards a post-growth economics is an exercise in continually challenging the conventional wisdom.

Does credit create a growth imperative?

Conventional wisdom suggests, for instance, that the mechanism of credit-creation by commercial banks delivers yet another growth imperative. According to this wisdom, the charging of interest on debt leads to instability in the absence of economic growth. Without growth, so the argument goes, it is impossible to service interest payments and repay debts, which would therefore accumulate unsustainably and eventually destabilise the economy.

This claim has been made, for instance, by the late ecological economist Richard Douthwaite. In *The Ecology of Money*, Douthwaite suggests that the 'fundamental problem with the debt method of creating money is that, because interest has to be paid on almost all of it, the economy must grow continuously if it is not to collapse.'[38]

Likewise, US degrowth activist Charles Eisenstein maintains that 'our present money system can only function in a growing economy. Money is created as interest-bearing debt: it only comes into being when someone promises to pay back even more of it.'[39]

We have already paid some attention to this debt-based money system and challenged its position in the economy of tomorrow. But if this argument is correct, the implications are profound. A post-growth economy simply could not live inside any recognisable form of capitalism. We would have to systematically dismantle one of the most fundamental aspects of capitalism – the charging of interest on debt – to have any chance of success. Though not of course impossible to contemplate, such a requirement certainly appears to push the post-growth economy beyond the dreams of all but the most utopian visionaries.

Strangely enough, the understanding itself has been subject to remarkably little in-depth economic scrutiny. There's a reason for this. Understanding the growth dynamics of credit creation requires an economic model capable of simulating the interaction between the monetary circuit and the real economy – exactly the kind of model that was conspicuous by its absence in the run-up to the financial crisis (Chapter 2).[40]

In recent years, there has been a renewed interest in models of this kind. Many of them build on the pioneering work of the late former UK Treasury economist, Wynne Godley, one of the few who was able to predict the financial crisis. In particular, Godley and his colleagues developed the concept of stock-flow consistent (SFC) economic models.[41]

The overall rationale of the SFC approach is to account consistently for all monetary flows between agents and sectors across the economy. The approach can be captured in three broad axioms: first, that each expenditure from a given actor (or sector) is also the income to another actor (or sector); second, that each sector's financial assets correspond to financial liabilities of at least one other sector, with the sum of all assets and liabilities across all sectors equalling zero; and finally, that changes in stocks of financial assets are consistently related to flows within and between economic sectors.

These simple understandings lead to a set of accounting principles that can be used to test any economic model or scenario prediction for consistency as a possible solution to financial flows in the real world. For this reason, SFC models are a powerful tool in the development of a post-growth macroeconomics. It's also why Peter Victor and I adopted this approach explicitly in our own modelling work.[42]

We decided to test the 'growth imperative' hypothesis ourselves directly. Does credit create a growth imperative? Does an interest-based money system necessarily require growth to remain stable? Using a simplified version of our own framework we set out to test the stability of a stationary, or quasi-stationary, economy, in the presence of interest-bearing debt and commercial credit creation.[43]

Somewhat to our surprise, we found not only that such a state is possible, but that it is stable across a wide range of different interest rate scenarios. We subjected our hypothetical economy to one-off shocks and to random fluctuations in the level of consumption, and the model remained stable. We also simulated a successful transition from a growth state to a stationary state without destabilising the economy.[44]

These findings don't exonerate a credit-based money system. As we saw in Chapter 8, this credit creation can lead to unsustainable levels of public and private debt, increased price and fiscal instability, speculative behaviour in relation to environmental resources, greater inequality in incomes and in wealth, and a profound and debilitating loss of sovereign power in the economy.

Monetary reform remains an essential component in the economy of tomorrow. But the results of our model suggest that it is not necessary to eliminate interest-bearing debt per se, if the goal is to achieve a resilient, stationary or quasi-stationary state of the economy. In short, one more impossibility theorem against a post-growth economics turns out to be false.

The stabilising role of government

There were some surprising corollaries to our overall finding. One of them was the absolutely critical importance of government fiscal policy. Just as Keynes predicted, government spending has the power to stabilise or to destabilise the economy.

One of our simulations explored the outcome of a 'strict austerity' policy.[45] Following a one-off consumption shock, government responds by cutting spending in order to try and reduce the fiscal deficit to zero. The result is a disaster. Consumption and investment both collapse and debts escalate uncontrollably, reinforcing the insights of all those who criticised austerity in the wake of the financial crisis (Chapter 2).

With the wrong policy, instability is entirely possible in a no-growth economy just as it is in a growth-based economy. Another of our simulations underlined this point. We explored what might happen when the 'animal spirits' of investors persuade firms to invest more or less readily depending on their expectations about the future.[46]

Figure 9.2 shows what happens. Scenario 1 represents the initial response of our stationary state economy to a one-off consumption shock. After an initially dramatic reversal, the economy begins to settle down again, supporting our claim that the stationary state is broadly stable under such a one-off event.

Scenario 2 shows what happens when animal spirits are exaggerated. The reluctance of firms to invest in the recession and their exuberance to do so when the economy bounces back sets up a boom-and-bust cycle of increasing amplitude, which will inevitably become unstable.[47]

Finally, however, Scenario 3 in Figure 9.2 illustrates the impact of a 'countercyclical' spending strategy. Government increases public spending when output is falling and reduces public spending when output is rising. This strategy has an immediate calming effect on the economy, bringing it back to a quasi-stationary state faster even than occurred (in Scenario 1) in the absence of exaggerated animal spirits.

We applied a similar principle to allow government spending to play a moderating role in the transition from a growth-based to a

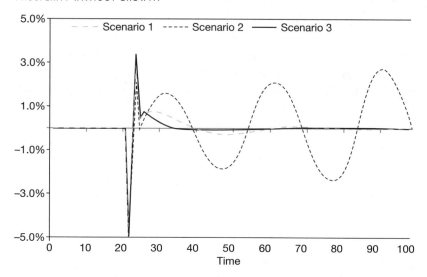

Figure 9.2 The stabilising role of countercyclical public spending
Source: Jackson and Victor (2015: figure 11).

stationary state economy. The principle proved remarkably robust. It appears that government spending provides the means to stabilise an unstable economy under a wide variety of conditions, in particular in those that lead ultimately to a stationary state.[48]

These findings would likely come as no surprise to Keynes or indeed to Hyman Minsky. Both economists saw fiscal policy as critical to the stability of the economy. Minsky in particular proposed a vital role for government as 'employer of last resort' spending directly into the economy to maintain high levels of employment and stabilise output in times of crisis.[49]

What's emerging here is that strategies of countercyclical spending, social investment and public sector employment play a vital role not just in the protection of social wellbeing but in the fundamental dynamics of the post-growth economy.

One final point is worth making. The capability of government to exercise these stabilising strategies depends on having an appropriate monetary policy. There may be no case for doing away with the charging of interest on debt altogether. But there is a strong case for government to have influence over its own power to invest in social welfare. This chapter underlines the importance of monetary reform to the economy of tomorrow.

Beyond the growth dilemma

My aim in this chapter has been first and foremost to make the case that a new post-growth macroeconomics is absolutely essential. We cannot entirely predict the growth potential of the economy of tomorrow. But the conditions of enterprise and of investment are certainly likely to reduce the growth potential of the economy, as conventionally measured, even as they also allow us to improve the quality of our society and protect the integrity of our environment.

I've also argued that building such a macroeconomics is a precise and definable task. Starting from clear first principles we can identify the underlying dimensions of this macroeconomy: the nature of enterprise, the quality of work, the structure of investment and the role of money within it.

The overarching goal for post-growth macroeconomics must be to show how these dimensions can be integrated into a coherent economic framework that delivers high levels of employment, allows for social investment, reduces inequality and protects financial stability.

In the conventional wisdom, these aims would all appear to be impossible. Economic stagnation is a recipe for high unemployment, rising inequality, escalating debt and increased financial instability, in this view. But this chapter has shown that a systematic approach to these challenges reveals surprising avenues of possibility.

Apparent growth imperatives dissolve under a closer scrutiny. Apparent impossibility theorems turn out to be no more than gatekeepers, standing guard over the transition to a post-growth economy, but armed mainly with false assumptions and outdated precepts. When challenged, they sometimes even turn tail and run.

There is a sense in which this should not surprise us. Economics is an artefact of human society. Its apparent intractability is a cultural construct. We devise the rules of the game and establish its mores. We build and regulate the institutions that serve it. Its gatekeepers are the characters in a drama of our own making. Rewriting their role lies entirely within our remit.

Integrating these insights into a consistent overarching theory is still very much a work in progress. But the overwhelming lesson from the exploration in this chapter is that a coherent 'post-growth' macroeconomics is entirely possible.

10

THE PROGRESSIVE STATE

The care of human life and happiness, and not their destruction, is the first and only object of good government.

Thomas Jefferson, 1809[1]

Achieving a lasting prosperity relies on providing capabilities for people to flourish – within certain limits. Those limits are not determined by us, but by the ecology and resources of a finite planet. Unbounded freedom to expand our material appetites just isn't sustainable. Governance is needed if we are to chart a path between rival dystopias and find a sustainable balance between aspiration and constraint.

Dismantling consumer capitalism doesn't look easy. Overthrowing it precipitously could drive us even faster along the road to ruin. But incremental changes on their own are unlikely to be enough. And even the most obvious changes seem hard to implement. Governments sometimes appear powerless to intervene, weakened by electoral cycles or captured by corporate interests.

Faced with this kind of intractability it's tempting to retrench. To cling more tightly to existing tenets. Or to resort to a kind of fatalism.

A place where we accept the inevitability of a changing climate, an unequal world, perhaps even the collapse of society. And concentrate all our efforts on looking after number one. In such circumstances, who would not look first towards their own and their family's security?

There are also those for whom revolution appears to be the answer. Or, if not the answer, then at least the inevitable consequence of continued social and ecological dysfunction. Let's break up the banks. Let's dismantle globalisation. Let's put an end to corporate power and overthrow corrupt governments. Let's demolish the old institutions and start anew.

But there are risks here, too. The spectre of a new barbarism lurks in the wings. Constrained for resources, threatened with climate change, struggling for economic stability: how long could we maintain civil society in such a world if we have already torn down every institutional structure we can lay our hands on? Both positions are understandable. But neither response is particularly constructive. Nor, as it happens, are they inevitable.

Is the vision of a captured, powerless, inefficient government the only one available to us? Or is it possible to conceive a renewed vision of the role of the state, fit for purpose in a resource-constrained and warming world? Can we define a clear set of tasks? Can we identify the resources that would be needed to govern for prosperity? The aim of this chapter is to explore these questions.

Contesting governance

There are dangers of venturing into such a contested terrain, of course. Debates over the role of the state, and in particular the question of whether we need 'more state' or 'less state', have been fiercely fought at times and have complex roots in history. Within the last century in particular, challenges against state governance have been vociferous and prolonged. Many of these recent challenges have often flowed from particular visions for the economy – most of them drawing on the supposed virtues of the 'free market'.

We touched on some of this in earlier chapters of the book. If the free and open market is the best instrument for the fair allocation of scarce resources and the most efficient means of provisioning for human needs, then it appears to follow that less government is better than more. The role of the state should be to get out of the way of markets so that they can operate without intervention.

This idea has achieved an almost unrivalled supremacy in contemporary economics and it has been used to particularly pernicious effect both in the liberalisation of financial markets and in defence of the subsequent austerity (Chapter 2).

In support of their views, proponents of laissez-faire capitalism will almost invariably draw on the failure of the most significant governance alternative of the last two centuries. The collapse of communism in the 1990s did nothing to persuade ordinary people that an active, interventionist state can be a good thing. The historical weaknesses of communism – the corruption of power, the erosion of autonomy, the destructive nature of its economic model – appear to underline the same message. Big government is bad for prosperity.

Quite often justification for this position is sought in the metaphor of the 'invisible hand' and the writings of Adam Smith. But it's useful to recall (Chapter 7) that Smith himself was intensely aware of the distorting power of corporate interests, and argued specifically that government was essential to keep these in check. The bigger the interests, the greater the power needed by government, to protect society against corruption and capture, according to Smith.[2]

By the middle of the twentieth century, two almost diametrically opposed conceptions of governance lay at the heart of debates about economics. These crystallised particularly clearly in the long-running dispute between the followers of the Austrian philosopher Friedrich Hayek and those of the British economist John Maynard Keynes.[3]

A vociferous defender of individual freedom of choice, Hayek warned of the lure of collectivism. He observed candidly the abuses of power that prevailed in the early communist countries and railed against central planning as a form of tyranny. For Hayek, government intervention was the first step on *The Road to Serfdom*.[4]

Keynes, for his part, was far from blind to the limitations of government. He was profoundly aware of the dystopian incarnations of communism (and of fascism) and wrote extensively about them. He would even complain privately about the short-sightedness of

Western politicians. But he saw nonetheless an absolutely fundamental role for government in maintaining economic and indeed social stability. Indeed for Keynes, social stability was one of the primary functions of macroeconomics.[5]

Of particular importance were Keynes' prescriptions about countercyclical spending. Government's influence over economic stability through its own ability to tax and spend lies at the heart of Keynes' macroeconomics. In Chapter 2, we saw how Keynesian ideas came naturally to the fore in the aftermath of the financial crisis in 2008 and prompted calls for a Green New Deal to revive the economy and invest in transition.

The importance of Keynes' ideas during the financial crisis has led some people to argue that the long-standing disputes over the role of government have changed profoundly in the last decade. 'The current financial crisis has also become a political crisis', wrote the political scientist Peter Hall, at the time. Financial instability 'is reconfiguring the role of government in the economy and conventional wisdom about the appropriate relationship between the public and the private sector', he argued.[6]

It would certainly be fair to say that the events of 2008 and 2009 rewrote the boundary between the public and the private sector and changed profoundly the landscape of twenty-first-century politics. Part-nationalisation of financial sector institutions was an almost shocking turn of events, particularly from a free-market perspective in which government is broadly seen as a distortion of the market.

And yet there was little disagreement anywhere about the role of the state in the circumstances. On the contrary, the only possible response when the economy stood on the brink of failure was for governments to intervene. Even the diehards agreed on this. 'Finance is inherently unstable', acknowledged *The Economist* in the early days of the crisis. 'So the state has to play a big role in making it safer by lending in a crisis in return for regulation and oversight.'[7]

A cynic might argue that, in leaping to the defence of financial institutions and in their partisan injections of financial stimulus, governments have in fact failed to respond to the lessons of the crisis. Far from reducing risk in financial markets and protecting the needs of the most vulnerable in society, state-sanctioned responses have shored up the balance sheets of financial institutions at the expense of social investment.

The broadly regressive nature of these responses has tended to reinforce a different kind of critique of government, namely that it is already captured by the interests of the few and broadly incapable of acting in the interests of the many. This view is often taken, for instance, by Marxian economists.

Some kind of state power is needed, even according to Hayek, just to sustain the legal structures which establish property rights and guarantee personal freedoms. 'But these rights have to be enforced', says the Marxist historian David Harvey, 'and it is at this point that the state, with its monopoly over the legitimate use of force and violence, is called upon to repress and police any transgressions against the personal property regime'.

Once this protective role of the state begins to privilege powerful corporations, as it has done at various points in history, not least in response to the financial crisis, then it corrupts the 'social bond between individual human rights and private property [which] lies at the centre of almost all contractual theories of government'.[8]

Perhaps the single most powerful way in which states have fallen prey to corporate interest is in relation to power over the money supply. As we saw in previous chapters, handing over control of the money supply to private interests has destabilised financial markets and distorted investment markets. But it has also disadvantaged the state in two additional ways. First, ideologically, by forcing them to protect financial institutions that are 'too big to fail'; and second, financially, by severely curtailing the potential for social investment, in particular when it is most needed, at times of crisis.

These critiques of government are potentially paralysing. It's almost as though the state can do nothing right, when the very idea of governance comes under attack from every side.

The right calls unashamedly on the state to rescue financial institutions during times of crisis, but the rhetoric of inefficiency and control is very quickly re-established to justify austerity in public spending and to resist regulation of markets, as soon as stability is restored. From the left, the state is regarded as a crucial agent in the protection of social goods, but it is broadly perceived as corrupted by private interest and impotent to act in the interests of ordinary citizens.

Governing the commons

More nuanced views of governance do, of course, exist. One of the most interesting of these belongs to the late Elinor Ostrom. Her work on the governance of the commons – grazing land, forests, fish stocks – earned her the honour of becoming the first woman ever to earn the Nobel prize for economics in 2009. Since many ecological resources (including the climate) can be classed as 'common pool resources', her work is of particular interest to the aims of this book.[9]

Working as a political scientist in the US, Ostrom had for some years been studying how small communities managed local resources when she happened to attend a lecture by the ecologist Garrett Hardin. It was 1968 – the same year in which Hardin published his landmark 'Tragedy of the commons'. Hardin's primary interest was in the problem of unchecked population growth. Like Malthus before him, he became convinced that the earth could not continue to provide resources at the same rate that the population was growing.[10]

Somewhere along the way, Hardin came across a couple of lectures first published in 1833 by the Victorian economist William Forster Lloyd. In the first of two lectures, Lloyd compares the quality of livestock on enclosed lands with those reared on common land. 'Why are the cattle on a common so puny and stunted?' he asks. 'Why is the common itself so bare-worn?' His answer lies in the different incentive structures that govern private land as opposed to commons.[11]

When animals are grazed on private land, the owner has an incentive to increase the number of livestock only to the point that the land itself can sustain. Beyond that point, the quality of both lifestock and land declines, and the landowner himself must bear the costs of overgrazing in terms of poor quality outputs, declining profits and degraded assets. The pursuit of profit finds a natural check in the desire to protect the underlying assets.

On common land things work differently. The land is owned by everyone and by no one at the same time. The fact that it is owned by everyone means that each farmer has an incentive to bring one more animal to graze there. The fact that it is owned by no one means that no one pays the associated costs.

Clearly, the commons cannot sustain an ever-increasing number of cows and so at some stage the animals suffer, the pasture becomes threadbare; the ecosystem fails. On private land, the risk of failure is borne by the landowner. But in the case of commons it's borne by society. Private profits lead to socialised losses – just as they did with the banking system during the financial crisis (Chapter 2).

The 'Tragedy' lies, in Hardin's view, in the inevitability with which common pool resources become degraded. And he offers only two possible solutions out of the dilemma. One is to place common pool resources under state ownership and management (nationalisation). The other is to assign individual property rights to them (privatisation). In an era when nationalisation was practically synonymous with communism, and communism was cast as the devil incarnate, it is perhaps not surprising that the mainstream economic response was to argue for the privatisation of commons.

Ostrom's response to the 'Tragedy' was different. Heavily influenced by Hayek, she resisted the idea that states know best. But neither did she sympathise with the rush to assign private property rights. Instead she drew on her empirical work to suggest another alternative.

In some circumstances, she insisted, there is no tragedy. Commons are owned by communities, often by people who live near each other and know each other well. Communities set up their own rules regarding access and create sanctions for those who violate them. And under certain conditions, this allows them to manage local resources successfully without recourse either to state ownership or to private enclosure.

Ostrom and her husband Vincent documented many hundreds of such cases and distilled from these examples a set of 'design principles' that led to successful common resource management. These included effective monitoring by the community, efficient dispute resolution and graduated sanctions schemes.

These principles also include an appeal to what Vincent Ostrom called 'polycentric governance' – a set of nested levels of governance from the most local to the most interconnected, each level taking some responsibility for the overall management of the system.

Many common pool resources – the oceans, the climate, even the money system, perhaps – are so interconnected that some need for higher levels of governance, at state or even at international level, is almost inevitable and sometimes desirable. A fascinating example of the 'desirability' of state governance of common pool resources is provided by the UK's attempt to sell off nationally owned forests in the wake of the financial crisis.

Ownership of the forests was formally vested in the Secretary of State for the Environment. Under pressure to achieve cost savings and reduce the deficit, the Department launched a consultation on the best way to sell off some of its assets. A public outcry ensued. The forests may have been the Minister's to own. But it turned out they were not the Minister's to sell. The community – in this case the general public – reacted vehemently to the idea and the scheme was abandoned.

Government as a commitment device

None of this is to suggest that governance for prosperity can be reduced to the community management of common pool resources. David Harvey has suggested that a 'political praxis' should strive for conditions under which the 'opposition between private property and state power is displaced as far as possible by common rights regimes'. When a Marxist economist begins to talk about dissolving 'the class opposition between capital and labour', there is clearly hope that the old ideological divisions are giving way to more practical visions of governance.[12]

But even within a polycentric approach to governance, there is still clearly some role for an effective state – for example, in establishing ecological limits and supporting common rights regimes; in using its power to tax and spend to stabilise economic cycles and achieve full employment; and finally in helping to shift the social logic that has us trapped in the 'iron cage' of consumerism (Chapter 6).

This last claim is clearly contentious in a modern democracy. Policy makers are (perhaps rightly) uncomfortable with the idea that they have any role in influencing people's values and aspirations. But the truth is that governments intervene constantly in the social logic of consumption, whether they like it or not.

One of the most dramatic ways in which this occurs is through social investment. Where (and how) governments invest has a huge influence on infrastructure, on technology, on access and ultimately on lifestyle. Health, education and public transport are archetypically public concerns, in which social investment is demonstrably vital.[13]

But government also plays a role in shaping technological innovation, as the Italian-born economist Mariana Mazzucato has pointed out. It's a common myth, she argues, to suppose that innovation is best suited to the private sector. On a closer inspection, the reality is very different. Private capital doesn't like risk and new technologies are inherently risky. Mazzucato documents example after example where government investment was vital to commercial success. '[E]very technology that makes the iPhone smart and not stupid owes its funding to both basic and applied research funded by the State', she points out.[14]

The influence of the state is not confined to technological innovation. A myriad different signals are sent out by the way in which education is structured, by the importance accorded to economic indicators, by public sector performance indicators, by procurement policies, by the impact of planning guidelines on public and social spaces, by the influence of wage policy on the work–life balance, by the impact of employment policy on economic mobility (and hence on family structure and stability), by the presence or absence of product standards (on durability for example), by the degree of regulation of advertising and the media, and by the support offered to community initiatives and faith groups.

In all these arenas, policy shapes and co-creates the social world. And the idea that it is legitimate for the state to intervene in changing the social logic of consumerism is far less problematic than is often portrayed.

At one level, the task here is as old as the hills. It is, in part at least, the task of balancing individual freedoms against the common good. Governance mechanisms emerged in human society for precisely this reason. The evolutionary basis for this is beginning to be understood. Societies capable of protecting social behaviour have a better chance of survival.[15]

The philosophical basis is provided by the concept of a 'social contract', an implicit arrangement between individuals and society to curb narrow individualism and support social behaviour. We hand over some of our individual freedoms. But in return we gain a certain security that our lives will be protected against the unbounded freedoms of others.[16]

Oxford economic historian Avner Offer provides a valuable extension of this idea in *The Challenge of Affluence*.[17] Left to our own devices, argues Offer, individual choices tend to be irredeemably myopic. We favour today too much over tomorrow, in ways which appear entirely 'irrational' under any reasonable discount rate. Economists call this the problem of 'hyperbolic' discounting.

It's not at all unfamiliar to bemoan the short-sightedness of human behaviour. Offer's unique contribution is to suggest that this fallibility has (or has in the past had) a social solution.

To prevent ourselves from trading away our long-term wellbeing for the sake of short-term pleasures, society has evolved a whole set of 'commitment devices': social and institutional mechanisms that moderate the balance of choice away from the present and in favour of the future.

Savings accounts, marriage, norms for social behaviour, government itself in some sense: all these can be regarded as commitment devices. Mechanisms which make it a little easier for us to curtail our appetite for immediate arousal and protect our own future interests. And indeed – although this is less obvious in Offer's exposition – the interests of affected others.

The idea that paternalistic interventions in the 'choice architecture' can help us counter short-termism and overcome social traps has been proposed by economist Richard Thaler and Harvard law professor Cass Sunstein in their enormously popular book *Nudge: Improving Decisions about Health, Wealth, and Happiness*. So, for example, by placing healthy foods rather than sweets near the checkout or making people opt out of pension fund contributions rather than having them opt in are seen as ways of 'nudging us' towards good long-term decisions and away from bad short-term ones.[18]

It's an appealing idea. *Nudge* did a lot to enhance the legitimacy of the idea that government has a role to play in helping people to live better lives. But it doesn't really go far enough in recognising the enormity of the constraints that people face, in their struggle to do the 'right thing'. Nor indeed does it fully recognise that some of the obstacles arise directly from the prevailing logic of consumer capitalism.

The trouble is, as Offer demonstrates, that the pursuit of affluence is itself eroding and undermining our commitment devices. Marriage, parenthood, community: all of these have come under attack in modern affluent countries. The explosion of debt, the decline of savings and the financial crisis itself reveal the erosion of economic prudence. And the hollowing out of government has left us ill-prepared to deal with this 'crisis of commitment'.[19]

Strikingly, Offer places a key responsibility for this erosion on the relentless pursuit of novelty in modern society. We explored this dynamic in Chapter 6. It is part of the social logic which perpetuates consumer capitalism. Novelty keeps us buying more stuff. Buying more stuff keeps the economy going. The end result is a society 'locked in' to consumption growth by forces outside the control of individuals.

Nature and structure conspire against us here. Lured by our evolutionary roots, bombarded with persuasion, and seduced by novelty: we are like children in a compulsory sweet shop, knowing full well that sugar is bad for us; but forced to stand in front of the overflowing shelves, and completely unable to resist the temptation.

At first sight this looks damning for the prospects that laissez-faire individualism is a sufficient governance mechanism for a lasting prosperity. Left to our own individual devices, it seems, there is not much hope that people will spontaneously behave sustainably. But we have seen already (Chapter 7) how this vision of human nature is a profound misconception. Taken together these insights point us towards a solution. The key lies in understanding more clearly the role that government – and 'governmentality' – plays in this dynamic.

The governmentality of growth

Social stability rests on economic stability. In a growth-based economy, economic stability rests on growth. So government finds itself needing to promote economic growth just in order to maintain stability. To do this, of course, it needs citizens to be consumers. More than that, it needs them to be a particular kind of individualistic and materialistic consumer with a continued appetite for consumer novelty. And this need persists even where it conflicts with the best intentions of government to protect or enhance social and ecological goods.

Social stability is, arguably, the highest of these goods. And to protect it, modern governments have engaged in an almost relentless rhetoric to promote the role of the citizen as consumer. These include appeals to individual freedom of choice and consumer sovereignty as well as the promotion of consumer novelty as a good in its own right.

But it goes beyond rhetoric. A complex network of institutions, regulations and market signals co-create the culture of consumerism. Concrete infrastructure determines the world of physical possibilities. Institutional structures constrain the possibilities for our social life. Social norms curtail the freedoms of the creative mind.

These constructions appear to us – and to government – as concrete, reified truths: 'laissez-faire policy is how markets work best'; 'de-regulation is what businesses want from government'; 'consumer choice is what people want'. We are even led to believe that citizens are, by nature, exactly what we need them to be: individualistic, hedonistic consumers in search of the good life – cashed out in increasingly materialistic ways.

The only trouble with this – aside from its implications in the ecological, social and financial crises that we face – is that it is patently false. As we saw in Chapter 7, it's completely mistaken to suppose that human motivations are all selfish; and ridiculous to call on evolutionary justifications for this. Evolution doesn't preclude moral, social and altruistic behaviours. On the contrary, social behaviours evolved in humans precisely because they offer selective advantages to the species.

This is not to suggest that human beings are angels. It's clear that both selfishness and altruism exist in all of us. But the balance between self- and other-regarding behaviours depends crucially on social structure. Where self-interest is rewarded, greed and selfishness thrive. But when social structures favour altruism, then empathy and kindness flourish and selfishness is penalised. The social structure of consumer capitalism is clearly in the former, rather than the latter category.

In understanding why this has happened, it's useful to draw on Michel Foucault's notion of governmentality – defined broadly as the 'art of government' – or as 'ways of governing'. Governmentality refers in particular to the set of organised practices and structures through which subjects are governed. It can be thought of as the way in which governments try to produce the citizen best suited to fulfil governments' own policies.[20]

The importance of Foucault's work is to suggest that governments find themselves drawn into specific ways of behaving, in part as a result of their own policies. This of course is exactly what we have identified in this chapter. Increasingly, it seems, the institutions of consumer society are designed to favour a particularly materialistic individualism and to encourage the relentless pursuit of consumer novelty because this is exactly what's needed to keep the economy going. The governmentality of the consumer society demands it.

The erosion of commitment is a structural requirement for growth as well as a structural consequence of affluence. Growth calls on us to be myopic, individualistic, novelty seekers, because that's exactly what's needed to perpetuate the economic system. And at the same time it propels us in this direction by undermining the commitment devices that support more altruistic and more conservative values.

The importance of governmentality lies in the recognition that this process doesn't just happen by itself. Government plays a crucial, indeed an active, role in it, precisely because it bears a responsibility for the stability of the macroeconomy. The individualistic pursuit of novelty is a key requirement in consumption growth and economic stability depends on consumption growth. Little surprise then that the drift of policy is in these directions.

Beyond the conflicted state

The principal role of government is to ensure that long-term public goods are not undermined by short-term private interests. It seems ironic then, tragic even, that governments across the world – and in particular in the liberal market economies – have been so active in championing the pursuit of unbounded consumer freedoms, often elevating consumer sovereignty above social goals and actively encouraging the expansion of the market into different areas of people's lives.

It is particularly odd to see this tendency going hand in hand with the desire to protect social and ecological goals. It's notable, for example, that the UK, one of the most fiercely liberal market economies, has also at times been a vociferous champion of sustainability, social justice and climate change policy. The UK's 2005 Sustainable Development Strategy received widespread international praise. Its 2008 Climate Change Act was a world-leading piece of legislation.

There is a real sense here of institutional schizophrenia. On the one hand, government is bound to the pursuit of economic growth. On the other, it finds itself having to intervene to protect the common good from the incursions of the market. The state itself is deeply conflicted, striving on the one hand to encourage consumer freedoms that lead to growth and on the other to protect social goods and defend ecological limits. This tension is what the historian Karl Polanyi called the 'double movement' of society.[21]

But the reason for this conflict becomes clear once we recognise the role that growth has conventionally played in macroeconomic stability. It arises directly from the governmentality of the growth-based society. With a vital responsibility to protect jobs and to ensure stability, the state is bound (under current macroeconomic understandings) to prioritise economic growth. And it is locked into this task, even as it seeks to promote sustainability and the common good. Government itself, in other words, is caught in the dilemma of growth.

Overcoming this dilemma is absolutely vital. The lessons from this study make it clear that without clear governance, change will be impossible. Individuals are too exposed to social signals and status competition. Businesses operate under market conditions. A transition from narrow self-interest to social behaviours, or from relentless novelty to a considered conservation of things that matter, can only proceed through changes in underlying structure. Changes that strengthen commitment and encourage social behaviour. And these changes require governments to act.

The thrust of policy over the last half-century – particularly in the liberal market economies – has been going in almost exactly the opposite direction. Governments have systematically promoted materialistic individualism and encouraged the pursuit of consumer novelty. This trend has been perpetrated, mostly deliberately, under the assumption that this form of consumerism serves economic growth, protects jobs and maintains stability. And as a result, the state has become caught up in a belief that growth should trump all other policy goals.

But this narrow pursuit of growth represents a horrible distortion of the common good and a misrepresentation of our underlying human values. It also undermines the legitimate role of government. A state framed narrowly as the protector of market freedom in the unbounded pursuit of consumerism bears no relation to any meaningful vision of social contract. At the end of the day, the state is society's commitment device, par excellence, and the principal agent in protecting our shared prosperity. A new vision of governance that embraces this role is critical.

Knowing that family, community, friendship, health and so on are vital influences on prosperity, and that the ability of the individual to protect these factors is being eroded in modern society, there would appear to be a strong argument in favour of a clearer and more active role for government in this regard.

Equally, accepting that unemployment, injustice and inequality have impacts not just at the individual level but at the level of aggregate wellbeing, there would appear to be an argument in favour of government intervening to protect employment, justice and equality.

Such a role would be, in a sense, a reinvigoration of the idea of the social contract. Within such a contract, a legitimate role for government would be to strengthen and protect commitment devices that prevent myopic choice and, equally importantly, to reduce the pernicious structural impacts of economic development that increase inequality and reduce wellbeing.

Of course, such a vision requires a democratic mandate. 'Political change comes from leadership and popular mobilisation. And you need both of them', argued a former UK Climate Change Secretary, Ed Miliband. Authoritarianism is damaging to human wellbeing in its own right. And in any case it is unlikely to succeed in modern pluralistic societies. A progressive State must engage actively with citizens both in establishing the mandate and delivering the change.[22]

But this doesn't absolve government from its own vital responsibility in ensuring a shared prosperity. The role of government is to provide the capabilities for its citizens to flourish – within ecological limits. The analysis here suggests that, at this point in time, that responsibility entails shifting the balance of existing institutions and structures away from materialistic individualism and providing instead real opportunities for people to pursue intrinsic goals of family, friendship, community, participation, creativity.

This view is by no means simply a luxury of advanced western economies. At a recent symposium on growth, I heard a young Singaporean minister propose a very similar view. Politicians are locked into a system that rewards them with power, he said. But then he insisted: it's not power but stewardship that constitutes good governance. Politicians should see themselves as stewards of human potential. Their role is to enable people to reach their full potential as human beings. To provide them with the skills and infrastructure to do so.[23]

For as long as economic stability depends on growth, the conflicted State will struggle to achieve this aim. Short-term electoral aims and short-term economic thinking will prevail. There will inevitably be a powerful tendency for governments to support social structures that reinforce materialistic, novelty-seeking individualism. Because that's what it takes to keep the economy afloat.

This is why the findings of the previous two chapters are so vital. Freeing the macroeconomy from the structural requirement for consumption growth will simultaneously free government to play its proper role in delivering social and environmental goods and protecting long-term interests. The same goal that's vital for a sustainable economy is essential to a progressive State.

Policies for a post-growth society

These considerations are the beginning rather than the end of a serious inquiry into governance for prosperity. They are the starting point for policy: the foundation for a post-growth social contract.

Elaborating on that foundation requires a wider public and policy dialogue than is possible here. Policy making is a social and political process. It must be informed by its constituencies. But it would be wrong to leave the question of policy hanging in the air completely.

And it's clearly possible already to establish some at least of the direction of travel. A step change in political will is probably essential to make progress in all of the proposals outlined below. But that too, I have argued, is surely possible – once the dilemmas that haunt the conflicted state are resolved.

In the following brief paragraphs, I highlight four broad policy themes for a post-growth society: establishing limits, countering consumerism, tackling inequality and 'fixing' economics.[24]

Establishing limits

The material profligacy of consumer society is depleting key natural resources and placing unsustainable burdens on the planet's ecosystems. Establishing clear resource and environmental limits is vital. Integrating these limits into both economic structure and social functioning is essential.

The work of the Stockholm Resilience Centre has done a lot to place this idea on the policy map. Its single biggest message is that planetary boundaries matter. It's fine of course to dispute exactly where they lie. And which ones are most important. And how we should respond to them. But simply to proceed as though limits were irrelevant to human endeavour is to invite disaster.[25]

If governance is to mean anything, it must inform itself about the constraints that nature imposes on us. Identifying clear resource and emission caps and establishing reduction targets under those caps is vital to a robust understanding of our own potential – and the threats to our survival.

This is of course exactly what the IPCC set out to establish in the case of greenhouse gas emissions. The Paris Agreement to 'pursue efforts' to restrict global warming to 1.5°C above the pre-industrial average establishes a precise set of carbon budgets. Meeting these budgets means adhering to rather precise emission pathways. We can enact (some countries have already enacted) legislation and policy that will lead our economies along those pathways. Or, of course, we can also fail to do so.[26]

As our scientific understanding of the environment improves, we learn more about the 'safe operating space' within which we should remain. We're at liberty to ignore or marginalise this knowledge. We also have the opportunity to integrate it into our decision-making. This is the first unavoidable step in establishing where we are. And the good news is, anyone can play.

Any government of any political colour or hue can allocate the relatively modest financial resources needed to measure and to monitor the material and ecological conditions on which our prosperity depends.

Whether it's carbon emissions and climate change, or deforestation and habitat loss, or the condition of genetic and biological diversity, of the quality of the soil, or the cleanliness of the ocean, or the resource quality of material deposits: a basic understanding of our position in relation to such planetary boundaries is entirely possible.

Uncertainty clearly exists. But the process of measuring and collating data informs our decision-making. We may still be many decades away from absolute resource scarcity. Or we may be considerably closer. We may be remarkably close to some production peaks. We may be slightly further away from others. But a scientific understanding of our best available information about these conditions is absolutely vital to proper economic planning.

The single most important message from the very early work on limits to growth (Chapter 1) was that early action is essential. Leaving our decision-making to the point where these changes are already upon us is a recipe for disaster. Addressing limits early is a key ingredient of success. The best possible scientific understanding of our fragile resource base is an absolute priority.

Countering consumerism

The social logic that locks us into the iron cage of consumerism is extremely powerful. But it's also detrimental to prosperity, both ecologically and psychologically. An essential prerequisite for a lasting prosperity is to free people from this damaging dynamic and provide opportunities for sustainable and fulfilling lives.

Governments are understandably reluctant to intervene in what is perceived as an arena of personal or social choice. But changing the social logic of consumption cannot simply be relegated to the realm of individual or community action. Whatever the latent desire for change, it's notoriously difficult for people simply to *choose* sustainable lifestyles. Even highly motivated individuals fall prey to conflict as they attempt to live better lives. The chances of wide-scale societal shifts in behaviour are negligible without changes in the social structure.

Conversely, of course, social structures can and do continually shift people's values and behaviours. Consumerism itself developed as a means of protecting consumption-driven economic growth. The culture of consumerism is conveyed through institutions, the media, social norms and a host of subtle and not so subtle signals encouraging people to express themselves, seek identity and search for meaning through material goods.

There's a very real, historical sense in which the consumer society is an artefact of modernity: co-created by marketeers, investors, advertisers, businesses and politicians. Dismantling these complex incentive structures requires a systematic attention to the myriad ways in which they were constructed, and are continually re-constructed.

Our first course of action must be to ask searching questions about the balance of the institutions that characterise modern society. Do they promote competition or cooperation? Do they reward self-serving behaviour or support those prepared to sacrifice personal gain in the service of others? What signals do schools, universities, business, the media and government itself send out to people? Which behaviours are supported by public investments and infrastructures and which are discouraged?

Perhaps the most critical task to hand is to identify (and correct) those aspects of this complex social structure that provide perverse incentives in favour of a materialistic individualism and undermine the potential for a shared prosperity.

Advertising is one of the most obvious targets for attention. Although advertising provides information, it is particularly pernicious in limiting people's mental and spiritual universe. A post-growth economy must refrain from manipulating our appetites in order to stimulate materialistic desire.

Particular concerns exist over the role of commercial advertising to children. Several countries (notably Sweden and Norway) have banned TV advertising to children under 12. The creation of commercial-free zones such as the one established by São Paulo's 'Clean City Law' is one way of protecting public space from commercial intrusion.[27]

Another is to provide systematic support for public media through state funding. As the Institute for Local Self-Reliance argues, 'communities should have the right to reserve spaces free of commercialism, where citizens can congregate or exchange ideas on an equal footing'.[28]

Stronger trading standards are needed to protect citizens both as workers and as consumers. The Fair Trade initiative is a good example of what can be achieved by companies prepared to act on a voluntary basis. But this approach isn't yet extensive enough to protect ecological and ethical standards along all supply chains. Or to ensure that these questions register on people's buying behaviours.[29]

Trading standards should also systematically address the durability of consumer products. Planned and perceived obsolescence is one of the worst afflictions of the throw-away society and undermines the rights and the legitimate interests of people both as consumers and citizens. Creating long-lasting, durable and serviceable products is essential.[30]

At the end of the day, unravelling the culture – and changing the social logic – of consumerism will require the kind of sustained and systematic effort it took to put it in place to start with. Crucially, though, this effort clearly won't succeed as a purely punitive endeavour. Dismantling consumerism simply isn't enough. Offering people viable alternatives to the consumer way of life is vital.

This means finding new ways to fulfil the social and psychological aspirations which have been given over to material consumption. One way to achieve this is through investment in public amenities and spaces that create opportunities for leisure and self-development. An equally important, complementary strategy lies in the strengthening of communities and the building of strong social ties that enrich human life without enlarging our ecological footprint.

We must nurture and support non-consumerist ways of understanding and being in the world. These ways can draw on a variety of traditions that have always opposed consumerism. They will in turn be strengthened by a retreat from market-driven growth, which inevitably inculcates values, beliefs and ways of being that favour success in the market environment.

What this means in practice requires a more detailed exploration than is possible here. It will certainly require a keener policy attention to what it means to flourish and how to measure this, particularly when it comes to questions of community, social participation and psychological wellbeing.

Crucially, these outcomes cannot be delivered in instrumental, ad hoc ways. Policy must pay closer attention to the structural causes of social alienation and anomie. It must have at its heart the goal of a meaningful and lasting prosperity. Progress depends on building the capabilities for people to flourish in less materialistic ways.

Tackling inequality

Systemic income inequalities increase anxiety, undermine social capital and expose lower income households to higher morbidity and lower life-satisfaction. In fact, the evidence of negative health and social effects right across unequal populations is mounting. Systemic inequality also drives positional consumption, contributing to a material 'ratchet' that drives resource flows through the economy.

Unproductive status competition increases material throughput and creates both psychological distress and social unrest. The British clinical psychologist Oliver James has argued that more unequal societies systematically report higher levels of distress than more equal societies.[31]

This same point has been made by epidemiologists Richard Wilkinson and Kate Pickett. *The Spirit Level* draws together astonishing evidence of the costs of inequality in terms of health and social problems. The broad hypothesis is clearly illustrated in Figure 10.1, which shows a high positive correlation between health and social problems and rising inequality in OECD nations.[32]

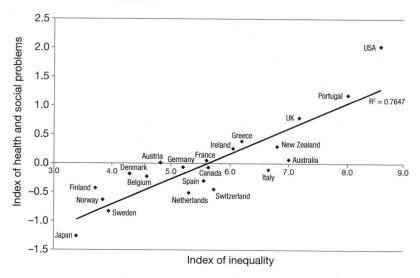

Figure 10.1 The health and social benefits of equality
Source: Data from the Equality Trust (see note 30)

Life expectancy, child wellbeing, literacy, social mobility and trust are all better in more equal societies. Infant mortality, obesity, teenage pregnancy, homicide rates and incidence of mental illness are all lower. Tackling systemic inequality is vital, argue Wilkinson and Pickett, and not just for the least well off. Society as a whole suffers in the face of inequality.

Tackling inequality would reduce social costs, improve quality of life and change the dynamic of status consumption. Little is currently being done to reverse the worsening trends, particularly in the liberalised market economies. But policies and mechanisms for reducing inequality and redistributing incomes are well documented.[33]

Potential policy measures include progressive tax structures, minimum and maximum income levels, improved access to education, anti-discrimination legislation and improving the local environment in deprived areas. Systematic attention to these policies is now vital.

The conditions of equity and ecological limits, taken together, suggest a key role for the model known as 'contraction and convergence' in which equal per capita allowances are established under an ecological cap that converges towards a sustainable level.[34] This approach has been applied, to some extent, for carbon. Similar caps could be established for the extraction of scarce non-renewable resources, for the emission of wastes (particularly toxic and hazardous wastes), for the drawing down of 'fossil' groundwater supplied and for the rate of harvesting of renewable resources.

A key point of influence will lie in the structure of incomes and wages. This balance has consistently rewarded competitive, individualistic and materialistic outcomes even when these are socially detrimental – as the lessons from the financial crisis made clear. Reducing the huge income disparities that result from this would send a powerful signal about what is valued in society.

Better recognition for those engaged in child care, care for the elderly or disabled and volunteer work would shift the balance of incentives away from status competition and towards a more cooperative, and potentially more altruistic, society. Some of these measures could be facilitated by forms of citizen's income, an idea that is now being explored in a variety of nations including Finland, the Netherlands, Canada and Switzerland.[35]

'Fixing' economics

An economy predicated on the continual expansion of debt–driven materialistic consumption is unsustainable ecologically, problematic socially and unstable economically. Changing this destructive dynamic requires the development of robust new economic thinking. Building a new post–growth macroeconomics is an urgent priority.

The shortcomings of the conventional system of national accounts (and the GDP as its central measure) are now well documented. The time is certainly ripe to make progress in developing a national accounting framework which provides a more robust measure of social progress and economic performance.[36]

But the task of fixing economics goes beyond simply adjusting our accounts. A new post–growth macroeconomics must address the dynamics of a slower, more labour-intensive economy, with a significantly changed portfolio of investment.

This new portfolio of investment demands a different financial landscape from the one that led to the collapse of 2008. Long-term security has to be prioritised over short-term gain and social and ecological returns must become as important as conventional financial returns. Reforming capital markets and legislating against destabilising financial practices are not just the most obvious response to the financial crisis; they are also an essential foundation for a new sustainable macroeconomy.

Social investment is likely to play a key role in the new portfolio. Increased investment in public goods and social infrastructure is an essential precursor to a less consumerist world. Enhanced public investment also sends a powerful signal about the balance between private interests and the common good.

This same balance has to be reflected in the politics of labour. The relentless pursuit of labour productivity growth is not necessarily adverse to prosperity. But it can dramatically undermine both the quality of work and the resilience of key economic sectors.

Alternative strategies clearly exist. One of these is to protect and support those sectors which are employment rich – many of which are threatened by austerity, declining social investment and the dynamics of Baumol's cost disease. Such a transition would involve protecting the quality and intensity of people's time in the workplace against incursions from the aggressive cost-cutting behaviour by the owners of capital.

This proposal is not a million miles from Minsky's suggestion that government should act as 'employer of last resort' in stabilising an unstable economy. As we've seen in Chapter 9, counter-cyclical public spending is, in general, a powerful tool for ensuring the stability of the post-growth economy.

Vital to government's ability to engage in this task is the nature of the monetary system itself. Increasing sovereign control over the money supply by removing (or reducing) the power of commercial banks to create money will have multiple advantages. Debt reduction, improved financial stability and enhanced social investment are the fruits of monetary reform.[37]

Governance for prosperity

Bringing all these components together is an enormous but exciting challenge. There are virtually no convincing precedents for a coherent and comprehensive vision of governance for the post-growth economy. But this new politics is neither the oppressive yoke of communism nor the evangelical laissez-faire of neoliberal market economics. It is a vital arena for improved political participation and renewed prosperity.

The myth of the powerless, conflicted state has taken a powerful hold over the collective imagination. Governance itself has been narrowly framed by pernicious half-truths, peddled by vested interests. But the conflicted state is, in large part, a casualty of the growth dilemma. And in rescuing the economy from that dilemma, government stands a chance, at least, of rescuing itself.

This chapter sees a positive, dynamic role for a 'progressive State'. One which is attentive both to changing social conditions and to the underlying needs of its citizens. One which collaborates actively in the design of the good life. One which is inclusive and considerate. One which invests vigorously in the common good. One which is entrepreneurial and innovative. The progressive State is dynamic, progressive and charismatic.

A prerequisite for its existence is freedom from the growth imperative. But the advantages to prosperity are legion. A more equal society will lower the importance of status goods. A less consumption-driven economy will reduce our impact on the planet. Enhanced investment in public goods will provide lasting returns to the common good. A less materialistic society will improve collective wellbeing.

In short, the progressive State is not just the instrumental means for ensuring social and economic stability in a low-growth environment. It is the basis for a renewed vision of governance. It is the foundation for a lasting prosperity.

11

A LASTING PROSPERITY

The people who are crazy enough to think they can change the world are the ones who do.

Steve Jobs, 1998[1]

Society is faced with a profound dilemma. To reject growth is to risk economic and social collapse. To pursue it relentlessly is to endanger the ecosystems on which we depend for long-term survival.

For the most part, this dilemma goes unrecognised in mainstream policy. It's only marginally more visible as a public debate. When reality begins to impinge on the collective consciousness, the best suggestion to hand is that we can somehow 'decouple' growth from its material impacts. And continue to do so while the economy expands exponentially.

The sheer scale of action implied by this is daunting. In a world of 10 billion people all aspiring to Western lifestyles, the carbon intensity of every dollar of output must be more than 200 times lower in 2050 than it is today. Long before the middle of the century, economic activity will need to be taking carbon out of the atmosphere rather than adding to it.[2]

Never mind that no one knows what such an economy looks like. Never mind that decoupling isn't happening at anything like that scale. Never mind that all our institutions and incentive structures continually point in the wrong direction. The dilemma, once recognised, looms so dangerously over our future that we are desperate to believe in miracles. Technology will save us. Capitalism is good at technology. So let's just keep the show on the road and hope for the best.[3]

This delusional strategy has reached its limits. Simplistic assumptions that capitalism's propensity for efficiency will stabilise the climate and solve the problem of resource scarcity are almost literally bankrupt. We now stand in urgent need of a clearer vision, braver policy making, something more robust in the way of a strategy with which to confront the dilemma of growth.

The starting place must be to unravel the forces that keep us in damaging denial. Nature and structure conspire together here. The profit motive stimulates a continual search for newer, better or cheaper products and services. Our own relentless search for novelty and social status lock us into an iron cage of consumerism. Affluence itself has betrayed us.

Affluence simultaneously breeds and feeds upon the continual production and reproduction of consumer novelty. But relentless novelty reinforces anxiety and weakens our ability to protect long-term social goals. In doing so it ends up undermining our own wellbeing and the wellbeing of those around us. Somewhere along the way, we lose the shared prosperity we sought in the first place.

None of this is inevitable. We can't change ecological limits. We can't alter human nature. But we can and do create and recreate the social world. Its norms are our norms. Its visions are our visions. Its structures and institutions shape and are shaped by our norms and visions. This is where transformation is needed.

This book has been dedicated to understanding and articulating such a transformation. The second half of the book, in particular, has set out practical steps that could be taken now to effect the transition to a sustainable economy.

This final chapter returns to some of the broader questions raised along the way. It summarises the key arguments. And it examines the wider implications of aspiring to achieve (or simply needing to deliver) prosperity without growth.

The sacred canopy

The starting point for all of this lies in a vision of prosperity as the ability to flourish as human beings – within the ecological limits of a finite planet.

This vision has undeniably material dimensions. It's perverse to talk about flourishing when there's inadequate food and shelter. And that is still the case for almost two billion people in the poorest parts of the world. But it's also plain to see that the simple equation of quantity with quality, of more with better, is false in general. Stuff on its own doesn't help us flourish. And sometimes it can even impede flourishing.

To do well is in part about the ability to give and receive love, to enjoy the respect of our peers, to contribute usefully to society, to have a sense of belonging and trust in the community, to help create the social world and find a credible place in it. In short, an important component of prosperity is the ability to participate meaningfully in the life of society.

These are primarily social and psychological tasks rather than material ones. The supreme success of the consumer society (and its simultaneous failure) has been to frame them almost entirely in terms of the ownership and possession of material commodities. We're certainly not the first society to endow mere stuff with symbolic meaning. But we are the first to hand over so much of our social and psychological functioning to materialistic pursuits.

Our sense of identity, our expressions of love, our search for meaning and purpose – even our dreams and desires – are articulated through the language of goods. The most fundamental questions we ask about the world and our place in it are played out through consumerism. Unlimited access to material goods stands in for our hopes of freedom. And sometimes even for immortality.

'The human animal is a beast that dies and if he's got money he buys and buys and buys,' says Big Daddy in Tennessee Williams' play *Cat on a Hot Tin Roof*. 'And I think the reason he buys everything he can is that in the back of his mind he has the crazy hope that one of this purchases will be life ever-lasting.'[4]

Here too delusion thrives. Of course material possessions offer novelty. Of course they comfort us and give us hope. Of course they connect us to those we love and seek to emulate. But these connections are fickle at best. They are as likely to impede as to facilitate. They fade and distort over time. Their promise is ultimately groundless.

This is the wisdom of the sages from time immemorial. It hasn't weakened over the years. It hasn't been diluted by our material wealth. But material wealth has made it harder and harder to see where real wealth lies. To distinguish what matters from what glitters. We're trapped in a labyrinth of material aspirations, seemingly destined to remain there until the spell breaks. And when it does, we're often lost. We wake to find foundations built on sand.

Some of the responses I've received from ordinary people underline this point graphically. A hospice manager wrote to me after reading an article I'd written on the illusory consolation of consumerism. He described how the diagnosis of terminal illness confronts people directly with this illusion. Those admitted to his care are suffering in all sorts of ways. Amongst the most difficult to negotiate is the crisis of meaning sparked by the realisation that the consumer dream in which they had been immersed so deeply is of no help to them whatsoever.

A community worker in the mental health sector made a similar point. He described mental breakdown as the equivalent of discovering that the emotional and cognitive dimensions of your life are breaking up. 'The person in crisis can no longer hold in balance a package of habitat, relationships, work, income, debt [and so on] with the skills, aspirations, meanings and purposes that they have evolved from their childhood.' Putting yourself back together again is as much about building new supportive relationships, new purposes and new meanings as it is about drugs or therapy, he told me.

An Augustinian sister reflected on the surprising absence of the concept of limits from our understandings of modernity: 'I suspect for very interesting reasons,' she said. Money offers us 'an imitation (albeit a fraudulent one) of eternity' because it seems as though it can increase without limit, she suggested. In other words, our steadfast allegiance to endless growth may be nothing more (nor less) than a response to our own mortality.

Perhaps none of this is so surprising. According to the psychologist Solomon Sheldon death anxiety motivates all we do and all we strive for as human beings. Death is the 'worm at the core' of human existence. It creates a kind of existential angst about ourselves, about our loved ones, about the fate of our society, about existence itself. It's at work in all societies. So it's not so surprising to find it at work in consumer capitalism.[5]

But this doesn't excuse the failings of consumerism. What's at stake here is not so much the existence of an underlying anxiety – which is common to every society – but rather the success or failure of each society, of each form of social organisation in responding to it.

The US sociologist Peter Berger articulates the challenge beautifully. Every society needs a framework within which to make sense of existence, he argues. This framework relates our temporal existence to some higher 'sacred' order. It provides the foundation for moral guidance and moral governance. And, by offering a transcendent reality, it allows us to confront the question of our own mortality and the loss of those we love.[6]

Berger calls this framework the 'sacred canopy'. His interest is mainly to understand religion: the sacred canopy, par excellence. But the need itself is endemic. It's a vital element in every kind of society we know about. The role of the sacred canopy is to keep us from despair, from the chaotic and sometimes meaningless void that lurks outside the neatly ordered structure of our lives, waiting to overturn our hopes and derail our best intentions.

Religion may offer some defence against this threat. But what should a society do, when religious belief is harder to come by? Or when its intellectual foundations have been shaken? Or when its manifestation entails increasingly fundamentalist (and inhuman) ideals? Is it so unlikely to suppose that some of these vital social functions are taken on by consumerism itself?

Material things comfort us. Sacred goods remind us of those we love, of dreams we hold, of our hopes for the future. Their seemingly endless availability consoles us for the temporary nature of our lives, for our disappointments and failures. It assures us that society holds out the promise of better lives (for us and for our children) into the future.

Seen in this light, consumerism isn't entirely empty. But it is patently flawed. Its sense of justice is tenuous, its framing and disbursement of rewards is iniquitous. It offers us a seductive sense of security, one that needs continually to be reinforced by engaging in yet more consumption. But even if it were sustainable, its success as a psychological strategy is fleeting at best. Pathological at worst.

Transforming a sacred canopy is no trivial task. Dismantling one is fraught with risk. Exhortation is clearly doomed to failure. Asking people to give up material commodities is like inviting a kind of social suicide. Worse still is to threaten our meaningful participation in society.

Unemployment is one such threat. Consumer capitalism may encourage us to define ourselves more as consumers – of goods, of time, of space – than through our role in the production of these things. But work still matters. Losing a job is still one of those situations that shakes our confidence and threatens our social world.[7]

This risk is heightened in a more unequal world. The stigma of unemployment is played out largely through social comparison. The sharper that comparison, the more debilitating the stigma. But in almost every society we've ever known, however equal, a social role of some kind matters. A thin lifeline to the sacred canopy.

Practical responses to this threat also point to reconstruction. And in particular to the advantages of simplicity – decluttering our lives and focusing on essentials. Consolidating the things that matter to us and reducing unnecessary commitments increases our resilience to external shocks and can even improve our quality of life.

Frugality seems harsh to us. But, as *Financial Times* columnist Harry Eyres points out, its linguistic roots don't lie in sacrifice and hardship at all but in the Latin word for fruit. 'Being "for the good fruit" means being honest and temperate, dedicated to long-term flourishing: as vital for human beings as for the earth itself.'[8]

In a world of limits, frugality recalls us to our membership in a wider community: 'Prosperity can only be conceived as a condition that includes obligations and responsibilities to others.' It's a view that's almost totally antithetical to a prevailing notion of prosperity through individual gain. A world constructed around the need to lionise selfishness and greed.[9]

We are encouraged to view the world myopically. Rainforests are 'a long way from here'. Extreme poverty may seem like someone else's problem. We peer at the future – and at those less fortunate than ourselves – through the wrong end of a powerful telescope. Everything seems so far away. But this narrow framing of the world undermines not only our own humanity but also the prospects for a fair and lasting prosperity.[10]

Our task here, as in more immediate and more personal crises, is one of reconstruction. Rebuilding prosperity from the bottom up is what's required. And though it may seem daunting, the reality is that we already know a lot about what's needed.

Prosperity transcends material concerns. Doing well consists in part in our ability to participate in the life of society, in our sense of shared meaning and purpose, in our capacity to create and to care and to dream.

We've become used to chasing all these goals through material stuff. Our challenge is to free ourselves from that constraint. But how should this happen? Is it a political task? Or is it an individual task? Is personal choice even relevant to our escape from the iron cage of consumerism?

Beyond the 'iron cage'

The rather strange answer to this crucial question is both yes and no. Yes, personal choice is possible. Day-to-day and moment-to-moment we make decisions about how to live. True, we are not always cognizant of them. True, they are heavily influenced by habit. By social norms. By the constraints of our past. By the demands of the present. By our expectations for the future. And yet ...

And yet to deny the validity of personal autonomy is to fly in the face of the evidence that people all over the world do in fact make decisions to live differently. This is neither a personal claim to the moral high ground nor a moral exhortation. Neither of these would be appropriate. It's simply an evidence-based reality.

It's possible to lead a healthier life, for instance. It's possible to eat better (or less) and exercise better (or more). It's possible to walk rather than ride. It's possible to own less stuff. It's possible to invest money more ethically. People do these things. For a variety of reasons. And sometimes they feel better for it.

It's possible to breathe more deeply. To spend more time with our family and friends. To volunteer in the community. It's possible to be more creative. To be more charitable. To be kinder to each other. It's possible to engage in totally random acts of unwarranted kindness.

People do all of these things. And strangely, all of them have been shown to have beneficial impacts on wellbeing. They cost nothing. They contribute nothing to the GDP. They have nothing to do with output or efficiency. They have everything to do with prosperity.

This is the 'yes' part of the answer. Yes, it is possible for individuals to prosper outside consumerism. To live better by consuming less. To have more fun with less stuff. Some people are sometimes already doing some of it.

Are these people crazy? Maybe. Are they crazy enough to think they can change the world? Possibly. Will they actually change the world? Who knows. To dare to think differently – even to act differently – is sometimes all that's needed. And sometimes it's nothing like enough for change to happen.

There is certainly a distinct likelihood that individual actions will never in themselves be sufficient to create widespread social change. Particularly in a social environment hostile to that change. Leaving things to personal choice won't work. Hoping it will happen by allowing the market free rein won't work. This is the 'no' part of the answer.

Nor will exhortation help. For one group of people (who already have both status and power) to attempt to persuade another group of people (without either status or power) to forgo material wealth is morally problematic. In today's society, it's tantamount to asking them to give up certain social and psychological freedoms. This cannot ultimately be the way forward.

Essential for change is the construction of credible alternatives. This task is a profoundly social one. The aim must be to provide real capabilities for people to flourish in less materialistic ways. It means investing and reinvesting in those capabilities: physically, financially, emotionally.

A core element here is the revitalisation of the notion of public goods. To renew our sense of public space, of public institutions, of common purpose. To invest money and time in shared goals, assets and infrastructures.

It sounds grand, but it needn't be. Green space, parks, recreation centres, sports facilities, libraries, museums, public transportation, local markets, retreats and 'quiet centres', festivals: these are some of the building blocks for a new vision of social participation.

Public services have increasingly been seen as a means of looking after those who couldn't afford such services privately. But, as the Harvard political philosopher Michael Sandel has pointed out, they 'are also traditionally sites for the cultivation of a common citizenship, so that people from different walks of life encounter one another and so acquire enough of a shared ... sense of a shared life that we can meaningfully think of one another as citizens in a common venture.'[11]

This sense of common endeavour is one of the casualties of consumer society. Little wonder that we've lost our connection to others. Little wonder that our sense of the future is hazy and uncommitted. Little wonder that our visions of prosperity have become blind to wider and more durable social goals. We've carved up our sense of shared endeavour – sometimes quite literally – so that we can sell off the pieces at market price just to keep our economies growing. In the process, we leave ourselves bereft of common meaning and purpose.

Countering consumerism must ultimately include creating the space to renew our vision. To rebuild the sacred canopy. To construct more robust frameworks of meaning and purpose. We must learn to nurture communities of meaning (outside the realm of the market) that offer credible answers to the deep foundational questions that continue to haunt us.[12]

Cinderella at the ball?

The loss of meaning and the decline in common endeavour are both an inevitable consequence of economies that feed, almost literally, on privatising our lives and commercialising our identities. A different kind of economy is essential for a different kind of prosperity. What do we know about this economy?

If we forget momentarily about the relentless pursuit of growth, we can concentrate on defining what an economy should look like. Surprisingly it boils down to a few obvious things. Capabilities for flourishing. The means to a livelihood. Participation in society. A degree of security. A sense of belonging. The ability to share in a common endeavour and yet to pursue our potential as individual human beings.

We know that resilience matters. Economies which collapse under perturbation directly threaten flourishing. We know that equality matters. Unequal societies drive unproductive status competition and undermine wellbeing not only directly but also by eroding our sense of shared citizenship.

Work – and not just paid employment – is vital to the economy of tomorrow, for all sorts of reasons. Work is more than just the means to a livelihood. It's part of our participation in the life of society. Through work we create and recreate the social world and find a credible place in it.

Beyond these basic principles, we also know quite a bit about the specific nature of the economic activities in such a society. They are likely to favour the delivery of service over the throughput of stuff. We want them to offer decent livelihoods. We need them to have lower material and energy throughput.

We know that it isn't just the outputs from these activities that must make a positive contribution to flourishing. It's the form and organisation of our systems of provision as well. Economic organisation needs to work with the grain of community and the long-term social good, rather than against it.

Where some have seen a radical transformation of human work through processes of robotisation, digitalisation and the 'internet of things', this book has outlined a rather different vision. Community-centred enterprise engaged in delivering local services, such as nutrition, education, care, maintenance and repair, recreation, craft, creativity, culture: these activities contribute to flourishing and are embedded in the community. They have the potential for low carbon footprints and they provide meaningful work.

There will still be some role for traditional economic sectors. Resource extraction will diminish in importance, as fewer materials are used and more are recycled. But manufacturing, construction, food and agriculture, retail, communication and financial intermediation will still be important.

Doubtless, the digital economy will transform many of these activities. Certainly, they will need to look rather different from the way they do right now. Agriculture will pay more attention to the integrity of the land and the welfare of livestock. Manufacturing will pay more attention to durability and repairability. Construction must prioritise refurbishment of existing buildings and the design of new sustainable and repairable infrastructures. The model of the 'circular economy' has much to offer here.[13]

Investment will be absolutely vital to achieve this transformation. And this represents a radical change in the nature of investment portfolios. Investment in resource extraction and in labour productivity growth will be diminished. Instead our investment portfolios must be geared towards energy and resource productivity, low carbon infrastructure, the protection of social and ecological assets.

This new portfolio calls up a different 'investment ecology'. Resource productivity will rise, but capital and labour productivities may stabilise or fall. Returns will probably be slower and delivered over longer timeframes. Though vital for prosperity, some investments may not generate returns in conventional monetary terms at all.

This means that social investment is crucial, not least in creating and maintaining public goods. An interesting reflection on Apple's 'think different' campaign (cited at the top of this chapter) is implicit in Mariana Mazzucato's analysis of the huge role played by the 'entrepreneurial state' in technological innovation.[14]

The crazy people who believe in the possibility of changing the world really matter. But theirs is not the only story. The progressive State (see Chapter 10) has a vital role to play in the dynamics of social change. This is not an appeal to an overbearing, centralised or bureaucratic government. It's a recognition of the proper role of government in supporting both collective and individual endeavour.

These ideas tend to be regarded at best as marginal distractions by mainstream economists and at worst as obstacles to growth. Sectors which make vital contributions to our quality of life, provide decent work and substantially reduce our material footprint are derided as 'stagnant' because they have a lower potential for labour productivity growth. Social investment is seen as irrelevant to the pursuit of profit.

In a growth-obsessed world we end up overlooking the parts of our economy that matter most. By concentrating instead on what matters, we are drawn inevitably to the features that must define the economy of tomorrow, the enterprise of tomorrow, the investment of tomorrow. A simple shift of focus opens out wide new horizons of possibility.

Realising those possibilities relies on developing an innovative palette of policy options. Beyond the conventional dichotomy between regulation and incentive, the progressive State must engage creatively and imaginatively in change. Universal basic income, sovereign money, capital taxation, pension restructuring, fiduciary reform, financial prudence: these have all received increasing attention in the years since the financial crisis. They are ideas whose time has come.[15]

At the end of the day, the task of elaborating the economy of tomorrow is precise, definable, meaningful and pragmatic. But it flies in the face of conventional wisdom. So we must expect the incumbent priests to confront us with a flurry of impossibility theorems. Economies must grow to survive. People are addicted to consumerism. Governments are powerless to intervene.

Impossibilism is the enemy of social change. Time and again, throughout this book, we've seen these axiomatic truths dissolve under a more careful scrutiny. A post-growth macroeconomics is after all conceivable. The state has a meaningful role to play in nurturing common endeavour. People can flourish without endlessly accumulating more stuff. Another world is possible. These are the rewards accorded to a careful analysis of the dilemma of growth.

The end of capitalism?

Does all this mean that capitalism is now finished? For many people, growth and capitalism go together. Growth is functional for capitalism. Capitalism demands growth. The idea of doing without growth is tantamount to doing away with capitalism, in this view.

One thing is pretty clear. The fundamental changes to the economy that I have advocated in this book are totally incompatible with the 'casino capitalism' or the 'consumer capitalism' that has characterised the richest economies in recent decades. But this is is not the same thing as saying that we have arrived at the end of capitalism entirely.

I've touched on this question in a number of places, throughout the book. Much depends on how, precisely, capitalism is defined. And as I've already intimated, the act of definition is itself so distorted by the inherently politicised nature of the debate as to be virtually impossible.

To make any kind of progress, we have to settle on a usable definition of the term. So let's start with Baumol's assumption that capitalistic economies are those where ownership and control of the means of production lies in private hands, rather than with the state. In general terms, this suggests there's a likelihood that the economy of tomorrow is going to be 'less capitalistic'.[16]

Longer-term, less productive investments will be essential for sustainability but less attractive to private capital. So the role of the progressive State in protecting these assets is going to be vital. Financing social investment without increasing public sector debt can only be achieved through higher taxation. Or through the public sector taking some ownership stake in productive assets. Or else by a reform of the monetary system in favour of sovereign money.

There are arguments in favour of each of these changes. The arguments from fairness are particularly telling and have been rehearsed increasingly in the aftermath of the financial crisis. Why should the taxpayer bear all the risk and reap none of the rewards of underwriting the financial sector, creating the investment needed for innovation or bearing the social costs of damaging industries and unsustainable debts?[17]

The mechanisms for generating state revenues from social investment are manifold. Natural assets provide essential ecological services, even when the monetary value of these services is inherently uncertain. Forestry, renewable energy technologies, local amenities, natural resources: all of these can be revenue-generating. Public and community sector investment in these assets should, as a point of principle, seek returns from their productive capabilities.

This in itself is not the end of capitalism. Even conventional economists accept that capitalistic economies often have some element of public ownership and control in the means of production. The reality is that pure state ownership and pure private ownership are just two variants in a quite wide spectrum of possibilities. Perhaps most interesting here are the various models of 'distributed' ownership and control which have a surprisingly long pedigree and are beginning to see something of a resurgence.

Employee ownership, for example, of both small and large enterprises, has received renewed attention in recent years, particularly in situations where more traditional capitalism has failed. Likewise, there are much more distributed models of public sector control. These examples erode the clear distinctions between capitalism and socialism even under a fairly conventional definition of these terms.[18]

Admitting a wide spectrum of ownership into a more flexible definition of capitalism may be one way to retain the concept in a post-growth world. For those for whom retaining capitalism is desirable. But are there perhaps more trenchant reasons to abandon the concept?

In Marxist traditions the answer to this question is clearly yes. Both Marx himself and many of his contemporaries believed that capitalism contains an inherent drive towards accumulation. Rosa Luxemburg, for example, suggested that this accumulative drive must eventually undermine and destabilise capitalism.[19]

Explanations of this accumulative drive often lie in the assumption that in a capitalist system, with interest-bearing debt, returns on investment can only be sustained through an expansion in demand. More recent work suggests that interest-bearing debt doesn't in itself create a growth imperative. But this finding doesn't eliminate the possibility of some other form of growth imperative inherent in capitalism.[20]

Another source for such an imperative, explored in some detail in this book, is the pursuit of increased labour productivity by the owners of capital. This imperative is substantially reduced in the Cinderella economy, precisely because the nature of its economic activities resists labour productivity growth. But realising these opportunities may also involve us in new distributions of ownership and lead to a different balance between the private and the public sector.

One way or another, the economy of tomorrow calls on us to revisit and reframe the concepts of productivity, profitability, asset ownership and control over the distribution of surpluses. It demands a revitalisation of social investment. It requires us to redress income and wealth inequality. It calls for a renegotiation of the role of the progressive State.

The question of what we call these new arrangements may well resolve itself over time. Certainly it's likely they won't bear a striking ressemblance to capitalism in its familiar and recent forms. But many of these are already bankrupt. Ripe for reformulation.

Perhaps we could agree to coin the terminology of a 'post-growth capitalism'. Perhaps not. Ultimately, there's little to be gained from rhetorical oversimplifications, motivated by ideological axioms, which do nothing to further understanding.

In the meantime, there is clearly plenty to do in terms of reforming economic structures and rebuilding social institutions without wasting our time on irresolvable turf wars. So perhaps we should not be overly respectful of traditional definition and received wisdom. Sometimes a healthy dose of disrespect is a stimulus to innovative thinking.

A little irreverance may help us expand the realm of the possible. A year or so after the first edition of this book was published, I was invited to participate in a debate on the future of capitalism in Berlin. Amongst my fellow discussants was a German artist called Christin Lahr. After the event she presented me with a certificate, which I still have.

The certificate is a printout of an online banking page. It shows the details of a transaction, a deposit of 1 euro cent, paid into the bank account of the German Federal Ministry of Finance. In the 'reason for payment' field are 108 characters taken from Chapter 1 of Karl Marx's *Das Kapital*.

Christin has been paying 1 euro cent into the same bank account every day since 31 May 2009, and importing a small portion of the text of *Das Kapital* as the 'reason for payment'. Her intention is that, over the next 38 years, the entirety of Marx's *magnum opus* will in this way be transcribed via online banking into the central account of the German government at the Federal Bank.

Christin makes a certificate from each transaction and presents each one to someone that she meets along the way. One of these she presented to me to mark my participation in the event. My own personal fragment of *Das Kapital* reads thus:

> –schaft beider Dinge vertritt: Ihren Wert, etwas rein Gesellschaftliches. Indem die relative Wertform einer Wa–

Which can be roughly translated as:

> –operty of both, something purely social, namely their worth. Since the relative form of value of a commod–

Of course, I can't deny that I would have preferred one of Marx's more famous and colourful sentences. Something like, for instance, 'Accumulate, accumulate! That is the Moses and the prophets!' But all the same, I am rather pleased with my gift – as I hope the German government is with theirs.

Not Utopia

The analysis in this book makes much of the potentially disruptive power of relentless consumer novelty. We've seen how the production and consumption of novelty drives the growth economy. Novelty both reinforces and is reinforced by the social logic of consumerism.

We've also seen how this dynamic has been deliberately reinforced by government, because of its role as a driver of growth. The fetishisation of novelty is on a par with the fetishisation of productivity. Indeed the two things are closely related.

Rejecting this obsession with novelty carries a risk: that novelty itself is demonised, while tradition or conservation is lionised for its own sake instead. It should be clear that this would be a mistake – for exactly the same reasons that it is a mistake to lionise novelty at the expense of tradition.

The tension between these two things exists for a reason. Innovation confers advantages in evolutionary adaptation – allowing us to respond flexibly to a changing environment. This ability is more critical now than ever. But tradition and conservation also serve our long-term interests. In evolutionary terms they allowed us to build security and establish a meaningful sense of posterity.

The point is not to reject novelty and embrace tradition. Rather it is to seek a proper balance between these vital dimensions of what it means to be human. A balance that has been lost in our lives, in our institutions and in our economy.[21]

The same point can be made about the concerns over hyper-individualism. To reassert the crucial importance of shared endeavour is not to demonise individual needs or personal dreams. The point is to redress the balance between the self and society – in a way that re-establishes the importance of public goods in working for the benefit of us all.

It's telling that our obsession with novelty bears such a key responsibility for undermining sustainability. Because the fundamental point about sustainability is that it's about longevity through time. Relentless novelty undermines our sense of a common endeavour embedded over time. And the social institutions that might correct for this have themselves been undermined by growth.

In short, the cultural drift that reinforces individualism at the expense of society, and supports innovation at the expense of tradition, is a distortion of what it means to be human.

This drift serves and is served by the pursuit of growth. But those who hope it will lead to a materialistic paradise are destined for disappointment. We simply don't have the ecological capacity to fulfil this dream. By the end of the century, our children and grandchildren will face a hostile climate, depleted resources, the destruction of habitats, the decimation of species, food scarcities, mass migrations and almost inevitably war.

Our only real choice is to transform the structures and institutions that shape the social world. To articulate a more credible vision for a lasting prosperity.

This book has highlighted the principal dimensions of that task. We must establish the ecological bounds on human activity. We must tackle the systemic inequalities which undermine social progress. We must fix the illiterate economics of relentless growth. We must transform the damaging social logic of consumerism.

We've seen how a faulty economics drives and is driven by a distorted social logic. But we've also seen that a different economics is achievable. A better and fairer social logic lies within our grasp.

This is not about overthrowing society. It's not about changing human nature. It's about taking simple steps towards the economy of tomorrow. Towards an economics fit for purpose. Towards a meaningful prosperity on a finite planet. At the heart of that economics we must place a more robust and a more realistic vision of what it means to be human.

That vision is not utopian. It's not a Western post–materialist fantasy. It's a vision based on a better scientific understanding of who we really are, more consistent with a deeper reality.

An African philosopher wrote to me following the publication of the first edition of this book, pointing out its similarities to the traditional African philosophy of Ubuntu, which celebrates our connectedness to each other and to the world. I am because we are, says Ubuntu.

Prosperity is a shared endeavour. The roots of this idea are broad and deep. And its foundations already exist. Inside each of us.

NOTES

Foreword and Prologue

1   McCloskey (1990).
2   The original report (Jackson 2009) is available online at www.sd-commission.
    org.uk/data/files/publications/prosperity_without_growth_report.pdf   or   at
    https://research-repository.st-andrews.ac.uk/bitstream/10023/2163/1/sdc-
    2009-pwg.pdf (accessed 16 October 2015).
3   There is of course a third choice – the colonisation of some other planet. But
    this was (for the moment!) outside the scope of our inquiry.
4   http://news.bbc.co.uk/1/hi/scotland/7970669.stm   (accessed   16   September
    2015).
5   The Federal Agency for Civic Education (Bundeszentrale für Politische Bildung)
    was the office that reprinted the German edition. On the terms of reference for
    the Study Commission, see German Bundestag Printed Paper 17/3853 Setting
    up of a Study Commission on "Growth, Wellbeing and Quality of Life – Paths
    to Sustainable Economic Activity and Social Progress in the Social Market
    Economy", 23/11/2010.
6   For a useful overview of Ecuador's *buen vivir* strategy, see Altmann (2014),
    Gudynas (2011). See also www.theguardian.com/sustainable-business/blog/
    buen-vivir-philosophy-south-america-eduardo-gudynas (accessed 23 October
    2015).

7   On the definition of *buen vivir*, see Walsh (2010), cited in Altmann (2014). On Ecuador's 'rights of nature' see, for example, http://therightsofnature.org/ecuador-rights/ (accessed 23 October 2015). Shortly after its constitution was signed into law, Ecuador also made history by defaulting on a proportion of its sovereign debt, on exactly the grounds being discussed during my visit to Greece; namely, that it was illegitimate or odious. See for example http://news.bbc.co.uk/1/hi/7780984.stm. (accessed 23 October 2015).

8   The concept of 'odious debt', also known in international law as 'illegitimate debt', is a legal theory dating back to 1927, which holds that public debt incurred by a regime for purposes that do not serve the best interests of the nation, should not be enforceable. See, for instance, UNCTAD (2007).

9   www.hradf.com/en/portfolio/small-ports-alimos-hydra-poros-epidavros (accessed 16 October 2015).

10   On renewable investment, see UNEP (2016). On the Sustainable Development Goals, see https://sustainabledevelopment.un.org/sdgs. On the Paris Agreement, see http://unfccc.int/resource/docs/2015/cop21/eng/l09.pdf (accessed 29 May 2016).

11   See the Hellenic Republic Asset Development Fund website www.hradf.com/en/portfolio/small-ports-alimos-hydra-poros-epidavros (accessed 16 October 2015).

12   For an overview of this work, see www.timjackson.org.uk; see also www.cusp.ac.uk; www.limits2growth.org.uk; www.prosperitas.org.uk (accessed 29 May 2016).

1 The limits to growth

1   Boulding made this comment at a hearing of the US Congress in 1973. See US Congress (1973).

2   It is a possibility worth considering – and I touch on it later – that this particular concept of progress as material betterment over time is itself a modern construction.

3   Global population will reach ten billion people by 2056, according to the median variant in the latest UN projections (UN 2015).

4   As we discuss in Chapter 6, the GDP can be thought of as simultaneously measuring the sum of all economic output (gross value added), the sum of all incomes (wages and dividends/profits) and the sum of all expenditures (consumption and investment). This latter is often referred to as aggregate demand. For a fascinating history of the GDP and its limitations, see Philipsen (2015).

5   In October 2015, the World Bank updated its poverty lines to reflect changes in purchasing power parity. Extreme poverty is now defined as living on less than $1.90 a day at 2011 purchasing power parity. Updated poverty data at different poverty lines can be calculated on the World Bank's PovCalNet

website: http://iresearch.worldbank.org/PovcalNet/index.htm?0 (accessed 7 November 2015).

6   This evocative phrase comes from the Indian ecologist Madhav Gadjil (Gadjil and Guha 1995).

7   Philipsen (2015).

8   'Be moderate in prosperity, prudent in adversity', advised Periander, the ruler of Corinth in 600 BC; 'Prosperity tries the fortunate; adversity the great', claimed Rose Kennedy, mother of JFK and RFK.

9   On income shares of the poor, see, for example, Milanovic (2011, 2012); see also his online presentation at www.ub.edu/histeco/pdf/milanovic.pdf, accessed 7 November 2015. Income of the top 1 per cent taken from Alvaredo et al. (2013); wealth of top 1 per cent from Credit Suisse (2015). On growing inequality see OECD (2015), Piketty (2014), UNDP (2013), UN (2013). On the impact of inequality see Stiglitz (2013), Wilkinson and Pickett (2009).

10 On doubling of income share see Alvaredo et al. (2013). On inequality since World War II, see UNDP (2013).

11 Piketty (2014), UNDP (2013).

12 On social recession and the turn to wellbeing see: Bacon et al. (2010), Easterlin (1974, 1995), Haidt (2007), Jackson (2008a), Layard (2005). On *buen vivir*, see Altmann (2014), Walsh (2010).

13 On Ecuador's 'rights of nature' see, for example, http://therightsofnature.org/ecuador-rights/ (accessed 23 October 2015).

14 World economic output is taken from the World Bank's World Indicators Database (http://data.worldbank.org/indicator/NY.GDP.MKTP.KD) for the years 1960 to 2014 and from Angus Maddison's database (www.ggdc.net/maddison/maddison-project/home.htm) for the earlier years. Adjusted to constant 2010 dollars, world GDP in 1950 was just under $7.3 trillion. In 2014 world GDP was $72 trillion. The average growth rate from 1950 to 2014 was 3.65 per cent. The same growth rate extended from 2014 to 2100 would lead to world economic output of $1,576 trillion, almost 22 times higher than in 2014 and 216 times higher than in 1950.

15 Wilhelm (2003).

16 Cited in King (2015).

17 Remarks at Convocation Ceremonies at University of South Carolina, 20 September 1983. Online at www.reagan.utexas.edu/archives/speeches/1983/92083c.htm (accessed 15 November 2015).

18 Berry (2008).

19 The first of six editions of the Essay was published in 1798 under the pseudonym Joseph Johnson (Malthus 1798). The final sixth edition was published more than a quarter of a century later (Malthus 1826). For a fuller discussion of Malthus' *Essay* and its relevance to sustainable development see Jackson (2002, 2003, 2013, 2015) and references therein. See also Bellamy Foster (1998), Brown et al. (1999).

20   Rousseau (1754).

21   Rousseau (1754).

22   This 'struggle for existence' was also enormously influential on Charles Darwin, who integrated it into his theory of natural selection (Jackson 2003).

23   Malthus (1798: 349).

24   For a Marxist critique of Malthus, see for instance Bellamy Foster (1998).

25   World population in 1800 was 1 billion people and GDP was around $700 billion measured in 1990 International Geary-Khamis dollars. World population in 2015 is 7.3 billion. World GDP is around $60 trillion, measured in the same currency. Historical statistics can be found on Angus Maddison's (archived) website at www.ggdc.net/MADDISON/oriindex.htm. See also Maddison (2008). The ongoing Maddison Project which aims to continue Maddison's historical work can be accessed at www.ggdc.net/maddison/maddison-project/home.htm (accessed 11 December 2015).

26   Club of Rome (1968).

27   Meadows et al. (1972, 2004). See also www.clubofrome.org/?p=375 (accessed 13 December 2015).

28   Sabin (2013). See also https://en.wikipedia.org/wiki/Simon%E2%80%93 Ehrlich_wager (accessed 14 December 2015).

29   MGI (2013); Grantham (2011); Sabin (2013). Commodity price data are from the Federal Reserve: https://research.stlouisfed.org/fred2/graph/?id=PALLFNFINDEXQ,# (accessed 15 December 2015).

30   Data from the Economist Commodity Price index.

31   For a discussion see Rogoff (2015).

32   Meadows et al. (1972: 126).

33   The G20 group warned of the threat of rising oil prices to global economic stability as early as 2005. See www.independent.co.uk/news/business/news/g20-warns-of-oil-price-threat-to-global-economic-stability-5348403.html (accessed 30 March 2016). The long-term concern was widely acknowledged. See, for example, the IEA's World Energy Outlook (IEA 2008) and the report of the Industry Taskforce on Peak Oil and Energy Security (ITPOES 2008).

34   Mohr et al. (2015: figure 5, for example).

35   Turner (2008, 2014). A second study (Pasqualino et al. 2015) puts the world on one of the *Limits* scenarios associated with enhanced technology; this scenario suggests that collapse will come from pollution rather than from resource depletion.

36   Ragnarsdottír and Sverdrup (2015), Sverdrup and Ragnarsdottír (2014).

37   Rockström et al. (2009); Steffen et al. (2015).

38   Stern (2007: xv). The widely cited conclusion was that 'if we don't act, the overall costs of and risks of climate change will be equivalent to losing at least 5% [and perhaps as high as 20%] of global GDP each year, now and forever'. By contrast, the report suggested, 'the costs of action can be limited to around 1% of GDP each year'. We'll return to this conclusion in Chapter 5.

39   NCE (2014), UNEP (2011).

40   Zeebe et al. (2016); see also Figure 5.2.

41   www.theguardian.com/environment/2016/jan/20/2015-smashes-record-for-hottest-year-final-figures-confirm (accessed 19 January 2016). See also Met Office (2015).

42   See, for example, http://climateactiontracker.org/global/173/CAT-Emissions-Gaps.html; www.nytimes.com/2015/09/28/world/limited-progress-seen-even-as-more-nations-step-up-on-climate.html; www.oxfam.org/sites/www.oxfam.org/files/file_attachments/ib-civil-society-review-climate-indcs-191015-en_2.pdf.

43   See UNFCCC (2015): The Paris Agreement, 12 December Draft. Online at http://unfccc.int/resource/docs/2015/cop21/eng/l09.pdf (accessed 29 December 2015).

44   IPCC (2014: 64, table 2.2). See also figure SPM 10, pp. SPM 18–19. For a discussion of the adequacy of this budget and an even more stringent estimate of the available carbon budget, see Rogelj et al. (2016).

45   Negative emission technologies include for instance: bio-energy with carbon capture and storage, biochar, direct air capture or enhanced weathering. On the challenges of these negative emission technologies, see for example Smith et al. (2016). Carbon dioxide emissions for 2015 were (estimated at) 35.7 Gt CO_2 (Lequéré et al. 2015: 374). In Chapter 5 we explore the implications of these targets for the carbon intensity of the economy, under different assumptions about economic growth.

46   See McGlade and Ekins (2015), Meinshausen et al. (2009). Bill McKibben quote is from McKibben (2007: 18).

47   See note 13.

48   Average income in high-income countries (HIC) more than trebled from $11,222 in 1960 to reach $38,652 per capita in 2014 (in constant 2010 US dollars), an average growth rate of 2.3 per cent per annum. At just 2 per cent average growth per annum, per capita income in HIC would reach $78,846 per capita in 2050 and $212,221 in 2100. According to the UN medium variant, the global population will reach 9.7 billion in 2050 and 11.2 billion in 2100 (UN 2015). The global size of an economy in which the entire population achieved HIC per capita incomes (including 2 per cent annual growth) would be $767 trillion in 2050 and £2,340 trillion in 2100.

49   See MEA (2005), TEEB (2010, 2012).

2 Prosperity lost

1   Keynes (1937), cited in Krugman (2015).

2   Felkerson (2011).

3   On rising inequality, see, for example, Credit Suisse (2014), Oxfam (2015), Piketty (2014). On health outcomes from austerity, see Stuckler and Basu (2014). See also www.theguardian.com/business/2015/oct/29/europes-politics-of-dystopia?CMP=Share_iOSApp_Other (accessed 12 March 2016).

4   See www.theguardian.com/uk/2009/jul/26/monarchy-credit-crunch (accessed 14 March 2016).

5   Turner (2015).

6   *Inside Job* (Sony Pictures, 2010).

7   On IMF prediction, see World Economic Outlook (IMF 2008: xiv); for OECD, see http://news.bbc.co.uk/1/hi/business/7430616.stm; on 'financial markets', see Soros (2008); on 'stagflation', see http://news.bbc.co.uk/1/hi/business/127516.stm; on food riots, see for example http://news.bbc.co.uk/1/hi/world/7384701.stm.

8   Reinhart and Rogoff (2013: figure 4).

9   See Hall and Soskice (2001). The authors also identified a group of countries which clustered together in a form they called Mediterranean capitalism.

10 Data on domestic private credit held by households and by non-financial institutions are taken from statistics held by the Bank for International Settlements; online at www.bis.org/statistics/totcredit/credpriv_doc.pdf (accessed 14 March 2016). Data on the national debt are taken from the Federal Reserve website: https://research.stlouisfed.org/fred2/series/GFDEGDQ188S/downloaddata (accessed 12 March 2016).

11 See, for example, Reinhart and Rogoff (2013: figure 2). For individual country data, see World Economic Outlook data (series GGXWDN_NGDP), available online at www.imf.org/external/pubs/ft/weo/2015/02/weodata/index.aspx (accessed 14 March 2016).

12 The following section is not strictly necessary to the flow of my argument, but provides a useful background to the way debt works.

13 Graeber (2014) also documents the concept of Jubilee – the periodic cancellation of debts in the earliest societies; a key mechanism in ensuring that debt doesn't de-stabilise society. See also Jackson and Dyson (2013), Ryan-Collins et al. (2012).

14 It's important to note that not all pension systems rely directly on personal savings and investments. The alternative is for state-provided pensions. But here the State acts essentially as a kind of savings intermediary. Taxation provides the channel between people's earnings (during their earning years) and their pensions (during retirement).

15 This role is contingent in itself, of course, on the nature of the society in which we live. It is in part a result of the particular model of home ownership in which as many people as possible aspire to own their own homes.

16 See, for instance, BoE (2014), Jackson and Dyson (2013), Godley and Lavoie (2007), Ryan-Collins et al. (2012), Wray (2012).

17   This description of the sovereign power of governments to spend does not apply directly in the case of countries with a shared currency, such as those in the Eurozone.

18   For example, the Maastricht Treaty prevents European central banks from buying government bonds directly from the government.

19   See Chapters 8 and 10. See also Connors and Mitchell (2013), Lakoff (2012) and Turner (2015).

20   Formally known as the public sector net debt, the national debt measures the 'financial liabilities issued by the public sector less its holdings of liquid financial assets, such as bank deposits' (see for example the ONS factsheet on Government and Public Sector Debt Measures; online at www.statistics.gov. uk/about/methodology_by_theme/public_sector_accounts/downloads/debt_ history.pdf).

21   This relationship is expressed in the so-called fundamental accounting identity $S - I = G - T + X - M$, where S is private sector savings, I is investment, G is government spending, T is taxation, X is exports and M is imports. The identity follows mathematically from the construction of the GDP as a measure of both incomes and expenditures (see for example Jackson and Victor 2013, 2015).

22   Reinhart and Rogoff (2013: 8, figure 3). At the end of 2015, the gross external debt of the US public and private sector was almost $18 trillion – higher than the GDP, see http://ticdata.treasury.gov/Publish/debta2015q3.html (accessed 15 March 2016).

23   Piketty (2014).

24   See, for instance, Credit Suisse (2014: 34).

25   The Basel III guidelines on capital adequacy were amongst these initiatives. See BIS (2011).

26   Minsky (1992, 1986).

27   See, for example, Barwell and Burroughs (2011). See also Bezemer (2010), Keen (1995, 2011), Wolf (2015).

28   See Greenspan (2008).

29   'A short history of modern finance', *The Economist*, 18 October 2008, p. 98.

30   Citibank quote is from the *Financial Times*, 10 July 2007. See also Turner (2015).

31   Citigroup had to be rescued by the US government on 23 November 2008, with an injection of $20 billion and the underwriting of more than $300 billion in risky assets.

32   Soros (2008: 81 et seq.), Summers (2014: 68).

33   Taken from a speech by the UK Prime Minister to the United Nations in New York, Friday 26 September 2008. See www.ft.com/cms/s/0/42cc6040-8bea-11dd-8a4c-0000779fd18c.html.

34   See, for example, www.guardian.co.uk/business/2008/dec/17/goldmansachs-executivesalaries (accessed 14 March 2016). Five years later, the bonus culture was still alive and well. Around 2,600 employees at British banks were paid a total of £3.4 billion in bonuses in 2013, an average £1.3 million pounds each

and almost 50 times the average annual salary in Britain. From 2015, however, the European Union has introduced a cap on bonuses, which may now at most be 100 per cent or exceptionally (with shareholder approval) 200 per cent of annual salary. The UK opposed the move but eventually accepted it; www.bbc. co.uk/news/business-30125780 (accessed 14 March 2016).

35   On capital adequacy, see BIS (2011). On reprivatisation of banks see, for example, www.bbc.co.uk/news/business-33769906 (accessed 14 March 2016). A survey of voters in the UK in 2013 revealed that almost two-thirds believed that the Royal Bank of Scotland, one of the banks bailed out by taxpayers during the crisis, should remain under public ownership.

36   'The green lining to this chaos', leading article in the *Independent on Sunday*, 12 October 2008.

37   GND (2013: 2). I'm grateful to Colin Hines, one of the co-authors of this report, for inspiring my section title!

38   Paul Krugman, 'Franklin Delano Obama?', *New York Times*, 10 November 2008. See also 'Finding a way out of the economic crisis', 14 November 2008, BBC reporter Nick Robinson's newslog and interview with Paul Krugman; online at www.bbc.co.uk/blogs/nickrobinson/2008/11/finding_a_way_out_of_the_economic_crisis.html (accessed 14 March 2016). In a definitive study of 1930s fiscal policy, US economist Cary Brown argues that this was largely because the federal public spending stimulus was undermined by spending cuts and tax hikes at local and state level.

39   See Gough (1979: chapter 6, Appendix A.2).

40   See, for example, *The Guardian*, 30 December 2008; online at www.guardian. co.uk/business/2008/dec/30/general-motors-gmac (accessed 14 March 2016).

41   'US porn industry seeks multi-billion dollar bailout', *Telegraph*, 8 January 2009; online at www.telegraph.co.uk/news/newstopics/howaboutthat/4165049/US-porn-industry-seeks-multi-billion-dollar-bailout.html (accessed 14 March 2016).

42   Cited in 'Global Green New Deal – UNEP Green Economy Initiative', press release at London Launch, 22 October 2008; online at www.unep.org/Documents. Multilingual/Default.asp?DocumentID=548&ArticleID=5957&l=en (accessed 16 March 2016).

43   DB (2008: 4).

44   PERI (2008: 10).

45   HSBC (2009).

46   Though most people associate Keynes' name with using public sector money to stimulate economic demand in times of crisis, his influence on today's macroeconomics runs much deeper than that and provides the basis for the idea that high street spending is the key to economic stability. As James Ahiakpor (2001) points out, 'Fundamental to Keynes's development of the multiplier concept … is the view that insufficient consumption spending is the principal limitation on the growth of aggregate demand, hence, income and employment creation.'

47   Reinhart and Rogoff (2010).

48   Krugman (2015). On the reworking of the Reinhart and Rogoff results, see Herndon et al. (2014). Herndon was a graduate student at Princeton when he discovered the errors in the Reinhart and Rogoff paper. See www.bbc.co.uk/news/magazine-22223190 (accessed 18 March 2016). See also Jayadev and Konczal (2010).

49   Quantitative easing is a way of injecting more liquidity into the economy and stimulating investment. The term refers mostly to the purchase by the Central Bank of government and corporate debt from financial institutions. See for instance BoE (2010). Suggestions for 'green quantitative easing' or 'people's quantitative easing' work slightly differently. See GND (2013), Positive Money (2013). On the scale of the US commitments, see Felkerson (2011).

50   Stuckler and Basu (2014).

51   For an overview (and collection of essays) on secular stagnation, see Teulings and Baldwin (2014); see also BIS (2015), Summers (2014). The term was originally coined in Alvin Hansen's Presidential Address to the American Economic Association in 1938. See Hansen (1939).

52   Gordon (2012, 2014, 2016).

53   Raw data on hours worked and GDP output were taken from the Total Economy Database; online at www.conference-board.org/data/economydatabase/ (accessed 3 March 2016). Labour productivity was calculated by dividing output by hours worked. Trend productivity growth was calculated from the raw productivity growth data by using an HP-filter, with lambda set to 100. See Hodrick and Prescott (1997). In the UK, the decline in labour productivity growth since the mid-1960s is even more striking. Trend labour productivity growth has been negative since 2013 (Jackson and Webster 2016: figure 3).

54   IMF (2015).

55   www.theguardian.com/business/2015/jul/08/china-stock-market-crisis-explained (accessed 17 October 2015).

56   www.mirror.co.uk/news/uk-news/stock-up-canned-food-after-6313506. See also www.theguardian.com/commentisfree/2015/nov/01/financial-armageddon-crash-warning-signs (accessed 4 November 2015).

57   See www.theguardian.com/business/live/2016/jan/20/davos-2016-day-1-economic-fears-markets-migration-robots-live#block-569f392ee4b0938bb7d2a069; www.theguardian.com/business/2016/jan/20/ftse-100-heads-closer-to-bear-market-amid-sharp-global-falls?CMP=Share_iOSApp_Other (accessed 15 March 2016).

3 Redefining prosperity

1   According to Herodotus, this quote was part of Solon's answer to Croesus, king of Greece from 560 to 545 BCE, on being asked by Croesus who was the happiest man alive. See for instance the translation of Herodotus' *History* by George

Rawlinson (1956). Book 1, from which this quote is adapted, can be found online at http://classics.mit.edu/Herodotus/history.1.i.html (accessed 19 January 2016).

2   One of the aims of the SDC's Redefining Prosperity project was to tease out some of these competing visions. See in particular the 'think-piece' contributions from Tim Kasser (2008), John O'Neill (2008), Avner Offer (2008), Hilde Rapp (2008), Jonathan Rutherford (2008), Zia Sardar (2008), Kate Soper (2008).

3   Townsend (1979: 31).

4   From a speech made by Robert Kennedy's at the University of Kansas in March 1968; www.theguardian.com/news/datablog/2012/may/24/robert-kennedy-gdp (accessed 20 May 2016).

5   Sardar (2008).

6   Dalai Lama and Cutler (2009); on happiness and compassion, see, for instance, Davidson and Begley (2012), Lyubomirsky et al. (2005). The quote from Davidson is cited in Dalai Lama and Cutler (2009: 30).

7   The literature on 'happiness' has exploded in recent years. See, for instance, Dalai Lama and Cutler (2009), Dolan (2015), Haidt (2007), Layard (2005), Lyubomirsky (2010).

8   Diener et al. (1995), Helliwell (2003), Inglehart et al. (2008), Kahneman and Krueger (2006).

9   Diener et al. (2011), Helliwell (2003).

10   See Inglehart et al. (2008), Kahneman et al. (2004).

11   Sardar (2008).

12   'The Living Standard' (Sen 1984) was originally published in *Oxford Economic Papers*, an economics journal, but is usefully reproduced (Sen 1998), along with excerpts from some of Sen's later essays on the subject, in Crocker and Linden (1998). See also Sen (1985, 1999).

13   Psychologists sometimes appeal to the concept of adaptation to explain why this phenomenon exists. We become accustomed to (adapt to) the pleasure something gives us and this leads us to expect the pleasure ahead of indulging in it. This expectation paradoxically diminishes the actual pleasure we receive from it, setting up a dynamic which has us continually searching for more.

14   See Sterling (2016) for a highly readable account of the neural design of our 'satisfaction circuits'.

15   Dalai Lama and Cutler (2009: 57).

16   Actually there is some disagreement as to whether the concept of utility is about the 'satisfactions' received from commodities or the desires for them (Sen 1998: 290), but this distinction need not concern us here.

17   This distinction led the economist Kelvin Lancaster (1966) to develop a sophisticated theory of 'attributes' which attempted to get round the difficulty that commodities are not the same as satisfactions. There is also an extensive and useful discussion of the relationship between satisfaction and material commodities in modern needs theories; see, for example, Doyal and Gough (1991), Ekins and Max Neef (1992), Jackson et al. (2004), Max Neef (1992).

18   See Chapter 6 for a fuller discussion of this dynamic. See also Jackson and Marks (1999), Jackson and Papathanasopoulou (2008).

19   This expenditure-based GDP also adds in net exports to account for trade. Thus the expenditure-based measure of GDP = C + I + G + X − M, where C is consumption, I is investment, G is government spending, X is exports and M is imports.

20   See note 4. For an overview of the formal literature on the limitations of the GDP, see Jackson and McBride (2005), Kubiszewski et al. (2012), Stiglitz et al. (2009). Defensive expenditures are those incurred as a result of the need to 'defend' against activity elsewhere in the economy. The costs of car accidents and cleaning up oil spills have this character. Positional expenditures can be seen as a special case, in which expenditures – on positional goods – are necessary mainly to defend our social position. Though these expenditures make sense at an individual level, it is perverse to count them cumulatively as an addition to wellbeing.

21   Stiglitz et al. (2009).

22   Daly and Cobb (1989).

23   GDP per capita data (in constant 2005$ are taken from the WDI database and converted to 2010 dollars; see Chapter 1, note 13); GPI data were compiled by Kubiszewski et al. (2012). The underlying measure – the Genuine Progress Indicator – adjusts the conventional GDP by subtracting a variety of defensive expenditures and external costs and adding in some traditionally non-monetised aspects of economic life such as housework and unpaid childcare. It also makes a provision for the depreciation of financial and natural capital. The existing GPI studies cover 18 countries representing around 50 per cent of the global economic output. The study extrapolates from these studies to construct a global indicator.

24   Daly (2014).

25   Layard (2005). The quote comes from Jeremy Bentham's 1776 *Fragment on Government*. Utilitarianism was further developed by Bentham's student John Stuart Mill, the father of classical economics (see Mill 1863).

26   Interestingly, this proposal to measure life-satisfaction was taken up by the UK government in 2006, following a recommendation by the Sustainable Development Commission. As Economics Commissioner, I was personally involved in setting up (and for my sins naming!) the Whitehall Wellbeing Working Group, which oversaw this process (see Defra 2007).

27   Easterlin (1974).

28   See Deaton (2008), Defra (2007), Easterlin (1995), Easterlin et al. (2010), Inglehart et al. (2008). In the Defra study, which explored satisfaction in different domains, higher income groups expressed lower satisfaction in the domain of community than lower income groups – an interesting reflection on the different dimensions of prosperity.

29   For UK, see http://news.bbc.co.uk/1/hi/programmes/happiness_formula/ 4771908.stm (accessed 20 January 2016). For Japan, see, for instance, http://

worlddatabaseofhappiness.eur.nl/hap_nat/nat_fp.php?cntry=6&name=
Japan&mode=3&subjects=190&publics=19 (accessed 21 January 2016).

30   Offer (2006). See also James (2007).

31   Angus Deaton, the author of a particularly influential study using data from 188
      countries across the world (Deaton 2008), recently received the Nobel Prize
      for his work.

32   Deaton's study suggests that each doubling of per capita income is associated
      with a constant increment in life-satisfaction (Deaton 2008: 57, figure 2). For
      the Gallup Poll data, each doubling of per capita income is associated with just
      over half a point on an 11-point life-satisfaction scale.

33   Inglehart et al. (2008). A rather similar graph is to be found in Angus Deaton's
      analysis of the results from Gallup's World Poll carried out in 2006. See Deaton
      (2008: 56, figure 1).

34   Inglehart et al. (2008: 279–280). 'The findings presented here are consistent
      with the interpretation that economic factors have a strong impact on SWB in
      low-income countries', write Inglehart and his colleagues (2008: 279), 'but that,
      at higher levels of development, evolutionary cultural changes occur in which
      people place increasing emphasis on self-expression and free choice'.

35   Easterlin's challenge to Inglehart's interpretation of the data in the World
      Values Survey is based on suggesting that the apparent shift in happiness in
      richer economies over time was an artefact of the way in which the question on
      happiness changed over successive surveys. The data on life-satisfaction don't
      show this change, he claims, because the life-satisfaction question was itself
      more robust over time. He then goes on to show, using data from the World
      Values Survey and elsewhere, that for a total of 37 countries (including both
      developed and developing nations) over periods of between 12 and 34 years,
      there is 'no significant relation between the improvement in life-satisfaction and
      the rate of economic growth' (Easterlin et al. 2010: 22463).

36   One of the difficulties in comparing the self-report measure against the GDP
      is that they are simply different kinds of scales. The GDP is (in principle at
      least) unbounded. It can (politicians hope) go on growing indefinitely. The
      life-satisfaction measure on the other hand is a bounded scale. You can only
      score from 0 to 10, however often you go on making the assessment. It is
      implicit in the definition of the self-report scale that utility itself is bounded.
      Statisticians say the two scales have different 'orders of integration' (see for
      example Ormerod 2008).

37   Kahnemann and Sugden (2005).

38   See, for instance, Csikszentmihalyi (1996, 1990). See also Ingelhart et al. (2008:
      279).

39   Offer (2008, 2006).

40   Sen (1998: 295).

41   In *Development as Freedom* (Sen 1999), for example, he argues explicitly that
      freedom is both the means and the end of development.

42   Robeyns and van der Veen (2007).
43   Nussbaum (2006).

4 The dilemma of growth

1   Former British Prime Minister Edward Heath: cited for example in a 2006 blog entitled 'Growth is Good' on the Conservative Home website: www. conservativehome.com/thetorydiary/2006/09/growth_is_good.html (accessed 22 January 2016). See also Douthwaite (1999: 20).
2   Whybrow (2015: 14).
3   Sterling (2016: 2). See also Sterling and Laughlin (2015). Sterling argues that the primary function of the 'pleasure circuit' is not pleasure per se but efficient learning.
4   See Bargh (1994), Jackson (2005a), Wood et al. (2002).
5   Sterling (2016: 2).
6   Becker (1973), Solomon et al (2014). The Becker quote is from Solomon et al. (2014: chapter 1).
7   For more insight on the symbolic role of consumer goods, see (for example): Baudrillard (1970), Bauman (2007), Dittmar (1992), Douglas and Isherwood (1996), McCracken (1990). On its relevance for sustainable consumption, see Jackson in particular (2005a, 2005b, 2006b, 2008b).
8   Berger (1969).
9   Belk et al. (2003).
10   Douglas (2006).
11   Mawdsley (2004).
12   McCracken (1990).
13   Offer (2006).
14   Wilkinson and Pickett (2009).
15   Marmot (2010: 34). See also Marmot (2005), Marmot and Wilkinson (2006), WHO (2012).
16   www.lho.org.uk/LHO_Topics/National_Lead_Areas/HealthInequalities Overview.aspx (accessed 18 March 2016).
17   Data are for the year 2014. Life expectancy data are taken from the Human Development Index database, online at http://hdr.undp.org/en/data (accessed 24 January 2016); GDP per capita data (in constant 2005$) are taken from the World Development Indicator database and converted to 2010 dollars (see Chapter 1, note 13).
18   This is partly of course because the x-axis is considerably longer in Figure 3.1 than in Figure 2.2, which used older income data measured on a different price basis. Once again, the best fit curve (shown in Figure 3.1) to the data is a logarithmic curve: $y = 4.2 \ln(x) + 36$ ($R^2 = 0.56$). This means, as was the case with life-satisfaction (see Chapter 3, note 32), that each doubling of

GDP is associated with a constant increase in life expectancy. In the case of life expectancy, each doubling of GDP is associated with $2.9 = 4.2 \times \ln(2)$ years of extra life.

19   UNICEF (2014). See also the World Health Organization's Global Health Observatory website: www.who.int/gho/child_health/mortality/mortality_under_five_text/en/ (accessed 26 January 2016).

20   Data are for 2014. Mortality rates are taken from the Human Development Indicator database; GDP per capita from the World Development Indicators database (see Chapter 1, note 13). See also UNICEF (2014).

21   Data are for 2014. Mean years of schooling are taken from the Human Development Indicator database; GDP per capita from the World Development Indicators database (see Chapter 1, note 13).

22   There are some wonderful recent developments in this field of study, in particular Hans Rosling's interactive GAPMINDER project, online at www.gapminder.org. See also Rosling's TED talk, online at www.ted.com/talks/hans_rosling_shows_the_best_stats_you_ve_ever_seen (accessed 25 January 2016).

23   See Stuckler and Basu (2014) for a thorough exploration of the health implications of different responses to economic hardship.

24   Time series data on life expectancy for individual countries are from the World Development Indicators database (series SP.DYN.LE00.IN).

25   Franco et al. (2007: 1374).

26   Stuckler and Basu (2014: 108 et seq.).

27   In the conventional model, resources are often excluded from the equation and the main dependencies are thought to be on labour, capital and technological innovation.

28   Aggregate demand refers to the 'expenditure' formulation of the GDP, namely the sum of private and public consumption plus business investment. See note 4 in Chapter 1.

29   IFS (2009).

30   It's important to qualify this claim with the recognition that short-run fluctuations in the growth rate are an expected feature of growth-based economies and there are some feedback mechanisms that bring the economy back into equilibrium. For instance, as unemployment rises, wages fall and labour becomes cheaper. This encourages employees to employ more people and increases output again. But increasing labour productivity without increasing output doesn't have this characteristic.

31   Friedman (2005).

32   The terminology of 'de-growth' (décroissance in the French) emerged in France in 2006. As a technical term is refers to (planned) reductions in economic output. As a social movement it seems to have convened a wider array of interests around political and social change. See, for example, Baycan (2007), d'Alisa et al. (2014), Demaria et al. (2013), Fournier (2008), Latouche (2007), Sippel (2009).

5 The myth of decoupling

1   Monbiot (2015). The quote is taken from the version of the article on Monbiot's website: www.monbiot.com/2015/11/24/false-promise/ (accessed 31 December 2015).

2   IPCC (2014: 64, table 2.2). See also figure SPM 10, pp. SPM 18–19. The estimate of current emissions is taken from Le Quéré (2015: 374).

3   Paul Krugman (2014).

4   See for example Breakthrough (2015), Füchs (2015), Pauli (2010), UNEP (2011).

5   Monbiot (2015).

6   I concentrate in what follows on historical trends in the consumption of certain finite resources and in emissions of greenhouse gases. These examples don't exhaust the concerns associated with a continually growing economy. But they are already of immediate concern and illustrate clearly the scale of the problem.

7   World primary energy consumption more or less doubled from just under 300 Exajoules (EJ – 1EJ equals 10^{18} Joules) in 1980 to just under 600 EJ in 2014. But the world economy expanded from around $28 trillion to over $72 trillion (in constant 2010 dollars) in the same period. Income data are taken from the World Bank's World DataBank available online at http://databank.worldbank. org/data/home.aspx (accessed 2 January 2016). Income data are extrapolated from two data series – constant 2005 dollars at market prices: NY.GDP.MKTP. KD; and current dollars at market prices: NY.GDP.MKTP.CD. Energy data are taken from the US Energy Information Administration's database, available online at www.eia.gov/cfapps/ipdbproject/iedindex3.cfm?tid=44&pid=44& aid=2&cid=ww,r1,r2,r3,r4,r6,r7,&syid=1980&eyid=2012&unit=QBTU (accessed 2 January 2016). Data for later years are extrapolated using implied energy consumption growth rates taken from the Enerdata Global Energy Statistical Yearbook 2015; online at www.enerdata.net/enerdatauk/press-and-publication/publications/world-energy-statistics-supply-and-demand.php (accessed 2 January 2016).

8   Energy intensity of the Chinese economy fell from 68 megajoules per 2010 dollar (MJ/$) in 1980 to less than 18 MJ/$ in 2014.

9   Data are from EIA International Energy Statistics database, online at: www.eia.gov/cfapps/ipdbproject/iedindex3.cfm?tid=44&pid=46&aid= 2&cid=regions&syid=1980&eyid=2012&unit=QBTU (accessed 2 January 2016).

10 Carbon intensities are calculated by dividing carbon emissions in thousands of metric tons (kT) from series EN.ATM.CO2E.KT in the World DataBank (see note 7) by the constant 2010 dollar output for the world and for each income region: high, middle and low. For the purposes of this exploration I have adopted a classification of income regions, based on the World Bank classification, but with some differences. Specifically, the middle income region

as defined here includes only the upper middle income (UMY) defined by the World Bank. And the low income region includes both low income countries (LIC) and the lower middle income countries (LMY) as defined by the World Bank. This corresponds to a more even distribution of the world's population across the three regions – see Jackson (2016) for more detail. For the latest year, global carbon emissions were extrapolated using emission growth rates taken directly from the Global Carbon Project data online at http://cdiac.ornl.gov/ GCP/ (accessed 9 January 2016). To get a regional breakdown, emissions for high and low income countries have been extrapolated using the trend in rate of growth of carbon intensity for the previous decade. Emissions for middle income countries are calculated as a residual.

11   See Jackson (2016) for a more detailed presentation of growth rates over time in GDP and carbon emissions across different regions.

12   Carbon dioxide emissions from the burning of fossil fuels and from industry (mainly the manufacture of cement) account for around 80 per cent of the greenhouse gas emissions responsible for climate change. So they are a good proxy for the challenge facing us. In the text here, I sometimes refer to carbon emissions rather than carbon dioxide emissions, and carbon intensity rather than carbon dioxide intensity. This is just a convenient shorthand. The data that I use to illustrate the problem refer specifically to carbon dioxide emissions and intensities.

13   The average rate of increase in global carbon dioxide emissions between 2010 and 2014 was 1.75 per cent per year. But in the high income countries, emissions declined at an average rate of 0.3 per cent.

14   See, for example, Druckman and Jackson (2009), Hoekstra and Wiedmann (2014), Carbon Trust (2006), Jackson et al. (2006).

15   A 17.5 per cent decline in UK greenhouse gas emissions between 1990 and 2007 was reported to the UN FCCC by the Department for Energy and Climate Change (DECC 2009). Druckman and Jackson (2009) report a 7 per cent rise in consumption-based emissions between 1990 and 2004. Defra (2015) report a further rise of 1.7 per cent over 2004 emissions by 2007, a total of 8.7 per cent rise over 1990 levels. Wiedmann et al. (2010) report an even higher rise of 13 per cent between 1992 and 2004.

16   See for example Goodall (2011), OECD (2011). Domestic material consumption is defined as the mass of raw materials used in the economy and is calculated as raw materials extracted in a country, plus raw materials imported, minus raw materials exported. Crucially however, this omits the raw materials used in overseas production processes which serve imports for domestic consumption and it assigns these instead to the country where the extraction took place.

17   OECD (2011: 5).

18   UNEP (2015), Wiedmann et al. (2015).

19   I am particularly grateful to Tommy Wiedmann, Tomas Marques, Neeyati Patel, Heinz Schandl, Janet Salem and Jim West for pointing me to the data

for these studies and for their thoughtful comments on the implications of it. Data for the material footprint and for the domestic material consumption between 1990 and 2010 are now publicly available online at www.uneplive. org/material#.Vo4EZlI3GQd (accessed 6 January 2016). For the years between 2010 and 2014, both indicators are estimated by using a linear regression on the resource intensity of GDP (for each indicator) over the preceding two decades and multiplying this by the GDP. Data on the GDP of the OECD countries were taken from the World Bank's World DataBank (series NY.GDP.MKTP. KD).

20   Source data from the US Geological Survey Statistical Summaries. Online since 2000 at http://minerals.usgs.gov/minerals/pubs/commodity/statistical_ summary/index.html#myb (accessed 7 January 2016). The curious drop in production in bauxite in 2014 was a result of massive drop in production in Indonesia from 55.7 million tonnes in 2013 to around half a million tonnes in response to a government ban on exporting bauxite and other unprocessed mineral ores that took effect in January 2014 as part of a law aimed at developing downstream processing facilities in Indonesia. The growth in earlier years represents stockpiling (particularly by China) in anticipation of this ban. See http://minerals.usgs.gov/minerals/pubs/commodity/bauxite/mcs-2015-bauxi. pdf (accessed 7 January 2016. On the footprint of metals, see Wiedmann et al. (2015).

21   See, for example, 'Digging for victory', *The Economist*, 15 November 2008, p. 69.

22   Krugman (2014), NCE (2014), Stern (2007) and UNEP (2011) are amongst the many proponents of this kind of argument.

23   This relationship is sometimes called the Environmental Kuznets Curve after the economist Simon Kuznets, who proposed that a similar inverted U-shaped relationship exists between incomes and income inequality. Evidence of the income Kuznets curve is also difficult to find (OECD 2008). For more discussion of the Environmental Kuznets Curve hypothesis, see, for example, Grossman and Krueger (1995), Jackson (1996), Rothman (1998).

24   Booth (2004: 73 et seq.). See also Dong et al. (2016).

25   The scenarios in this section have been extensively revised for this edition of the book, in part to account better for regional differences between poorer and richer countries and in part to take on board the demands of the 1.5°C target, agreed in Paris in December 2015.

26   Ehrlich and Holdren (1971). See also Kaya and Yokoburi (1997). Also called the IPAT equation, the Ehrlich–Holdren equation states that Impact (I) = Population (P) x Affluence (A) x Technology T (hence IPAT). On a closer inspection this relationship turns out to an identity rather than an equation. It is by definition true. Much has been written about the predictive power (or lack thereof) of this relationship, but it remains a useful device for coming to terms with the arithmetic of growth.

27   It follows from the IPAT equation that the average annual growth in emissions r_i over any given period satisfies the equation: $1+r_i = (1+r_p) \times (1+r_a) \times (1+r_t)$, where r_p is the average population growth rate, r_a is the average growth in per capita income and r_t is the average growth (or decline) in carbon intensity. Multiplying out the factors on the right hand side of the equation gives the approximate 'rule of thumb': $r_i \approx r_p + r_a + r_t$. This approximation works very well for small percentage changes (a few per cent per annum). It needs more care in application when the rates of change exceed this. It can also be shown that when per capita income and population rates are positive, the estimated technology improvement rate is always slightly higher than the actual rate. So the rule of thumb provides a robust indication of a sufficient rate of improvement to achieve target reductions.

28   The error term in calculating the technological improvement rate using the rule of thumb is 0.001 per cent. The actual rate is very slightly higher than the estimate. Rates of change were calculated using data sources for income and carbon emissions taken from the World Bank's online WorldData statistical database (series NY.GDP.MKTP.KD and EN.ATM.CO2E.KT respectively) and for population from UN (2015).

29   This follows from inverting the formula for compound growth $E_n = E_0 \ast (1+r)^n$, where E_n are emissions in year n, E_0 emissions in year 0 and r the rate of compound growth. Solving for the rate of growth r, we find that $r = (E_n/E_0)^{(1/n)} - 1$. With $E_n/E_0 = 0.1$, and $n = 36$ we find $r = -6.2$ per cent.

30   In the first calculation we have: $0.8 + 1.3 - 0.6 = 1.5$ per cent. In the second we have $r_t \approx 0.8 + 1.3 + 6.2 = 8.3$ per cent.

31   See Jackson (2016) for a full description of the carbon dioxide emissions pathways summarised here.

32   The average rate of change in global carbon intensity between 1964 and 2014 was -0.87 per cent per year. Between 2004 and 2014 it was -0.16 per cent per year.

33   Negative emission technologies include, for instance, bio-energy with carbon capture and storage, biochar, direct air capture or enhanced weathering. On the challenges of these negative emission technologies, see, for example, Anderson (2015), Smith et al. (2016). For more on the emission pathways described here see Jackson (2016).

34   Growing at 2 per cent per annum between now and 2050, the average per capita income of high income countries would about double from $39,000 to $79,000 a year. The per capita income of middle income countries (as defined here) would need to increase 14-fold, and of low income countries 60-fold, to reach $79,000 by 2050.

6 The 'iron cage' of consumerism

1   Extract from 'Pack behaviour', an article about the vulnerability of banking giant Santander, *The Economist*, 15 November 2008, p. 96.

2   Numerous commentators over the course of the last century or more have picked up on this anxiety, both as an epidemiological fact and as a systemic aspect of modern life. Notable contributions include: Alain de Botton (2004), Emile Durkheim (1903), Fred Hirsch (1977), Oliver James (2007), Kierkegaard (1844), Jonathon Rutherford (2008), Tibor Scitovski (1976).

3   The term 'iron cage' was first coined by Max Weber (1958) in *The Protestant Ethic and the Spirit of Capitalism* to refer to the bureaucracy that he saw emerging as a constraint on individual freedoms in capitalism. But there are also elements in Weber's work where he uses the same concept to characterise consumerism itself as the following quote shows: 'In Baxter's view, the care for external goods should only lie on the shoulders of the "saint like a light cloak, which can be thrown aside at any moment". But fate decreed that the cloak should become an iron cage' (1958: 181). This theme has been picked up and applied to consumerism more explicitly by sociologist George Ritzer (2004).

4   For a brief introduction to the history of capitalism, see Fulcher (2004). An economy is 'capitalistic' according to Baumol et al. (2007) when 'most or at least a substantial proportion of its means of production are in private hands, rather than being owned and operated by the government'. For a deliciously irreverent introduction to the history of capitalism, see Goodwin (2012).

5   For Marxian definitions, see, for instance, Harvey (2010, 2014). See also Marx (1867) and Luxemburg (1913). Some recent approaches extend the idea of capital to natural assets such as the soil, the wetlands, the oceans or the atmosphere (natural capital), to technological and intellectual expertise (human capital) and to processes of community and relational resilience (social capital). See, for example, the 'five capitals' approach pioneered by international development theorists such as Chambers and Conway (1992) and popularised by Forum for the Future (Porritt 2005).

6   Baumol and his colleagues distinguish between: 'state-guided capitalism, in which government tries to guide the market most often by supporting particular industries that it expects to become "winners"; oligarchic capitalism, in which the bulk of the power and wealth is held by a small group of individuals and families; big firm capitalism, in which the most significant economic activities are carried out by established giant enterprises; entrepreneurial capitalism, in which a significant role is played by small, innovative firms' (2007: 60 et seq.). 'About the only thing these systems have in common is that they recognise the right of private ownership of property', the authors write. 'Beyond that they are very different.'

7   Hall and Soskice (2001).

8   Smith (1776).

9   See, for instance, Baumol et al. (2007).

10 See, for instance, Hart (2007), Füchs (2015), Jørgensen et al. (2015), Porritt (2005).

11 For a more formal exposition of the basic economics here, see, for example, Anderton (2000), Begg et al. (2003), Hall and Papell (2005). For its relevance to the environment, see Booth (2004), Daly (1996), Jacobs (1991), Victor (2008a, 2008b).

12 This is probably the one place where the standard economic model pays any attention to the physical reality of keeping activity going. The gradual degradation of capital goods is foreseen explicitly by the laws of thermodynamics.

13 It's important to note that capital is not the only requirement here. Management practice, organisational changes and training are also critical in increasing productivity in the firm (see, for example, Freeman and Shaw, 2009). The commonest way to increase capital productivity has been to increase the capital utilisation factor, making sure that machinery and buildings are fully utilised, for example through continuous batch processing and other process design changes (see, for example, Lientz and Rea 2001, Reay et al. 2008).

14 For an exploration of national trends in labour productivity and their impact on growth, see Maddison (2007: 304 et seq.), Timmer et al. (2007). For a discussion on productivity at firm level, see Freeman and Shaw (2009), and for UK firms, see Oulton (1996).

15 See The Conference Board (2015: 7).

16 Timmer et al. (2007: figure 2A).

17 The hypothesis that technological change is a key driver of growth is a key component of the so-called Solow–Swan growth model. Production output depends on three so-called 'factors of production': labour, capital and materials. Early growth theories suggested that growth could be predicted mainly on the basis of how much labour and capital was available. But these models failed to account for the 'residual' growth after expansions in capital and labour had been factored in. In 1956, economists Robert Solow and Trevor Swan independently argued that this residual could be explained by technological progress (Solow 1956, Swan 1956).

18 On rebound, see: Chitnis et al. (2014), Druckman et al. (2011), Sorrell (2007).

19 See Jackson (1996: chapter 1) for a more detailed discussion of this point; see also Georgescu-Roegen (1972), Daly (1996).

20 See Schumpeter (1934, 1950, 1954). For more detailed discussion of the relevance of Schumpeter's work in this debate, see Beinhocker (2007), Booth (2004), Bouder (2008), Rutherford (2008), Wall (2008).

21 Perez (2003: 25).

22 Baumol (2012: chapter 2).

23 Lewis and Bridger (2001).

24 Belk et al. (1989, 2003), Csikszentmihalyi and Rochberg-Halton (1981), Hill (2011).

25 Belk (1988).
26 Dichter (1964).
27 See Armstrong and Jackson (2008, 2015), Arndt et al. (2004), Belk et al. (1989), Jackson (2013), Jackson and Pepper (2010).
28 This point has been made in various ways by numerous authors. See in particular: Baudrillard (1970), Booth (2004), Bourdieu (1984), Campbell (2004, 2005, 2015), Hirsch (1977), Veblen (1898).
29 Armstrong and Jackson (2015), Belk (1988), Campbell (2004), McCracken (1990).
30 Armstrong and Jackson (2015), Cushman (1990: 599), Dittmar et al. (2014).
31 Booth (2004: 37).

7 Flourishing – within limits

1 Elise Boulding cited in APO News November 2007. Online at www.apo-tokyo.org/publications/wp-content/uploads/sites/5/2007_Nov_p4b.pdf (accessed 21 May 2016).
2 Data on household sector debt are taken from the UK National Accounts (series NNRE) published by the Office for National Statistics (ONS). The savings ratio shown in Figure 7.1 uses the cash savings ratio recently defined by the ONS for the years 1990–2016. The cash savings ratio is defined by excluding the imputed value of housing (which is largely an accounting item that householders never actually see) from disposable income before making the savings rate calculation (ONS 2016). The cash savings ratio prior to 1997 is extrapolated using the conventional data (series RVGL) from the National Accounts database and the ratio of the two measures in 1997. Data are available from the ONS online database at www.ons.gov.uk/ons/datasets-and-tables/index.html (accessed 20 February 2016).
3 Lebow (1955: 7).
4 'Enormous shopping complex opens'; BBC news, 30 September 2008, online at http://news.bbc.co.uk/1/hi/england/london/7699209.stm (accessed 28 February 2016).
5 Cited in Pyszczynski et al. (2003: chapter 5, 'Black Tuesday: the psychological impact of 9/11').
6 Bookchin was writing under the pseudonym Lewis Herber (1962); see Putnam (2001).
7 Lane (2001), Norman (2010), Norman et al. (2007), Pieters (2013), Rutherford (2008).
8 ESS (2015), Eurofund (2011, 2013, 2014), Inglehart et al. (2008), NEF (2009).
9 Dorling et al. (2008). Mark Easton's BBC report (including Prof Dorling's quote) is at http://news.bbc.co.uk/1/hi/uk/7755641.stm (accessed 28 February 2016). The index measures a weighted average of the numbers of non-married adults, one-person households, recent inhabitants (people who have moved to

their current address within the last year) and people renting privately. Strictly, speaking this is an index of 'aloneness' rather than 'loneliness'. But as an indicator of the degree of fragmentation of communities it is a useful tool

10 Smith (1937 (1776): 821).
11 Sen (1984, 1998: 298).
12 Mill (1848).
13 Soper (2008).
14 See also Bunting (2005) on the work–life balance.
15 Kasser (2008, 2002).
16 Dittmar et al. (2014).
17 See Hamilton (2003).
18 Richard Gregg (Gandhi's student) originally published his paper on 'Voluntary Simplicity' in the Indian Journal *Visva Bharati Quarterly*. For more on voluntary simplicity and downshifting, see Elgin (1991), Etzioni (1998 (2006)), Hamilton (2003), Schor (1998), Wachtel (1983), amongst many others; for a detailed examination of the pros and cons of the idea of living better by consuming less, see Evans (2011), Evans and Abrahamse (2008), Jackson (2005b); for social psychological evidence, see Dittmar et al. (2014), Kasser (2008, 2002), and references therein.
19 Csikszentmihalyi (1990, 2000, 2003, 2014).
20 Findhorn Foundation: www.findhorn.org/; Plum Village: www.plumvillage. org/ (accessed 28 February 2016).
21 www.simplicityforum.org/index.html (accessed 28 February 2016).
22 On downshifting, see Drake (2000); Ghazi and Jones (2004). Australian data on downshifting are from Hamilton and Mail (2003). US data from the Merck Family Fund poll (1995); see also Hamilton (2003), Huneke (2005), Schor (1998).
23 Honoré (2005).
24 Hopkins (2008), Peters et al. (2010).
25 Hopkins (2011). For an overview of the movement and a discussion of its social and political ambitions, see Coke (2014).
26 See Brown and Kasser (2005), Coke (2014), Dittmar et al. (2014), Evans and Abrahamse (2008), Gatersleben et al. (2008), Kasser (2008).
27 See, for example, Armstrong and Jackson (2008), Evans and Abrahamse (2008), Hobson (2006), Jackson (2005b), Pepper et al. (2009), SDC (2006b).
28 On wage disparities see, for example, Bradley (2006). On discounted long-term costs, see Stern (2007). On signalling status, see Bunting (2005), Schor (1998). On the 'shopping generation', see NCC (2006).
29 For a wonderfully balanced discussion of the emergence of modern conceptions of selfishness, see Midgley (2010).
30 The poem was first published in 1705 under the title of *The Grumbling Hive*. De Mandeville rewrote the poem several times between 1705 and 1732 (de Mandeville 1989).

31   Smith (1937 (1776): book IV, chapter 2). Online at www.econlib.org/library/
      Smith/smWN13.html (accessed 27 February 2016).
32   Robinson (1948: 276). Variations of this quotation have been attributed
      to John Maynard Keynes, of whom Robinson was a close colleague. But
      these attributions appear to have no foundation. See for instance http://
      quoteinvestigator.com/2011/02/23/capitalism–motives/.
33   Darwin (1892: 68).
34   It's worth remembering, however, that the economic hypothesis preceded the
      evolutionary one in the complex history of economic ideas, and the former
      was clearly influential on the latter – not least through Malthus's influence on
      Darwin. For more on this complex history of ideas, see, for example, Cronin
      (1991), Jackson (2002, 2003), Mirowski (1989), Rose and Rose (2000), Wright
      (1994).
35   The existence of 'group selection' has been fiercely contested ever since
      Darwin's proposals. Darwin (1892: 257).
36   Hamilton (1963, 1964).
37   See, for example, Ridley (1994, 1996), Sterling (2016), Whybrow (2015),
      Wright (1994).
38   Dawkins (1976), Wilson (1975). On the controversy, see (for instance) Rose
      and Rose (2000).
39   Schwartz (1999, 2006).
40   Axelrod (1984).

8 Foundations for the economy of tomorrow

1   Shaw (1903).
2   Raworth (2012: 7).
3   This is not to suggest that nutrition is the only service that food provides. Food
     is not just fodder; human beings don't just feed – as Fine and Leopold (1994)
     have pointed out. Enjoyment, ritual, sociality: all of these are also mediated by
     food.
4   See, for example, Orsdemir et al. (2015), White et al. (1999).
5   In fact, the biggest contributor to growth over the last decade, across the EU
     as a whole, was the IT sector. Of the EU 15, only the UK placed its emphasis
     more firmly in the financial and business sector (see Timmer et al. 2007: figure
     2A). This underlines the fact that there are different versions of capitalism
     even within the advanced economies. But none of them has so far achieved
     significant progress in relation to 'dematerialised services'.
6   When accounted for using a consumption-based perspective: see Druckman
     and Jackson (2008, 2009), Jackson et al. (2007), Tukker et al. (2007).
7   Services as a way of transforming enterprise for sustainability was the core
     concept in a book I published two decades ago (Jackson 1996). The book

synthesised the findings from a five-year research programme I led at the Stockholm Environment Institute (Jackson 1993). But the concept can be traced back considerably further, at least to a paper published in 1966 by the economist Kelvin Lancaster, entitled 'Goods are not goods', in which he argued that goods are really bundles of 'attributes' that have value to consumers (Lancaster 1966).

8   See Alperovitz (2013), Jackson and Victor (2013), McKibben (2007), Schor (2010), Schumacher (1973), and references therein.

9   I'm grateful to Brian Davey at FEASTA (Foundation for the Economics of Sustainability) for suggesting the terminology of the Cinderella economy.

10   Ayres (2008: 292). See also BERR (2008).

11   On circular economy, see www.ellenmacarthurfoundation.org/circular-economy (accessed 26 March 2016). See also Allwood and Cullen (2015), Stahel and Jackson (1993).

12   ILO (2015: 19).

13   Keynes (1930). For some recent proposals to reduce working hours, see Hayden (1999), NEF (2013), Skidelsky and Skidelsky (2013).

14   It's interesting to note that these trends have been reversed somewhat during the last decade, with working hours increasing and labour productivity growing more slowly (Chapter 2). Data are from the OECDStat database, online at http://stats.oecd.org/Index.aspx?DatasetCode=ANHRS (accessed 30 March 2016). See also Victor (2008a: 157–158).

15   Astonishingly, in 2008, when I was writing the first edition of this book, Victor's work stood out as an almost unique attempt to develop any kind of model of a non-growing economy. It is, in short, a worthy pioneer of the idea of an ecological macroeconomics. The model is described in more detail in his book *Managing Without Growth* (Victor 2008a). In subsequent work together Peter Victor and I have explored a twin strategy of work sharing and a shift to more labour intensive sectors (Jackson and Victor 2011, 2015, Jackson et al. 2016).

16   See www.nytimes.com/2010/08/04/business/global/04dmark.html?ref=business&_r=0.

17   For a conceptual model of these twin strategies and their efficacy in maintaining employment as demand stabilises, see Jackson and Victor (2011). See also Jackson (2012), Victor (2008a).

18   Appleby et al. (2014), Lombardo and Eyre (2011).

19   Baumol and Bowen (1966).

20   The intensities shown in Figure 8.1 were calculated as the greenhouse gas intensity of final demand using an input–output methodology for the Canadian economy. See Jackson et al. (2014). Similar results hold for other advanced economies. See, for instance, Druckman and Jackson (2008).

21   See Castel et al. (2011); see also www.thenews.coop/article/co-operatives-make-happy-place-work.

22   Stuckler and Basu (2014: 'Conclusion: healing the body economic').

23   Sandel (2009).

24 See, for instance, www.huffingtonpost.com/ellen-dorsey/philanthropy-rises-to-the_b_4690774.html (accessed 28 March 2016).

25 www.theguardian.com/environment/2015/jun/05/norways-pension-fund-to-divest-8bn-from-coal-a-new-analysis-shows (accessed 28 March 2016).

26 IEA (2015: 4–5). The IEA suggest that spending $13.5 trillion between 2015 and 2030 would be sufficient to meet the Intended Nationally Determined Commitments. But these would only achieve an increase in the percentage of low carbon technologies in the energy portfolio from around 20 per cent to 25 per cent. The 1.5°C target would mean achieving net zero carbon emissions before 2030 (see Chapter 5). On a simple pro-rata basis, the capital costs of achieving this could be as high as $216 trillion (i.e. 16 times the $13.5 trillion). Even this may be an underestimate if the low-hanging fruit of easier, cheaper renewable technologies are exhausted rather quickly.

27 GND (2008: 3).

28 UNEP (2008). See also HSBC (2009), Krugman (2014), NCE (2014), UNEP (2011). In a paper published in 1997, ecological economists Robert Costanza and his colleagues estimated that the value of global ecosystem services amounted to around $33 trillion per year, almost twice the global GDP at the time (Costanza et al. 1997). A more recent meta-study – based on the TEEB (2010, 2012) reports – collates values for ecosystem services ranging from 490 int$ per hectare per year for 'the total bundle of ecosystem services that can potentially be provided by an "average" hectare of open oceans' to almost 350,000 int$ per hectare per year for 'the potential services of an "average" hectare of coral reefs' (de Groot et al. 2012).

29 UNEP (2011). In response, however, see Victor and Jackson (2012).

30 This version of the quote appears to be a paraphrase of a passage originally published in Henry Ford's autobiography (Ford 1922: chapter 7).

31 Useful critiques of debt-based money can be found in Daly (2014), Farley et al. (2013), Huber and Robertson (2000), Jackson and Dyson (2013), Sigurjónsson (2015), Wolf (2014), as well as the groundbreaking early work from Douthwaite (1999). The idea of eliminating banks' ability to create money can be traced to Frederick Soddy (1931); for a useful historical overview, see Dittmer (2015).

32 See, for example, BoE (2014), Jackson and Dyson (2013), Ryan-Collins et al. (2012), Wray (2012).

33 See Capital Institute (2012). The Patient Capital Collaborative is an innovative United States-based initiative to help 'angel investors' nurture and fund start-up companies aiming to have a positive social and environmental impact in the world.

34 www.spear.fr (accessed 30 March 2016).

35 www.unifiedfieldcorporation.com/ (accessed 30 March 2016).

36 See, for example, Birch (2012). See also www.washingtonpost.com/news/wonk/wp/2014/08/05/about-100-million-americans-are-now-using-credit-unions-should-you-join-them/ (accessed 30 March 2016).

37 www.triodos.co.uk/en/about-triodos/who-we-are/mission-principles/why-different/. Another similar example is Merkur Bank in Denmark: www.merkur.dk/om-merkur/english/ (accessed 30 March 2016).
38 Friedman (1948).
39 Benes and Kumhof (2012).
40 Huber (2017). See also: http://tribune.com.pk/story/1004991/the-swiss-referendum-on-sovereign-money/ (accessed 30 March 2016).
41 Turner (2013).

9 Towards a 'post-growth' macroeconomics

1   Robinson (1955).
2   Mill (1848).
3   Keynes (1930). Aggregate demand refers to the consumption-based formulation of GDP = C + G + I + X − M (see Chapter 3, note 19).
4   Daly (1977).
5   Macroeconomics is, quite simply, the study of the economy as a whole. In conventional economics it is distinguished from microeconomics, which studies individual markets and or individual decision-makers. This call for a robust, ecologically literate macroeconomics is probably one of the most important recommendations to emerge from the first edition of this book. It has also been the motivation for much of the research work that has occupied me, in particular in my collaboration with Peter Victor, during recent years. See, for instance, Jackson and Victor (2011, 2013, 2015, 2016), Jackson et al. (2014, 2016), Victor and Jackson (2012). See also www.prosperitas.org.uk (accessed 4 April 2016).
6   See, for instance, D'Alisa et al. (2014), Fournier (2008), Kallis (2011, 2015), Latouche (2007). See also, the contributions from those who speak of a 'post-growth' economy, such as Blewitt and Cunningham (2015).
7   http://newint.org/blog/2015/05/14/degrowth-federico-demaria/ (accessed 29 October 2015). See also D'Alisa et al. (2014). Quotes are taken from Kallis (2015).
8   See Kallis (2015).
9   Keynes (1930).
10 See, for example, Füchs (2015), NCE (2014), Pauli (2010), UNEP (2011); see also www.oecd.org/greengrowth/oecdworkongreengrowth.htm (accessed 24 April 2016).
11 Daly (1977: 119).
12 Sandel (2013).
13 For an entertaining vision of such a world, see Porritt (2013).
14 See www.triodos.com/en/investment-management/who-we-are/growth/ (accessed 7 April 2016).

15   NCE (2014), UNEP (2011).

16   Responding to the UK Law Commission, in 2014, the Association of British Insurers wrote: 'Research continues to demonstrate that active stewardship and integration of [environmental, social and governance] factors within investment decisions can lead to improved risk-adjusted performance (Law Commission 2014: 97).

17   For instance, Carbon Tracker (2013). See also www.parliament.uk/documents/commons-committees/environmental-audit/Letter-from-Mark-Carney-on-Stranded-Assets.pdf (accessed 11 April 2016).

18   See, for example, Eurosif (2014). For an example of such outperforming funds, see www.alliancetrustinvestments.com/global/documents/3301/A-Guide-to-SRI (accessed 11 April 2016).

19   It's been suggested that a declining EROI may be one factor that has contributed to secular stagnation. At some critical point, certainly, it's likely that the EROI of fossil fuel resources will fall below that of renewables (Mohr et al. 2015, Hall et al. 1992, Hall and Klitgaard 2012).

20   Gough (1979: especially chapter 6 and Appendix A.2).

21   See Timmer et al. (2007: table 1).

22   Baumol (1967, 2012), Baumol and Bowen (1966). See also Nordhaus (2006).

23   Nordhaus (2006: 37).

24   See www.theguardian.com/stage/theatreblog/2012/nov/20/repertory-theatre-ian-mckellen (accessed 10 April 2016). Another potential fate for these services, as they disappear from the economy, is that they move into the amateur or voluntary sector. Although in some cases this can be advantageous to local communities, there are other situations in which society is deprived of professional expertise and training, and the quality of the service declines as a result.

25   For instance, Baumol (1967: 897).

26   The quote is from Baumol (2012: chapter 2). There's a worrying corollary to this finding. As Baumol himself points out, many of the so-called progressive sectors are themselves potentially problematic, implicated as they are either in militaristic spending or in environmental damage (Baumol 2012: chapter 7).

27   Baumol (1967: 419). What Baumol means here by 'balanced growth' is that the proportion of real services delivered in the economy remains constant. In our exploration, we would be looking even to increase this real proportion of service activities.

28   Nordhaus (2006: 38).

29   The analysis in Figure 9.1 was based on raw data from the Bank of England (Hills et al. 2010). The trend line was estimated using the Hodrick-Prescott (HP) filter (https://en.wikipedia.org/wiki/Hodrick%E2%80%93Prescott_filter) with the multiplier λ set to 100.

30 NEF (2013, 2010), Victor (2008a). See also www.lejdd.fr/Politique/Rocard-Hamon-Duflot-150-personnalites-appellent-a-travailler-moins-pour-travailler-tous-et-mieux-783977 (accessed 8 May 2016).

31 Jackson and Victor (2011, 2015, 2016).

32 Credit Suisse (2015), OECD (2008), Oxfam (2014, 2015).

33 Piketty (2014).

34 www.theguardian.com/business/video/2014/may/02/thomas-piketty-capital-rock-star-economist-video (accessed 4 May 2016).

35 Friedman (2005).

36 See Piketty (2014: 168 et seq.). Piketty's second law of capitalism can be written as: $\alpha \to r\frac{s}{g}$ as $t \to \infty$. For a summary of the argument, see Jackson and Victor (2016).

37 Jackson and Victor (2016). The interested reader can find a usable version of our simulation model online at www.prosperitas.org.uk/SIGMA (accessed 9 May 2016).

38 Douthwaite (1999, 2006).

39 Eisenstein (2012). For another similar view, see Farley et al. (2013).

40 A notable exception is a paper by the German economist Mathias Binswanger (2009), which appears to confirm the hypothesis. But, by his own admission, Binswanger's analysis is incomplete. In particular, Binswanger's paper 'does not aim to give a full description of a modern capitalist economy'. In particular, he notes that his model 'should be distinguished from some recent modelling attempts in the Post Keynesian tradition' which set out to provide what Wynne Godley called '"comprehensive, fully articulated, theoretical models" that could serve as a "blueprint for an empirical representation of a whole economic system" (Godley 1999, p394)' (Binswanger 2009: 711). A recent symposium on the 'growth imperative' has contributed several new perspectives on Binswanger's original hypothesis, but these papers also fall short of providing a full analysis of this kind (Binswanger 2015, Rosenbaum 2015).

41 Godley (1999), Godley and Lavoie (2007).

42 Jackson et al. (2016). See also the suite of models and working papers available at www.prosperitas.org.uk (accessed 9 May 2016).

43 Jackson and Victor (2015).

44 The interested reader can see the outcome of our scenarios in the online version of the FALSTAFF model at www.prosperitas.org.uk/falstaff_steadystate (accessed 9 May 2016). It should be noted that our study didn't explicitly model certain microeconomic behaviours that might be expected to lead both to a heightened monetary expansion and also to aggregate demand growth or perhaps instability. For instance, it is clear that competitive (positional) behaviour by firms through profit maximisation could expand investment (particularly when finance is cheap) in order to stimulate demand (Gordon and Rosenthal 2003). Neither do we attempt here to model Minsky-like behaviour in which

progressive overconfidence amongst lenders leads to an expansion of credit, over-leveraging and eventual financial instability (Keen 2011; Minsky 1994).

45   See Jackson and Victor (2015: figure 8).

46   It was Keynes who introduced the idea that economic behaviour is in part the result of 'a spontaneous urge to action' rather than a fully considered rational response to circumstances. When things are going well, 'animal spirits' can lead to overinvestment. When things are going badly, they can lead to underinvestment. The interplay of these behaviours is one of the causes of business cycles (Keynes 1936: 161–162).

47   We simulated this phenomenon by increasing the 'accelerator coefficient' in our investment function, so that firms invest more readily when they expect future growth and less readily when they expect a recession (Jackson and Victor 2015).

48   See Scenario 8 in our online version of the FALSTAFF model: www.prosperitas. org.uk/FALSTAFF (accessed 10 May 2016).

49   Minsky (1986, 1992).

10 The progressive State

1   Letter to the Republican Citizens of Washington County, Maryland. See Washington (1871: 165).

2   Smith (1776).

3   A light-hearted take on the Keynes v. Hayek confrontation can be found online at www.youtube.com/watch?v=d0nERTFo-Sk. A slightly more serious discussion on the BBC's Radio 4 can be found here: www.bbc.co.uk/news/ business-14366054 (accessed 8 March 2016).

4   Hayek (1944).

5   See, for instance, Keynes (1978). See also Keynes (1926, 1936).

6   From an article for the Huffington Post by Peter Hall – Professor of European Studies at Harvard and co-author of *Varieties of Capitalism*; online at www. huffingtonpost.com/2008/10/13/global-economic-crisis-li_n_134393.html (accessed 8 March 2016).

7   'Redesigning global finance', *The Economist* leader, 15 November 2008, p. 13.

8   See, for instance, Harvey (2014: chapter 3).

9   Ostrom (1990). See also Wall (2014).

10   Hardin (1968). See also Harford (2013).

11   Lloyd (1833).

12   Harvey (2014: epilogue).

13   See Stuckler and Basu (2014) for a discussion of the impact of social investment in mitigating the impacts of the financial crisis.

14   Mazzucato (2015: 4).

15   For background on the evolution of social behaviours, see Axelrod (1984), Sober and Wilson (1998), Wright (1994).

16   The idea of the social contract was first articulated in Hobbes' *Leviathan* in 1651, and developed further by John Locke and Jean-Jacques Rousseau in the late seventeenth and eighteenth centuries. For further discussion on the relevance of the social contract to modern environmental debates, see Hayward and O'Brien (2010), Jackson (2008a), O'Brien et al. (2009).

17   See Offer (2006).

18   For instance, Thaler and Sunstein (2009). A similar view, named 'choice editing', was put forward by the UK Sustainable Consumption Round Table (SDC 2006a). See also Kahneman (2011).

19   On savings rates and household debts see Figure 7.1. On parenthood, see Offer (2006: chapter 14).

20   Foucault (1991, 2008), Mayhew (2004).

21   Polanyi (1942).

22   On authoritarianism, see Doyal and Gough (1991), Inglehart et al. (2008). The Ed Miliband quote is from 'People power vital to climate deal', *Guardian*, 8 December 2008; online at www.guardian.co.uk/environment/2008/dec/08/ed-miliband-climate-politics-environment (accessed 10 March 2016).

23   www.youtube.com/watch?v=VWSCErK0OLw&index=4&list=PLqRdItpbj_2I8uBMYAOqscTfDk4D8Rxlp (accessed 14 May 2016).

24   In the first edition of this book I identified 12 specific policy areas within three overarching themes. In the second edition, I've chosen to focus more clearly on the underlying narrative, while teasing out broad areas on which policies for a post-growth economy must focus. These broad areas show some resonance with other overviews of this emerging policy focus such as the one recently been published by the Melbourne Sustainable Society Institute (Alexander 2016) and the work of the Green House think-tank in the UK (Blewitt and Cunningham 2015).

25   Rockström et al. (2009), Steffen et al. (2015).

26   For instance, see Chapters 1 and 5 and IPCC (2014).

27   See, for example, 'Sweden pushes its ban on children's ads', *Wall Street Journal*, 29 May 2001; 'The Norwegian action plan to reduce commercial pressure on children and young people', Ministry of Children and Equality; online at www.regjeringen.no/en. On São Paolo's *Lei Limpa Cuidade*, see 'São Paulo: a city without ads', David Evan Harris, Adbusters, September–October 2007.

28   See ILSR (2014).

29   See www.fairtrade.org.uk/ (accessed 14 May 2016).

30   Cooper (2010), EMF (2015).

31   James (2007: appendix 1 and 2).

32   Data are taken from the Spirit Level data (Wilkinson and Pickett 2009) published on the Equality Trust website at www.equalitytrust.org.uk/civicrm/contribute/transact?reset=1&id=5 (accessed 11 May 2016). The index of 'health and social problems' on the y-axis in Figure 10.1 includes life expectancy, literacy, infant mortality, homicide, imprisonment, teenage births, trust, obesity, mental

illness (including alcohol and drug addiction) and social mobility. The index of inequality is an average of the 20:20 income inequality index published in the United Nations Development Program Human Development Reports over recent years. See also Wilkinson (2005).

33 Oxfam (2014, 2015).

34 Meyer (2004).

35 See, for instance, Lord (2003), RSA (2015).

36 A recent leader in *The Economist* magazine argued that it's time to ditch the GDP as a measure of prosperity; online at www.economist.com/news/leaders/21697834-gdp-bad-gauge-material-well-being-time-fresh-approach-how-measure-prosperity?fsrc=scn/tw/te/pe/ed/howtomeasureprosperity (accessed 14 May 2016). Further examples of critiques of the GDP include the OECD's *Beyond GDP* initiative, http://ec.europa.eu/environment/beyond_gdp/index_en.html (accessed 30 March 2016); and the report from the Sen-Stiglitz Commission (Stiglitz et al. 2009).

37 See the discussion on this point in Chapter 8. See also Benes and Kumhof (2012), Jackson and Dyson (2013). Versions of the sovereign money proposal are currently being debated in several advanced economies including Switzerland and Iceland.

11 A lasting prosperity

1 This line was part of an Apple advertising campaign entitled *Think Differently* launched in 1998. Steve Jobs and Richard Dreyfus both made recordings of the voiceover. On the day of the release, Jobs decided against using his voiceover, arguing that the campaign was about Apple, rather than about him. Jobs' recording is, however, still online, for instance, at http://geekologie.com/2011/10/touching-steve-jobs-voicing-apples-iconi.php (accessed 2 June 2016).

2 See Figure 5.6.

3 It would be wrong to dismiss entirely the potential for technological breakthroughs. The fact is, we already have at our disposal a range of options that could begin to deliver effective change: renewable, resource-efficient, low carbon technologies capable of weaning us from our dangerous dependence on fossil fuels. These options have to provide the technological platform for the transition to a sustainable economy. But the idea that they will emerge spontaneously by giving free rein to the competitive market is patently false.

4 Williams (1954).

5 Solomon et al. (2014).

6 Campbell (2003) called these three functions of the sacred canopy cognitive meaning, moral meaning and emotional meaning.

7 See, for instance, Bauman (1998, 2007).

8   Eyres (2009).
9   The first quote is from Sardar (2008).
10   The quote is from Burningham and Thrush (2001).
11   Online at http://downloads.bbc.co.uk/rmhttp/radio4/transcripts/20090609_
     thereithlectures_marketsandmorals.rtf (accessed 29 March 2016). It's telling that
     the most common experience of shared public space in the consumer society is
     the shopping mall. The commercialised and individualised nature of activities in
     that space works directly against a sense of shared endeavour.
12   For a fuller discussion of these points, see Armstrong and Jackson (2015),
     Jackson (2006b, 2013), Jackson and Pepper (2010).
13   See EMF (2015), Jackson (1996), Stahel and Jackson (1993), Webster (2015).
14   Mazzucato (2015).
15   See, for example, Alexander (2016), Piketty (2014), Raventos (2007), RSA
     (2015), Turner (2015).
16   Baumol et al. (2007). See also Chapter 6.
17   See, for instance, Mazzucato (2015), Piketty (2014).
18   See, for example, Harvey (2014). On employee ownership, see Abrams (2008),
     Erdal (2008), Nuttall (2012).
19   Luxemburg (1913).
20   See Chapter 9 and in references cited therein, in particular Jackson and Victor
     (2015).
21   This idea is close to what Zia Sardar (2008) has called transmodernity.

References

Abrams, John 2008. *Companies We Keep: Employee Ownership and the Business of Community and Place*. Chelsea Green Publishing Company.

Ahiakpor, James 2001. 'On the mythology of the Keynesian multiplier'. *American Journal of Economics and Sociology* 60: 745–773.

Alexander, Sam 2016. 'Policies for a post-growth economy'. Melbourne: Melbourne Sustainable Society Institute. Online at http://simplicitycollective.com/policies-for-a-post-growth-economy (accessed 11 May 2016).

Allwood, Julian and Jonathan Cullen 2015. *Sustainable Materials – Without the Hot Air*. Cambridge: UIT Cambridge.

Alperovitz, Gar 2013. *What Then Must We Do: Straight Talk About the Next American Revolution*. White River Junction, VT: Chelsea Green Publishing.

Altman, Philipp 2014. 'Good life as a social consilience: proposal for natural resource use: the indigenous movement in Ecuador'. *Consilience: The Journal of Sustainable Development* 12(1): 82–94.

Alvaredo, Facundo, Anthony Atkinson, Thomas Piketty and Emmanuel Saez 2011. The top 1 per cent in international and historical perspective. *Journal of Economic Perspectives* 27(3): 3–20.

Anderson, Keven 2015. 'Duality in climate science'. *Nature Geoscience* 8: 898–900.

Anderton, Alain 2000. *Economics*, 3rd edition. Ormskirk, UK: Causeway Press.

Appleby, John, Amy Galea and Richard Murray. 2014. 'The NHS productivity challenge: experience from the front line'. London: The Kings Fund. Online at   www.kingsfund.org.uk/sites/files/kf/field/field_publication_file/the-nhs-productivity-challenge-kingsfund-may14.pdf (accessed 27 March 2016).

Armstrong, Alison and Tim Jackson 2015. 'The mindful consumer: mindfulness training and the escape from consumerism'. Online at www.foe.co.uk/sites/default/files/downloads/mindful-consumer-mindfulness-training-escape-from-consumerism-88038.pdf.

Armstrong, Alison and Tim Jackson 2008. 'Tied up in "nots": an exploration of the link between consumption and spirituality'. Paper presented to the European Sociological Association conference, Helsinki, August 2008.

Arndt, Jamie, Sheldon Solomon, Tim Kasser and Kay Sheldon 2004. 'The urge to splurge: a terror management account of materialism and consumer behaviour'. *Journal of Consumer Psychology* 14(3): 198–212.

Axelrod, Robert 1984. *The Evolution of Cooperation*, reprinted 2006. London: Basic Books.

Ayres, Robert 2008. 'Sustainability economics: where do we stand'. *Ecological Economics* 67: 281–310.

Bacon, Nicola, Marcia Brophy, Nina Mguni, Geoff Mulgan and Anna Shandro 2010. *The State of Happiness. Can Public Policy Shape People's Wellbeing and Resilience?* London: The Young Foundation.

Bargh, John 1994. 'The four horsemen of automaticity: awareness, intention, efficiency, and control in social cognition'. In R. Wyer and T. Skrull (eds), *Handbook of Social Cognition,* 2nd edition, vol. *1, Basic Processes.* Hillsdale, NJ: Lawrence Erlbaum, pp. 1–40.

Barwell, Richard and Oliver Burrows 2011. *Growing Fragilities – Balance Sheets in the Great Moderation.* London: Bank of England.

Baudrillard, Jean 1970. *The Consumer Society – Myths and Structures*, reprinted 1998. London: Sage Publications.

Bauman, Zygmunt 2007. *Consuming Life.* Cambridge: Polity Press.

Bauman, Zygmunt 1998. *Work, Consumerism and the New Poor.* Buckingham: Open University Press.

Baumol, William 2012. *The Cost Disease: Why Computers Get Cheaper and Health Care Doesn't.* New Haven and London: Yale University Press.

Baumol, William 1967. 'Macroeconomics of unbalanced growth: the anatomy of urban crisis'. *American Economic Review* 57(3): 415–426.

Baumol, William and William Bowen 1966. *Performing Arts: The Economic Dilemma.* New York: Twentieth Century Fund.

Baumol, William, Robert Litan and Carl Schramm 2007. *Good Capitalism, Bad Capitalism, and the Economics of Growth and Prosperity.* Newhaven and London: Yale University Press.

Baycan, Baris Gencer 2007. 'From limits to growth to degrowth within French green politics'. *Environmental Politics* 16(3): 513–517.

Becker, Ernest 1973. *The Denial of Death*, reprinted 1997. New York: Simon and Schuster.

Begg, David, Stanley Fischer and Rudiger Dornbusch 2003. *Economics*, 7th edition. Maidenhead: McGraw-Hill.

Beinhocker, Eric 2007. *The Origin of Wealth: Evolution, Complexity, and the Radical Remaking of Economics*. London: Random House.

Belk, Russell 1988. 'Possessions and the extended self'. *Journal of Consumer Research* 15: 139–168.

Belk, Russell, Guliz Ger and Søren Askegaard 2003. 'The fire of desire – a multi-sited inquiry into consumer passion'. *Journal of Consumer Research* 30: 325–351.

Belk, Russell, Melanie Wallendorf and John F. Sherry 1989. 'The sacred and the profane in consumer behavior: theodicy on the Odyssey'. *Journal of Consumer Research*, 16: 1–38.

Bellamy Foster, John 1998. 'Malthus essay on population at age 200: a Marxian view'. *Monthly Review* 50(7). Online at http://monthlyreview.org/1998/12/01/malthus-essay-on-population-at-age-200/ (accessed 11 December 2015).

Benes, J. and M. Kumhof 2012. 'The Chicago Plan Revisited'. Washington: International Monetary Fund. Online at www.imf.org/external/pubs/ft/wp/2012/wp12202.pdf (accessed 7 March 2016).

Bentham, Jeremy 1776. *A Fragment on Government*, reprinted 2010. Cambridge: Cambridge University Press.

Berger, Peter 1969. *The Sacred Canopy – Elements of a Sociological Theory of Religion*. New York: Anchor Books.

BERR 2008. *Smart Business – Sustainable Solutions for Changing Times*. Report of the UK Government's Business Taskforce on Sustainable Consumption and Production. London: Department for Business, Enterprise and Regulatory Reform.

Berry, Wendell 2008. Faustian Economics – hell hath no fury. Harper's Magazine. Online at http://harpers.org/archive/2008/05/faustian-economics/ (accessed 16 May 2016).

Bezemer, Dirk 2010. 'Understanding financial crisis through accounting models'. *Accounting, Organizations and Society* 35(7): 676–688.

Binswanger, Mathias 2015. 'The growth imperative revisited. A rejoinder to Gilanyi and Johnson'. *Journal of Post Keynesian Economics* 37(4): 648–660.

Binswanger, Mathias 2009. 'Is there a growth imperative in capitalist economies? A circular flow perspective'. *Journal of Post Keynesian Economics*, 31: 707–727.

Birch, Ray 2012. 'US credit unions reach new record: $1 trillion in assets'. *Credit Union Journal* 16(15): 1, 26.

BIS 2015. *Secular Stagnation, Debt Overhang and Other Rationales for Sluggish Growth, Six Years on*. BIS Working Paper 482. Geneva: Bank for International Settlements. Online at www.bis.org/publ/work482.pdf (accessed 4 November 2015).

BIS 2011. Basel III: 'A global regulatory framework for more resilient banks and banking systems. Basel Committee on Banking Supervision/Bank for International Settlements'. Online at www.bis.org/publ/bcbs189.pdf (accessed 15 March 2016).

Blewitt, John and Ray Cunningham (eds) 2015. *The Post-Growth Project: How the End of Economic Growth Could Bring a Fairer and Happier Society*. London: London Publishing Partnership.

BoE 2014. 'Money in the modern economy: an introduction'. *Bank of England Quarterly Bulletin*, Q1 London: Bank of England. Online at www.bankofengland.co.uk/publications/Documents/quarterlybulletin/2014/qb14q101.pdf (accessed 30 March 2016).

Booth, Douglas 2004. *Hooked on Growth – Economic Addictions and the Environment*. New York: Rowman and Littlefield.

Bouder, Frederic 2008. 'Can Decoupling Work?' Thinkpiece contributed to the SDC Workshop 'Economy Lite – can decoupling work?' February. London: Sustainable Development Commission. Online at www.sd-commission.org.uk/pages/redefining-prosperity.html.

Bourdieu, Pierre 1984. *Distinction – A Social Critique of the Judgement of Taste*. London: Routledge and Kegan Paul.

Bradley, S 2006. *In Greed we Trust: Capitalism Gone Wrong*. Victoria, BC: Trafford.

Breakthrough 2015. *An Ecomodernist Manifesto*. Orlando, CA: The Breakthrough Institute.

Brown, Kirk and Tim Kasser 2005. 'Are psychological and ecological well-being compatible? The role of values, mindfulness, and lifestyle'. *Social Indicators Research* 74(2): 349–368.

Brown, Lester, Gary Gardner and Brian Halweil 1999. *Beyond Malthus: Nineteen Dimensions of the Population Challenge*. New York: W. W. Norton & Co.

Bunting, Madeleine 2005. *Willing Slaves: How the Overwork Culture is Ruining Our Lives*. London: HarperPerennial.

Burningham, Kate and Diana Thrush 2001. *Rainforests are a Long Way from Here: The Environmental Concerns of Disadvantaged Groups*. York: York Publishing Services Ltd.

Campbell, Colin 2015. 'The curse of the new: how the accelerating pursuit of the new is driving hyper-consumption', in Karin Ekström (ed.) *Waste Management and Sustainable Consumption: Reflections on Consumer Waste*. London: Routledge, chapter 2.

Campbell, Colin 2005. *The Romantic Ethic and the Spirit of Modern Consumerism*. Oxford: Basil Blackwell.

Campbell, Colin 2004. 'I shop therefore (I know that) I am: the metaphysical foundations of modern consumerism', in Karin Ekstrom and Helen Brembeck (eds), *Elusive Consumption*. Oxford: Berg.

Campbell, Colin 2003. 'A new age theodicy for a new age', in P. Berger (ed.), *The De-Secularisation of the World*. New York: Basic Books.

Capital Institute 2012. *The Patient Capital Collaborative – Field Study No. 3: A Field guide to Investment in a Regenerative Economy*. New York: Capital Institute. Online at http://fieldguide.capitalinstitute.org/uploads/1/3/9/6/13963161/ppcepub.pdf (accessed 7 March 2016).

Carbon Tracker 2013. 'Unburnable Carbon: wasted capital and stranded assets'. London: Carbon Tracker. Online at www.carbontracker.org/wp-content/uploads/2014/09/Unburnable-Carbon-2-Web-Version.pdf (accessed 23 July 2016).

Carbon Trust 2006. *The Carbon Emissions in All That We Consume.* London: Carbon Trust.

Castel, D., C. Lemoine and A. Durand-Delvigne 2011. 'Working in cooperatives and Social Economy: Effects on Job Satisfaction and the Meaning of Work'. *Perspectives interdisciplinaires sur le travail et la santé* 13(2). Online at http://pistes. revues.org/2635.

Chambers, Robert and Gordon Conway 1992. 'Sustainable rural livelihoods: practical concepts for the 21st century'. IDS Discussion Paper 296. Brighton: Institute for Development Studies. Online at www.ids.ac.uk/publication/sustainable-rural-livelihoods-practical-concepts-for-the-21st-century (accessed 3 February 2016).

Chitnis, M., S. Sorrell, A. Druckman, S Firth and T. Jackson 2014. 'Who rebounds most? Estimating direct and indirect rebound effects for different UK socioeconomic groups'. *Ecological Economics* 106: 12–32.

Club of Rome 1968. 'The predicament of mankind. A quest for structured responses to growing worldwide complexities and uncertainties'. Rome: Club of Rome. Online at http://quergeist.net/Christakis/predicament.pdf (accessed 13 December 2015).

Coke, Alexia 2014. 'Where do we go from here? Transition strategies for a low carbon future'. PASSAGE Working Paper 14-03. Guildford: University of Surrey. Online at www.prosperitas.org.uk/assets/wp_14-03_acoke-transition-strategies.pdf (accessed 26 February 2016).

Common, Michael and Sigrid Stagl 2005. *Ecological Economics – An Introduction.* Cambridge: Cambridge University Press.

Conference Board 2015. *Productivity Brief 2015: Global Productivity Growth Stuck in the Slow Lane with No Signs of Recovery in Sight.* New York: Conference Board. Online at www.conference-board.org/retrievefile.cfm?filename=The-Conference-Board-2015-Productivity-Brief.pdf&type=subsite (accessed 15 February 2016).

Connors, Elisabeth and William Mitchell 2013. 'Framing modern money theory'. Working Paper 06-13. Casuarina, NT: Centre of Full Employment and Equity.

Cooper, Tim (ed.) 2010. *Longer-Lasting Products: Alternatives to the Throw-Away Society.* London: Routledge.

Costanza, Robert et al. 1997. 'The value of the world's ecosystem services and natural capital'. *Nature* 387: 256, table 2.

Credit Suisse 2015. *Global Wealth Report 2015.* Geneva: Credit Suisse. Online at https://publications.credit-suisse.com/tasks/render/file/?fileID=F2425415-DCA7-80B8-EAD989AF9341D47E (accessed 18 October 2015).

Credit Suisse 2014. Global Wealth Report 2014. Geneva: Credit Suisse. https://publications.credit-suisse.com/tasks/render/file/?fileID=60931FDE-A2D2-F568-B041B58C5EA591A4 (accessed 15 march 2016).

Crocker, David and Toby Linden (eds) 1998. *The Ethics of Consumption*. New York: Rowman and Littlefield.

Cronin, H, 1991. *The Ant and the Peacock—Sexual Selection from Darwin to Today*. Cambridge: Cambridge University Press.

Csikszentmihalyi, Mihaly 2014. *Flow and the Foundations of Positive Psychology: The Collected Works of Mihaly Csikszentmihalyi*. Dordrecht: Springer.

Csikszentmihalyi, Mihaly 2003. 'Materialism and the evolution of consciousness', in T. Kasser and A. Kanner (eds), *Psychology and Consumer Culture – The Struggle for a Good Life in a Material World*. Washington, DC: American Psychological Association, chapter 6.

Csikszentmihalyi, Mihaly 2000. 'The costs and benefits of consuming'. *Journal of Consumer Research* 27(2): 262–272. Reprinted in T. Jackson (2006a), chapter 24.

Csikszentmihalyi, Mihaly 1996. *Creativity: Flow and the Psychology of Discovery and Invention*. New York, NY: Harper Perennial.

Csikszentmihalyi, Mihaly 1990. *Flow: The Psychology of Optimal Experience*. New York: Harper and Row.

Csikszentmihalyi, Mihaly and Eugene Rochberg-Halton 1981. *The Meaning of Things – Domestic Symbols and the Self*. Cambridge and New York: Cambridge University Press.

Cushman, Philip 1990. 'Why the self is empty: toward a historically situated psychology'. *American Psychologist* 45: 599–611.

Dalai Lama and Howard Cutler 2009. *The Art of Happiness,* 10th anniversary edition. London: Hodder and Stoughton.

D'Alisa, Giacomo, Federico Damaria and Giorgos Kallis (eds) 2014. *Degrowth: A Vocabulary for a New Era*. London: Routledge.

Daly, Herman 2014. *From Uneconomic Growth to a Steady-State Economy*. Advances in Ecological Economics. Northampton, MA: Edward Elgar.

Daly, Herman 1996. *Beyond Growth*. Washington, DC: Beacon Press.

Daly, Herman 1977. *Steady State Economics*. New York: W. H. Freeman and Co Ltd.

Daly, Herman and John Cobb 1989. *For the Common Good – Redirecting the Economy Toward Community, the Environment and a Sustainable Future*. Boston: Beacon Press.

Darwin, Charles 1892. *The Autobiography of Charles Darwin and Selected Letters*, ed. Francis Darwin, reprinted 1958. New York: Dover.

Davidson, Richard and Sharon Begley 2012. *The Emotional Life of Your Brain: How Its Unique Patterns Affect the Way You Think, Feel, and Live – and How You Can Change Them*. London: Penguin.

Dawkins, Richard 1976. *The Selfish Gene*. Oxford and New York: Oxford University Press.

DB 2008. *Economic Stimulus: The Case for 'Green' Infrastructure, Energy Security and 'Green' Jobs*. New York: Deutsche Bank.

de Botton, Alain 2004. *Status Anxiety*. Oxford: Oxford University Press.

de Groot, Rudolf, Luke Brander, Sander van der Ploega, Robert Costanza, Florence Bernardd, Leon Braate, et al. 2012. 'Global estimates of the value of ecosystems and their services in monetary units'. *Ecosystem Services* 1(1): 50–61.

de Mandeville, Bernard 1989. *The Fable of the Bees*. London: Penguin.

Deaton, Angus 2008. 'Income, health and wellbeing around the world: evidence from the Gallup World Poll'. *Journal of Economic Perspectives* 22(2): 53–72.

DECC 2009. 'UK Greenhouse Gas Inventory, 1990 to 2007: annual report for submission under the Framework Convention on Climate Change'. London: Department for Energy and Climate Change. Online at http://uk-air.defra.gov.uk/assets/documents/reports/cat07/0905131425_ukghgi-90-07_main_chapters_Issue2_UNFCCC_CA_v5_Final.pdf (accessed 4 January 2016).

Defra 2015. 'UK's carbon footprint 1997–2012'. London: Department of Environment, Food and Rural Affairs. Online at www.gov.uk/government/uploads/system/uploads/attachment_data/file/414180/Consumption_emissions_Mar15_Final.pdf (accessed 4 January 2016).

Defra 2007. *Sustainable Development Indicators in Your Pocket*. London: TSO.

Demaria, Federico, Francois Schneider, Filka Sekulova and Joan Martinez-Alier 2013. 'What is degrowth? From an activist slogan to a social movement'. *Environmental Values* 22(2): 191–215.

Dichter, E 1964. *The Handbook of Consumer Motivations: The Psychology of Consumption*, New York: McGraw-Hill.

Diener, Ed, M. Diener and C. Diener 1995. 'Factors predicting the subjective wellbeing of nations'. *Journal of Personality and Social Psychology* 69: 851–864.

Diener, Ed, Louis Tay and David Myers 2011. 'The religion paradox: if religion makes people happy, why are so many dropping out?' *Journal of Personality and Social Psychology* 101(6): 1278–1290.

Dittmar, Helga 1992. *The Social Psychology of Material Possessions – To Have Is to Be*. New York: St Martin's Press.

Dittmar, Helga, Rod Bond, Megan Hurst and Tim Kasser 2014. 'The relationship between materialism and personal well-being: a meta-analysis'. *Journal of Personal and Social Psychology* 107: 879–924.

Dittmer, K. 2015. '100 per cent reserve banking: a critical review of green perspectives'. Ecological Economics 109: 9–16.

Dolan, Paul 2015. *Happiness by Design: Finding Pleasure and Purpose in Everyday Life*. London: Penguin.

Dong, Boamin, Fei Wang and Guo 2006. 'The global EKCs'. *International Review of Economics and Finance*. In press. Available at http://dx.doi.org/10.1016/j.iref.2016.02.010.

Dorling, Danny, Dan Vickers, Bethan Thomas, John Pritchard and Dimitris Ballas 2008. 'Changing UK: The way we live now'. Sheffield: University of Sheffield. Online at http://sasi.group.hef.ac.uk/research/changingUK.html (accessed 23 July 2016).

Douglas, Mary 2006 (1976). 'Relative poverty, relative communication', in A. Halsey (ed.), *Traditions of Social Policy*. Oxford: Basil Blackwell, reprinted in Jackson (2006a), chapter 21.

Douglas, Mary and Baron Isherwood 1996. *The World of Goods*, 2nd edition. London: Routledge.

Douthwaite, Richard 2006. *The Ecology of Money*. Cambridge: Green Books. Online at www.feasta.org/documents/moneyecology/pdfs/chapter_one.pdf (accessed 16 March 2016).

Douthwaite, Richard 1999. *The Growth Illusion – How Economic Growth Has Enriched the Few, Impoverished the Many and Endangered the Planet*. Totnes, Devon: Green Books.

Doyal, Len and Ian Gough 1991. *A Theory of Human Needs*. Basingstoke: Palgrave Macmillan.

Drake, John 2001. *Downshifting: How to Work Less and Enjoy Life More*. San Francisco: Berrett-Koehler.

Druckman, A., M. Chitnis, S. Sorrell and T. Jackson 2011. 'Missing carbon reductions? Exploring rebound and backfire effects in UK households'. *Energy Policy* 39: 3572–3581.

Druckman, Angela and Tim Jackson 2009. 'Mapping our carbon responsibilities: more key results from the Surrey Environmental Lifestyle Mapping (SELMA) Framework'. RESOLVE Working Paper 02-09. Guildford: University of Surrey. Online at http://resolve.sustainablelifestyles.ac.uk/sites/default/files/RESOLVE_WP_02-09_0.pdf (accessed 4 January 2016).

Druckman, Angela and Tim Jackson 2008. 'The Surrey Environmental Lifestyle Mapping (SELMA) Framework – development and key results to date'. RESOLVE Working Paper 08-08. Guildford: University of Surrey. Online at http://resolve.sustainablelifestyles.ac.uk/sites/default/files/RESOLVE_WP_08-08_0.pdf (accessed 4 January 2016).

Durkheim, Emile 1903. *Suicide*, reprinted 2002. Routledge Classics. London: Routledge.

Easterlin, Richard 1995. 'Will raising the incomes of all increase the happiness of all?' *Journal of Economic Behaviour and Organization*, 27: 35–47.

Easterlin, Richard 1974. 'Does economic growth improve the human lot? Some empirical evidence', in D. David and M. Reder (eds), *Nations and Households in Economic Growth*. Stanford: Stanford University Press.

Easterlin, Richard, Laura Angelescu McVey, Malgorzata Switek, Onnicha Sawangfa and Jacqueline Smith Zweig 2010. 'The happiness–income paradox revisited'. *Proceedings of the National Academy of Science* 107(52): 22463–22468.

Eisenstein, Charles 2012. 'We can't grow ourselves out of debt, no matter what the Federal Reserve does'. Guardian, 13 September. Online at www.theguardian.com/commentisfree/2012/sep/03/debt-federal-reserve-fixation-on-growth (accessed 16 March 2016).

Ekins, Paul and Manfred Max Neef (eds) 1992. *Real-Life Economics: Understanding Wealth Creation*. London: Routledge.

Elgin, Duane 1981. *Voluntary Simplicity – Towards a Way of Life That is Outwardly Simple, Inwardly Rich*, reprinted 1993. New York: William Morrow.

EMF 2015. *Towards a Circular Economy: Business Rationale for an Accelerated Transition*. Cowes, Isle of Wight: Ellen McArthur Foundation. Online at www.ellenmacarthurfoundation.org/assets/downloads/TCE_Ellen-MacArthur-Foundation_9-Dec-2015.pdf (accessed 4 June 2016).

Erdal, David 2008. *Local Heroes: How Loch Fyne Oysters Embraced Employee Ownership and Business Success*. London: Viking.

ESS 2015. Europeans' Personal and Social Wellbeing. Topline Results from Round 6 of the European Social Survey. London: City University. Online at www.europeansocialsurvey.org/docs/findings/ESS6_toplines_issue_5_personal_and_social_wellbeing.pdf (accessed 20 February 2016).

Etzioni, Amitai 1998. 'Voluntary simplicity: characterisation, select psychological Implications and societal consequences'. *Journal of Economic Psychology* 19(5): 619–643, reprinted in T. Jackson (2006a), chapter 12.

Eurofund 2014. *Social Cohesion and Wellbeing in the EU*. Dublin: Eurofound. Online at www.eurofound.europa.eu/publications/report/2014/quality-of-life-social-policies/social-cohesion-and-well-being-in-the-eu (accessed 20 February 2016).

Eurofund 2013. *Political Trust and Civic Engagement During the Crisis. 3rd EQLS Briefing*. Luxembourg: Publications Office of the European Union.

Eurofund 2011. *Participation in Volunteering and Unpaid Work. 2nd EQLS Briefing*. Luxembourg: Publications Office of the European Union.

Eurosif 2014. 'Eurosif SRI Study 2014'. Online at www.eurosif.org/publication/european-sri-study-2014/ (accessed 11 April 2016).

Evans, David 2011. 'Consuming conventions: sustainable consumption, ecological citizenship and the worlds of worth'. *Journal of Rural Studies* 27(2): 109–115.

Evans, David and Wokje Abrahamse 2008. 'Beyond rhetoric: the possibilities of and for "sustainable lifestyles"'. RESOLVE Working Paper Series 06-08. Guildford: University of Surrey.

Eyres, Harry 2009. 'The sour smell of excess'. *Financial Times*, Saturday 23 May.

Farley, Josh, M. Burke, G. Flomenhoft, B. Kelly, D. Forrest Murray, S. Posner et al. 2013. 'Monetary and fiscal policies for a finite planet'. *Sustainability* 5: 2802–2826.

Felkerson, James 2011. '$29,000,000,000,000: a detailed look at the Fed's bailout by funding facility and recipient'. Levy Economics Institute Working Paper 658. New York: Levy Economics Institute. Online at www.levyinstitute.org/pubs/wp_698.pdf (accessed 2 November 2015).

Fine, Ben and Ellen Leopold 1993. *The World of Consumption*. London: Routledge.

Ford, Henry 1922. 'My life and work: the autobiography of Henry Ford'. Reprinted by Digireads, www.digireads.com (accessed 4 April 2016).

Foucault, Michel 2008. *The Birth of Biopolitics: Lectures at the Collège de France*. French edition 2004, ed. Michel Senellart; English trans. Graham Burchell (2008).

Foucault, Michel 1991. 'Governmentality', trans. Rosi Braidotti and revised by Colin Gordon, in Graham Burchell, Colin Gordon and Peter Miller (eds), *The Foucault Effect: Studies in Governmentality*. Chicago: University of Chicago Press, pp. 87–104.

Fournier, Valérie 2008. 'Escaping from the economy: the politics of degrowth'. *International Journal of Sociology and Social Policy* 28(11–12): 528–545.

Franco, Manuel, Pedro Orduñez, Benjamín Caballero, José A. Tapia Granados, Mariana Lazo, José Luís Bernal et al. 2007. 'Impact of energy intake, physical activity, and population-wide weight loss on cardiovascular disease and diabetes mortality in Cuba, 1980–2005'. *Journal of Epidemiology* 166: 1374–1380.

Freeman, Richard and Kathryn Shaw 2009. *International Differences in the Business Practices and Productivity of Firms*. Proceedings of a Conference held at the National Bureau of Economic Research 2006. Chicago: University of Chicago Press (forthcoming). Online at www.nber.org/books/free07-1.

Friedman, Benjamin 2005. *The Moral Consequences of Economic Growth*. New York: Alfred A Knopf.

Friedman, Milton 1948. 'A monetary and fiscal framework for economic stability'. *American Economic Review* 38: 245–264.

Füchs, Ralf 2015. *Green Growth, Smart Growth: A New Approach to Economics, Innovation and the Environment*. London and New York: Anthem Press.

Fulcher, James. 2004. *Capitalism – A Very Short Introduction*. Oxford: Oxford University Press.

Gadjil, Madhav and Ramachandra Guha 1995. *Ecology and Equity – The Use and Abuse of Nature in Contemporary India*. New York: Routledge.

Gatersleben, Birgitta, Jesse Meadows, Wokje Abrahamse and Tim Jackson 2008. 'Materialistic and environmental values of young volunteers in nature conservation projects'. RESOLVE Working Paper 07-08. Guildford: University of Surrey.

Georgescu-Roegen, Nicholas 1972. *The Entropy Law and the Economic Process*. Cambridge, MA: Harvard University Press.

Ghazi, Polly and Judy Jones 2004. *Downshifting: A Guide to Happier, Simpler Living*. London: Hodder and Stoughton.

GND 2013. *A National Plan for the UK: From Austerity to the Age of the Green New Deal*. London: Green New Deal Group. Online at www.greennewdealgroup. org/wp-content/uploads/2013/09/Green-New-Deal-5th-Anniversary.pdf (accessed 17 March 2016).

GND 2008. 'A Green New Deal: joined up policies to solve the triple crunch of the credit crisis, climate change and high oil prices'. The first report of the Green New Deal Group. London: NEF.

Godley, W. 1999. 'Seven unsustainable processes'. Special Report to the Levy Institute. Online at www.levyinstitute.org/pubs/sevenproc.pdf (accessed 21 March 2016).

Godley, Wynne and Marc Lavoie 2007. *Monetary Economics – An Integrated Approach to Credit, Money, Income, Production and Wealth* London: Palgrave Macmillan.

Goodall, Chris 2011. '"Peak Stuff". Did the UK reach a maximum use of material resources in the early part of the last decade?' Online at http://static1. squarespace.com/static/545e40d0e4b054a6f8622bc9/t/54720c6ae4b06f326a850 2f9/1416760426697/Peak_Stuff_17.10.11.pdf (accessed 4 January 2016).

Goodwin, Michael 2012. *Economix: How Our Economy Works (and Doesn't Work) in Words and Pictures.* New York: Abrams Comicarts.

Gordon, Myron and Jeffrey Rosenthal 2003. 'Capitalism's growth imperative'. *Cambridge Journal of Economics* 27: 25–48.

Gordon, Robert 2016. *The Rise and Fall of American Growth: The US Standard of Living since the Civil War.* Princeton: Princeton University Press.

Gordon, Robert 2014. 'The turtle's progress: secular stagnation meets the headwinds'. In Teulings and Baldwin, pp. 47–60.

Gordon, Robert 2012. 'Is US economic growth over? Faltering innovation confronts the six headwinds'. NBER Working Paper 18315. Cambridge, MA: National Bureau of Economic Research. Online at www.nber.org/papers/w18315.pdf (accessed 17 October 2015).

Gough, Ian 1979. *The Political Economy of the Welfare State.* Basingstoke: Palgrave Macmillan.

Graeber, David 2014. *Debt: The First Five Thousand Years,* revised 2nd edition. New York: Melville House Publishing.

Grantham, Jeremy 2011. 'Resource limitations 2. Quarterly letter July 2011'. Online at https://davidruyet.files.wordpress.com/2011/08/jgletter_resource limitations2_2q11.pdf (accessed 16 December 2015).

Greenspan, Alan 2008. *The Age of Turbulence: Adventures in a New World.* London: Penguin.

Grossman, Gene and Alan Krueger 1995. 'Economic growth and the environment'. *Quarterly Journal of Economics* 110: 353–378.

Gudynas, Eduardo 2011. 'Buen vivir: today's tomorrow'. *Development* 54(4): 441–447.

Haidt, Jonathan 2006. *The Happiness Hypothesis: Putting Ancient Wisdom and Philosophy to the Test of Modern Science.* London: Arrow Books.

Hall, Charles, Cutler Cleveland and Robert Kaufmann 1992. *Energy and Resource Quality: The Ecology of the Economic Process.* Niwot: University of Colorado Press.

Hall, Charles and Kent Klitgaard 2012. *Energy and the Wealth of Nations: Understanding the Biophysical Economy.* New York and London: Springer.

Hall, Peter and David Soskice 2001. *Varieties of Capitalism: The Institutional Foundations of Competitive Advantage.* Oxford: Oxford University Press.

Hall, Robert and David Papell 2005. *Macroeconomics: Economic Growth, Fluctuations and Policy.* New York: W.W. Norton.

Hamilton, Clive 2003. 'Downshifting in Britain. A sea-change in the pursuit of happiness'. Discussion Paper No 58. Canberra: The Australia Institute.

Hamilton, Clive and L. Mail 2003. 'Downshifting in Australia: a sea-change in the pursuit of happiness'. Discussion Paper No. 50. Canberra: The Australia Institute.

Hamilton, William 1964. 'The genetical evolution of social behaviour'. *Journal of Theoretical Biology* 7: 1–52.

Hamilton, William 1963. 'The evolution of altruistic behaviour'. *American Naturalist* 97: 354–356.

Hansen, Alvin 1939. 'Economic progress and declining population growth'. *American Economic Review* 29(1): 1–15.

Hardin, Garrett 1968. 'The tragedy of the commons'. *Science* 162(3859): 1243–1248. doi:10.1126/science.162.3859.1243.

Harford, Tim 2013. 'Do you believe in sharing? The undercover economist'. Online at http://timharford.com/2013/08/do-you-believe-in-sharing/ (accessed 9 March 2016).

Hart, Stuart 2007. *Capitalism at the Crossroads*, 2nd edition. New Jersey: Wharton School of Publishing.

Harvey, David 2014. *Seventeen Contradictions and the End of Capitalism*. London: Profile Books.

Harvey, David 2010. *A Companion to Marx's Capital*. London: Verso.

Hayden, Anders 1999. *Sharing the Work, Sparing the Planet – Work Time, Consumption and Ecology*. London: Zed Books.

Hayek, Friedrich 1944. *The Road to Serfdom*. London: Routledge.

Hayward, Bronwyn and Karen O'Brien 2010. 'Security of What for Whom? Rethinking social contracts in a changing climate', in K. L. O'Brien, A. St. Clair and B. Kristoffersen (eds), *Climate Change, Ethics, and Human Security*. Cambridge: Cambridge University Press.

Helliwell, John 2003. 'How's life? Combining individual and national variables to explain subjective wellbeing'. *Economic Modelling* 20(2): 331–360.

Herber, Lewis 1962. *Our Synthetic Environment*. New York: Alfred A Knopf. Online at http://dwardmac.pitzer.edu/Anarchist_Archives/bookchin/syntheticenviron/osetoc.html (accessed 26 February 2016).

Herndon, Thomas, Michael Ash and Robert Pollin 2014. 'Does high public debt consistently stifle economic growth? A critique of Reinhart and Rogoff'. *Cambridge Journal of Economics* 38(2): 257–279. doi:10.1093/cje/bet075.

Hill, Julie 2011. *The Secret Life of Stuff: A Manual for a New Material World*. London: Random House.

Hills, Sally, Ryland Thomas and Nicholas Dimsdale 2010. *The UK Recession in Context – What do Three Centuries of Data Tell Us?* London: Bank of England.

Hirsch, Fred 1977. *Social Limits to Growth*, revised edition 1995. London and New York: Routledge.

Hobson, K., 2006. 'Competing discourses of sustainable consumption: does the rationalisation of lifestyles make sense?' In Jackson (2006a), pp. 305–327.

Hodrick, Robert and Edward Prescott 1997. 'Postwar US business cycles: an empirical investigation'. *Journal of Money, Credit, and Banking* 29(1): 1–16.

Hoekstra, Arjen and Thomas Wiedmann 2014. 'Humanity's unsustainable environmental footprint'. *Science* 344(6188): 1114–1117.

Honoré, Carl 2005. *In Praise of Slow: How a Worldwide Movement Is Challenging the Cult of Speed*. London: Orion Books.

Hopkins, Rob 2011. *The Transition Companion: Making Your Community More Resilient in Uncertain Times*. Totnes, Devon: Green Books.

Hopkins, Rob 2008. *The Transition Handbook: From Oil Dependency to Local Resilience*. Totnes, Devon: Green Books.

HSBC 2009. A Climate for Recovery. *The Colour of Stimulus Goes Green*. London: HSBC Global Research.

Huber, J. and J. Robertson 2000. *Future Money*. London: New Economics Foundation.

Huneke, M. 2005. 'The face of the un-consumer: an empirical examination of the practice of voluntary simplicity in the United States'. *Psychology and Marketing* 22(7): 527–550.

IEA 2015. *Energy and Climate Change*. World Energy Outlook Special Briefing for COP 21. Paris: International Energy Agency. Online at www.iea.org/media/news/WEO_INDC_Paper_Final_WEB.PDF (accessed 29 March 2016).

IEA 2008. *World Energy Outlook 2008*. Paris: International Energy Agency.

IFS 2009. The IFS Green Budget January 2009. London: Institute for Fiscal Studies.

ILO 2015. *Global Employment Trends for Youth 2015. Scaling up Investments in Decent Jobs for Youth*. Geneva: International Labour Organisation. Online at www.ilo.org/global/research/global-reports/youth/2015/lang--en/index.htm (accessed 22 March 2016).

ILSR 2014. *Building Community; Strengthening Economies*. 40th Anniversary Annual Report. Washington, DC: Institute for Local Self-Reliance. Online at https://ilsr.org/annual-report-2014/ (Accessed 14 May 2016).

IMF 2015. *World Economic Outlook 2015*. Washington, DC: International Monetary Fund. Online at www.imf.org/external/pubs/ft/weo/2015/02/ (accessed 17 October 2015).

IMF 2008. *World Economic Outlook 2008*. Washington DC: International Monetary Fund. Inglehart, Ronald, Roberto Foa, Christopher Peterson and Christian Welzel 2008. 'Development, freedom and rising happiness: a global perspective (1981–2007)'. *Perspectives on Psychological Science* 3(4): 264–285.

IPCC 2014. *Climate Change 2014: Synthesis Report. Contributions of Working Groups I, II and III to the Fifth Assessment Report of the Intergovernmental Panel on Climate Change*. Geneva: IPCC.

ITPOES 2008. *The Oil Crunch: Securing the UK's Energy Future*. First Report of the Industry Taskforce on Peak Oil and Energy Security. London: ITPOES.

Jackson, Andrew and Ben Dyson 2013. *Modernising Money: Why Our Monetary System is Broken and How it Can be Fixed*. London: Positive Money.

Jackson, Tim 2016. 'Emission pathways in historical perspective: an analysis of the challenge of meeting the 1.5°C target'. PASSAGE working paper 16/01. Guildford: Centre for the Understanding of Sustainable Prosperity.

Jackson, Tim 2015. 'Commentary on Marxism and ecology: common fonts of a great transition. Great transition initiative'. Online at www.greattransition.org/commentary/tim-jackson-marxism-and-ecology-john-bellamy-foster (accessed 26 May 2016).

Jackson, Tim 2013. '*Angst essen Seele auf* – escaping the "iron cage" of consumerism'. In *Wuppertal Spezial* 48: 53–68. Wuppertal: Wuppertal Institute for Climate, Environment and Energy. Online at www.sustainablelifestyles.ac.uk/sites/default/files/newsdocs/tj_2014_-_angste_essen_seele_auf_in-_ws_48.pdf (accessed 11 December 2015).

Jackson, T. 2012. 'Let's be less productive'. *New York Times*, 27 May 2012. Online at www.nytimes.com/2012/05/27/opinion/sunday/lets-be-less-productive.html?_r=0 (accessed 7 March 2016).

Jackson, Tim 2009. *Prosperity without Growth? The Transition to a Sustainable Economy*. London: Sustainable Development Commission.

Jackson, Tim 2008a. 'Where is the wellbeing dividend? Nature, structure and consumption inequalities'. *Local Environment* 13(8): 703–723.

Jackson, Tim 2008b. 'The challenge of sustainable lifestyles', in *State of the World 2008: Innovations for a Sustainable Economy*. Washington, DC: WorldWatch Institute, chapter 4.

Jackson, Tim (ed.) 2006a. *Earthscan Reader in Sustainable Consumption*. London: Earthscan.

Jackson, Tim 2006b. 'Consuming paradise? Towards a social and cultural psychology of sustainable consumption', in T. Jackson (ed.) (2006a), chapter 25.

Jackson, Tim 2005a. *Motivating Sustainable Consumption – A Review of Evidence on Consumer Behaviour and Behavioural Change*. London: SDRN.

Jackson, Tim 2005b. 'Live better by consuming less? Is there a double dividend in sustainable consumption. *Journal of Industrial Ecology* 9(1–2): 19–36.

Jackson, Tim 2003. 'Sustainability and the "struggle for existence": the critical role of metaphor in society's metabolism'. *Environmental Values* 12: 289–316.

Jackson, Tim 2002. 'Consumer culture as a failure in theodicy', in T. Cooper (ed.), *Consumption, Christianity and Creation*, Proceedings of an Academic Seminar, 5 July, Sheffield Hallam University, Sheffield.

Jackson, Tim 1996. *Material Concerns: Pollution, Profit and Quality of Life*. London: Routledge.

Jackson, Tim (ed.) 1993. *Clean Production Strategies – Developing Preventive Environmental Management in the Industrial Economy*. Boca Raton, FL: Lewis Publishers.

Jackson, Tim, Ben Drake, Peter Victor, Kurt Kratena and Marc Sommer 2014. 'Foundations for an ecological macroeconomics: literature review and model development'. WWWforEurope Working Paper no. 65. Online at www.foreurope.eu/fileadmin/documents/pdf/Workingpapers/WWWforEurope_WPS_no065_MS38.pdf (accessed 23 July 2016).

Jackson, Tim, Wander Jager and Sigrid Stagl 2004. 'Beyond insatiability – needs theory and sustainable consumption', in L. Reisch and I. Røpke (eds), *Consumption – Perspectives from Ecological Economics*. Cheltenham: Edward Elgar.

Jackson, Tim and Nic Marks 1999. 'Consumption, sustainable welfare and human needs – with reference to UK expenditure patterns 1954–1994'. *Ecological Economics* 28(3): 421–442.

Jackson, Tim and Eleni Papathanasopoulou 2008. 'Luxury or lock-in? – an exploration of unsustainable consumption in the UK 1968–2000'. *Ecological Economics* 68: 80–95.

Jackson, Tim, Eleni Papathanasopoulou, Pete Bradley and Angela Druckman 2007. 'Attributing UK carbon emissions to functional consumer needs: methodology and pilot results'. RESOLVE Working Paper 01-07, University of Surrey. Online at www.surrey.ac.uk/resolve/Docs/WorkingPapers/RESOLVE_WP_01-07.pdf.

Jackson, Tim, Eleni Papathanasopoulou, Pete Bradley and Angela Druckman 2006. 'Attributing carbon emissions to functional household needs: a pilot framework for the UK'. International Conference on Regional and Urban Modelling, Brussels, Belgium, 1–2 June.

Jackson, Tim and Miriam Pepper 2010. 'Consumerism as theodicy – an exploration of religions and secular meaning functions', in L. Thomas (ed.), *Consuming Paradise*. Oxford: Palgrave-Macmillan.

Jackson, Tim and Peter Victor 2016. 'Does slow growth lead to rising inequality? Some theoretical reflections and numerical simulations'. *Ecological Economics* 121: 206–219. Online at http://dx.doi.org/10.1016/j.ecolecon.2015.03.019 (accessed 19 January 2016).

Jackson, Tim and Peter Victor 2015. 'Does credit create a growth imperative? A quasi-stationary economy with interest-bearing debt'. *Ecological Economics* 120: 32–48. Online at http://dx.doi.org/10.1016/j.ecolecon.2015.09.009 (accessed 18 March 2016).

Jackson, Tim and Peter Victor 2013. *Green Economy at Community Scale*. Toronto: Metcalf Foundation.

Jackson, Tim and Peter Victor 2011. 'Productivity and work in the new economy – some theoretical reflections and empirical tests', in *Environmental Innovation and Societal Transitions* 1(1): 101–108.

Jackson, T., P. Victor and A. Asjad Naqvi 2016. 'Towards a stock-flow consistent ecological macroeconomics'. WWW for Europe Working Paper no. 114. Online at www.foreurope.eu/fileadmin/documents/pdf/Workingpapers/WWWforEurope_WPS_no114_MS40.pdf (accessed 23 July 2016).

Jackson, Tim and Robin Webster 2016. 'Limits revisited: a review of the limits to growth debate'. Guildford: Centre for the Understanding of Sustainable Prosperity. Online at http://limits2growth.org.uk/wp-content/uploads/2016/04/Jackson-and-Webster-2016-Limits-Revisited.pdf (accessed 24 April 2016).

Jacobs, Michael 1991. *The Green Economy*. London: Pluto Press.

James, Oliver 2007. *Affluenza*. London: Vermillion.

James, Oliver 1998. *Britain on the Couch: Why We're Unhappier Compared to 1950 Despite Being Richer*. London: Arrow Books.

Jayadev, Arjun and Mike Konczal 2010. 'The boom not the slump: the right time for austerity'. Roosevelt Institute briefing paper. Online at www.excellentfuture. ca/sites/default/files/not_the_time_for_austerity.pdf (accessed 18 March 2016).

Jørgensen, Sven Erik, Brian Fath, Søren Nors Nielsen, Federico Pulselli, Daniel Fiscus and Simone Bastianoni. 2015. *Flourishing within Limits to Growth*. London: Routledge.

Kahneman, Daniel 1991. *Thinking Fast and Slow*. London and New York: Penguin.

Kahneman, Daniel and Alan Krueger 2006. 'Developments in the measurement of subjective well-being'. *Journal of Economic Perspectives* 20(1): 3–24.

Kahneman, Daniel, Alan Krueger, David Schkade, N. Schwartz and A. Stone 2004. 'A survey method for characterizing daily life experience: the day reconstruction method'. *Science* 3: 1776–1780.

Kahneman, Daniel and Robert Sugden. 2005 'Experienced utility as a standard of policy evaluation'. *Environmental and Resource Economics* 32: 161–181.

Kallis, Giorgos 2015. 'The degrowth alternative, essay for the great transition initiative'. Online at www.greattransition.org/publication/the-degrowth-alternative (accessed 14 October 2015).

Kallis, Giorgos 2011. 'In defence of degrowth'. *Ecological Economics* 70(5): 873–880.

Kasser, Tim 2008. *A Vision of Prosperity*. London: Sustainable Development Commission. Online at www.sd-commission.org.uk/publications.php?id=740 (accessed 19 January 2016).

Kasser, Tim 2002. *The High Price of Materialism*. Cambridge, MA: MIT Press.

Kaya, Yoichi and Keiichi Yokoburi 1997. *Environment, Energy, and Economy: Strategies for Sustainability*. Tokyo: United Nations University Press.

Keen, Steve 2011. *Debunking Economics*, revised and expanded edition. London and New York: Zed Books.

Keen, Steve 1995. 'Finance and economic breakdown: modelling Minsky's "financial instability hypothesis"'. *Journal of Post Keynesian Economics* 17(4): 607–635.

Keynes, John Maynard 1978. *Collected Writings of John Maynard Keynes*, vol. 17. Cambridge: Cambridge University Press.

Keynes, John Maynard 1937. *The Collected Writings of John Maynard Keynes*, vol. 21, *World Crises and Policies in Britain and America*, reprinted 2012. Cambridge: Cambridge University Press.

Keynes, John Maynard 1936. *The General Theory of Employment, Interest and Money*, reprinted 2007. London: Macmillan.

Keynes, John Maynard 1930. 'Economic possibilities for our grandchildren'. *Essays in Persuasion*. New York: W. W. Norton & Co.

Keynes, John Maynard 1926. *The End of Laissez Faire: The Economic Consequences of the Peace*. London: Hogarth Press.

Kierkegaard, Søren 1844. *The Concept of Anxiety: A Simple Psychologically Orienting Deliberation on the Dogmatic Issue of Hereditary Sin*, reprinted as *Kierkegaard's Writings*, vol. 8. Princeton: Princeton University Press.

King, Ursula 2015. *Spirit of Fire: The Life and Vision of Teilhard de Chardin*, 2nd edition. New York: Orbis Books.

Krugman, Paul 2015. 'The austerity delusion'. *Guardian*, 29 April. Online at www.theguardian.com/business/ng-interactive/2015/apr/29/the-austerity-delusion (accessed 18 March 2016).

Krugman, Paul 2014. 'Could fighting global warming be cheap and free?' *New York Times*, 18 September. Online at www.nytimes.com/2014/09/19/opinion/paul-krugman-could-fighting-global-warming-be-cheap-and-free.html?_r=1 (accessed 31 December 2015).

Kubiszewski, Ida, Robert Costanza, Carla Franco, Philip Lawn, John Talberth, Tim Jackson et al. 2013. 'Beyond GDP: Measuring and achieving global genuine progress'. *Ecological Economics* 93: 57–68.

Lakoff, George 2012. 'All in the mind'. *Progress Magazine*. Online at www.progressonline.org.uk/2012/09/12/all-in-the-mind-2/ (accessed 15 March 2016).

Lancaster, Kelvin 1966. 'A new approach to consumer theory'. *Journal of Political Economy* 174: 132–157.

Lane, Robert 2001. *The Loss of Happiness in Market Democracies*. New Haven, CN: Yale University Press.

Latouche, Serge 2007. 'De-growth: an electoral stake?' *International Journal of inclusive Democracy* 3(1) (January). Online at www.inclusivedemocracy.org/journal/vol3/vol3_no1_Latouche_degrowth.htm.

Law Commission 2014. 'Fiduciary duties of financial intermediaries'. Law Com 350. London: House of Commons. Online at www.lawcom.gov.uk/wp-content/uploads/2015/03/lc350_fiduciary_duties.pdf (accessed 8 May 2016).

Layard, Richard 2005. *Happiness*. London: Penguin.

Le Quéré, C. et al. 2015. 'Global carbon budget 2015'. *Earth Systems Science Data* 7: 349–396. Online at www.earth-syst-sci-data.net/7/349/2015/essd-7-349-2015.html (accessed 8 January 2016).

Lebow, Victor 1955. 'Price competition in 1955'. *Journal of Retailing* 31(1): 5–10.

Lewis, David and Darren Bridger 2001. *The Soul of the New Consumer: Authenticity – What We Buy and Why in the New Economy*. London: Nicholas Brealey.

Lientz, Bennet and Kathryn Rea 2001. *The 2001 Professional's Guide to Process Improvement: Maximizing Profit, Efficiency, and Growth*. Colorado: Aspen Publishers Inc.

Lloyd, William Forster 1833. 'Two lectures on the checks to population'. Online at https://archive.org/details/twolecturesonch00lloygoog (accessed 9 March 2016).

Lombardo, Barbara and Caryl Eyre 2011. 'Compassion fatigue: a nurse's primer'. *OJIN: The Online Journal of Issues in Nursing* 16(1). Online at www.nursingworld.org/MainMenuCategories/ANAMarketplace/ANAPeriodicals/OJIN/

TableofContents/Vol-16-2011/No1-Jan-2011/Compassion-Fatigue-A-Nurses-Primer.html (accessed 27 March 2016).

Lord, Clive 2003. *A Citizen's Income – A Foundation for a Sustainable World*. Charlbury, Oxford: Jon Carpenter Publishing.

Luxemburg, Rosa 1913. *The Accumulation of Capital*, reprinted 2003. London: Routledge Classics.

Lyubomirsky, Sonja 2010. *The How of Happiness: A Practical Guide to Getting The Life You Want*. London: Piatkus.

Lyubomirsky, Sonja, Ken Sheldon and David Schkade 2005. 'Pursuing happiness: the architecture of sustainable change'. *Review of General Psychology* 9(2): 111–131.

McCloskey, D 1990. 'Storytelling in economics', in Christopher Nash (ed.), *Narratives in Culture: The Uses of Storytelling in the Sciences, Philosophy and Literature*. London: Routledge.

McCracken, Grant 1990. *Culture and Consumption*, Bloomington and Indianapolis: Indiana University Press.

McGlade, Chris and Paul Ekins 2015. 'The geographical distribution of fossil fuels unused when limiting global warming to 2°C'. *Nature* 517: 187–190.

McKibben, Bill 2007. *Deep Economy – The Wealth of Communities and the Durable Future*. New York: Henry Holt & Co.

Maddison, Angus, 2008. 'Historical statistics for the world economy. Online at www.ggdc.net/maddison/.

Maddison, Angus 2007. *Contours of the World Economy 1 – 2030: Essays in Macroeconomic History*. Oxford: Oxford University Press.

Malthus, T. 1826. *An Essay on the Principle of Population; or, a View of its Past and Present Effects on Human Happiness; an Inquiry into Our Prospects Respecting the Future Removal or Mitigation of the Evils which it Occasions*, 6th edition. London: Munay.

Malthus, T. 1798. *An Essay on the Principle of Population, as it Affects the Future Improvement of Society, with Remarks on the Speculations of Mr Godwin, M. Condorcet and Other Writers*. London: J. Johnson.

Marmot, Michael 2010. 'Fair society, healthy lives'. Marmot Review of Health Inequalities. Online at www.instituteofhealthequity.org/projects/fair-society-healthy-lives-the-marmot-review (accessed 24 January 2016).

Marmot, Michael 2005. *Status Syndrome – How Your Social Standing Directly Affects Your Health*. London: Bloomsbury.

Marmot, Michael and Richard Wilkinson (eds) 2006. *Social Determinants of Health*, 2nd edition. Oxford: Oxford University Press.

Marx, Karl 1867. *Capital: A critique of Political Economy*, reprinted 2004. London: Penguin.

Mayhew, Susan 2004. 'Governmentality', in Mayhew, ed., *A Dictionary of Geography*. Oxford: Oxford University Press.

Mawdsley, Emma 2004. 'India's middle classes and the environment'. *Development and Change* 35(1): 79–103.

Mazzucato, Mariana 2015. *The Entrepreneurial State: Debunking Public and Private Sector Myths*. New York: Public Affairs Books.

Max Neef, Manfred 1992. *Human-Scale Development: Conception, Application and Further Reflection*. London: Apex Press.

MEA 2005. *Ecosystems and Human Wellbeing: Current States and Trends*. Washington, DC: Island Press.

Meadows, Donella, Dennis Meadows, Jørgen Randers and William Behrens 1972. *The Limits to Growth*. New York: Universe Press.

Meadows, Donella, Jørgen Randers and Dennis Meadows 2004. *Limits to Growth – The 30 Year Update*. London: Earthscan.

Meinshausen, Malte, Nicolai Meinshausen, William Hare, Sarah Raper, Katja Frieler, Reto Knutti et al. 2009. 'Greenhouse-gas emission targets for limiting global warming to 2°C'. *Nature* 458: 1158–1162.

Met Office 2015. 'Global climate in context as the world approaches 1°C above pre-industrial for the first time'. Exeter: Met Office. Online at www.metoffice.gov. uk/media/pdf/7/6/OneDegree2015.pdf (accessed 29 December 2015).

Meyer, Aubrey 2004. 'Briefing: contraction and convergence'. *Engineering Sustainability* 157(4): 189–192.

MGI 2013. *Resource Revolution: Tracking Global Commodity Markets*. London and New York: McKinsey Global Institute.

Midgley, Mary 2010. *The Solitary Self – Darwin and the Selfish Gene*. Dublin: Acumen Press.

Milanovic, Branco 2012. *Global Income Inequality by the Numbers*. World Bank Research Paper. Washington, DC: World Bank. See Milanovic's presentation online at www.ub.edu/histeco/pdf/milanovic.pdf (accessed 7 November 2015).

Milanovic, Branco 2011. *The Haves and the Have Nots*. New York: Basic Books.

Mill, John Stuart 1863. *Utilitarianism*. London: Parker, Son & Bourn, reprinted 1972. London: HarperCollins.

Mill, John Stuart 1848. *Principles of Political Economy with Some of Their Applications to Social Philosophy*, book 4, chapter 6, 'Of the Stationary State'. London: Longman's Green and Co. Online at www.econlib.org/library/Mill/mlP61.html (accessed 26 February 2016).

Minsky, Hyman 1994. 'Financial instability and the decline of banking: public policy implications'. Hyman P. Minsky Archive (Paper 88). Online at http://digital commons.bard.edu/hm_archive/88 (accessed 18 July 2016).

Minsky, Hyman 1992. 'The Financial Instability Hypothesis'. Working Paper no. 74. Annandale-on-Hudson: Levy Economics Institute. Online at www.levyinstitute. org/pubs/wp74.pdf (accessed 15 March 2016).

Minsky, Hyman 1986. *Stabilizing an Unstable Economy*. New York: McGraw Hill.

Mirowski, Philip 1989. *More Heat than Light – Economics as Social Physics, Physics as Nature's Economics*. Cambridge: Cambridge University Press.

Mohr, S., J. Wang, G. Ellem, J. Ward and D. Giurco 2015. 'Projection of world fossil fuels by country'. *Fuel* 141: 120–135.

Monbiot, George 2015. 'False promise'. Online at www.monbiot.com/2015/11/24/ false-promise/. Published in *Guardian,* 24 November 2015, as 'Consume more or conserve more: sorry but we just can't do both'. Online at www.theguardian. com/commentisfree/2015/nov/24/consume-conserve-economic-growth-sustainability (accessed 31 December 2015).

NCC 2006. *Shopping Generation.* London: National Consumer Council.

NCE 2014. *Better Growth, Better Climate: The New Climate Economy Report: The Synthesis Report.* Washington, DC: World Resources Institute/Global Commission on the Economy and the Climate. Online at http://2014.newclimateeconomy.report/ wp-content/uploads/2014/08/BetterGrowth-BetterClimate_NCE_Synthesis-Report_web.pdf (accessed 15 October 2015).

NEF 2013. *Time on Our Side: Why We All Need a Shorter Working Week.* London: New Economics Foundation.

NEF 2010. *21 Hours: Why a Shorter Working Week Can Help Us All to Flourish in the 21st Century.* London: New Economics Foundation. Online at http://b.3cdn. net/nefoundation/f49406d81b9ed9c977_p1m6ibgje.pdf (accessed 8 May 2016).

NEF 2009. *National Accounts of Wellbeing – Bringing Real Wealth into the Balance Sheet.* London: New Economics Foundation. 12218. Cambridge, MA: National Bureau of Economic Research.

Norman, Jesse 2010. *The Big Society – The Anatomy of the New Politics.* Buckingham: University of Buckingham Press.

Norman, Jesse, Kitty Ussher and Danny Alexander 2007. *From Here to Fraternity: Perspectives on Social Responsibility.* London: CentreForum.

Nussbaum, Martha 2006. *Frontiers of Justice: Disability, Nationality and Policy Design.* Cambridge: Cambridge University Press.

Nuttall, Graeme 2012. 'Sharing success – the Nuttall review of employee ownership'. London: Department of Business, Innovation and Skills. Online at www.gov.uk/ government/publications/nuttall-review-of-employee-ownership (accessed 23 July 2016).

O'Brien, Karen, Bronwyn Hayward and Berkes, F. 2009. 'Rethinking social contracts: building resilience in a changing climate'. *Ecology and Society.* 14(2), online, 17pp.

O'Neill, John 2008. *Living Well – Within Limits: Wellbeing, Time and Sustainability.* London: Sustainable Development Commission. Online at www.sd-commission. org.uk/publications.php?id=781 (accessed 19 January 2016).

OECD 2015. *In it Together: Why Less Inequality Benefits All.* Paris: Organization for Economic Cooperation and Development. Online at www.oecd.org/social/in-it-together-why-less-inequality-benefits-all-9789264235120-en.htm (accessed 8 November 2015).

OECD 2011. *Resource Productivity in the G8 and the OECD.* Paris: Organization for Economic Cooperation and Development. Online at www.oecd.org/env/ waste/47944428.pdf (accessed 4 January 2016).

OECD 2008. *Growing Unequal? Income Inequality and Poverty in OECD Countries.* Paris: Organization for Economic Cooperation and Development.

Offer, Avner 2008. *A Vision of Prosperity.* London: Sustainable Development Commission. Online at www.sd-commission.org.uk/publications.php?id=741 (accessed 19 January 2016).

Offer, Avner 2006. *The Challenge of Affluence.* Oxford: Oxford University Press.

ONS 2016. 'National Accounts articles: alternative measures of real households disposable income and the saving ratio: June 2016'. London: Office for National Statistics. Online at www.ons.gov.uk/economy/nationalaccounts/uksectoraccounts/articles/nationalaccountsarticles/alternativemeasuresofreal householddisposableincomeandthesavingratiojune2016 (accessed 23 June 2016).

Ormerod, Paul 2008. *Is the Concept of 'Wellbeing' Useful for Policy Making?* London: Sustainable Development Commission. Online at www.sd-commission.org.uk/publications.php?id=782 (accessed 19 January 2016).

Oulton, Nicholas 1996. 'Competition and the dispersion of labour productivity amongst UK companies'. NIESR Paper no. 103. London: National Institute of Economic and Social Research.

Orsdemir, Adem, Vinayak Deshpande and Ali Parlakturk 2015. 'Is servicization a win–win strategy? Profitability and environmental implications of servicization'. Available at SSRN: http://ssrn.com/abstract=2679404 or http://dx.doi.org/10.2139/ssrn.2679404 (accessed 26 March 2016).

Ostrom, Elinor 1990. *Governing the Commons: The Evolution of Institutions for Collective Action.* Cambridge: Cambridge University Press.

Oxfam 2015. 'Wealth: having it all and wanting more'. Oxfam Issue Briefing, January. Oxford: Oxfam.

Oxfam 2014. 'Working for the few'. 178 Oxfam Briefing Paper. Oxford: Oxfam international. Online at http://oxf.am/KHp (accessed 18 October 2015).

Pasqualino, Roberto, Aled Jones, Irene Monasterolo and Alexander Phillips 2015. 'Understanding global systems today – a calibration of the World3 Model between 1995 and 2012'. *Sustainability* 7(8): 9864–9889.

Pauli, Gunther 2010. *The Blue Economy: 10 Years, 100 Innovations, 100 Million Jobs.* Taos, New Mexico: Paradigm Publications.

Pepper, Miriam, Tim Jackson and David Uzzell 2009. Values and Sustainable Consumer Behaviours. *International Journal of Consumer Studies.* Special issue on Sustainable Consumption. Forthcoming.

Perez, Carlota 2003. *Technological Revolutions and Financial Capital: The Dynamics of Bubbles and Golden Ages.* Cheltenham: Edward Elgar.

PERI 2008. *Green Recovery: A Program to Create Good Jobs and Start Building a Low-Carbon Economy.* A report by the Political Economy Research Institute, University of Massachusetts, Amherst, September 2008. Washington, DC: Center for American Progress.

Peters, Michael, Shane Fudge and Tim Jackson (eds) 2010. *Low Carbon Communities: Imaginative Approaches to Combating Climate Change Locally*. Cheltenham: Edward Elgar.

Philipsen, Dirk 2015. *The Little Big Number: How GDP Came to Rule the World and What to Do About It*. Princeton: Princeton University Press.

Pieters, Rik 2013. 'Bidirectional dynamics of materialism and loneliness: not just a vicious cycle'. *Journal of Consumer Research* 40(4): 615–631.

Piketty, Thomas 2014. *Capital in the 21st Century*. Harvard: Harvard University Press.

Polanyi, Karl 1942. *Great Transformation – The Political and Economic Origins of Our Time*, reprinted 2002. Uckfield: Beacon Press.

Porritt, Jonathon 2013. *The World We Made: Alex McKay's Story from 2050*. London: Phaidon Press.

Porritt, Jonathon 2005. *Capitalism – As if the World Matters*. London: Earthscan.

Positive Money 2013. 'Sovereign money'. London: Positive Money. Online at http://positivemoney.org/wp-content/uploads/2013/11/Sovereign-Money-Final-Web.pdf (accessed 18 March 2016).

Putnam, Robert 2001. *Bowling Alone: The Collapse and Revival of American Community*. New York: Simon and Schuster.

Pyszczynski, Tom, Sheldon Solomon and Jeff Greenberg 2003. *In the Wake of 9/11: The Psychology of Terror*. Washington, DC: American Psychological Association.

Ragnarsdottír, Vala and Harald Sverdrup 2015. 'Limits to growth revisited'. *Geoscientist* online. Online at www.geolsoc.org.uk/Geoscientist/Archive/October-2015/Limits-to-growth-revisited (accessed 17 December 2015).

Rapp, Hilde 2008. *Fulfillment and Prosperity: A Neo-Gandhian Vision*. London: Sustainable Development Commission. Online at www.sd-commission.org.uk/publications.php?id=737 (accessed 19 January 2016).

Raventos, Daniel 2007. *Basic Income – The Material Conditions of Freedom*. London: Pluto Press.

Rawlinson, George 1956. *The History of Herodotus*. San Diego, CA: Tudor Publishing Company.

Raworth, Kate 2012. 'A safe and just space for humanity. Can we live within the doughnut?' Oxfam Discussion Paper. Oxford: Oxfam. Online at www.oxfam.org/sites/www.oxfam.org/files/file_attachments/dp-a-safe-and-just-space-for-humanity-130212-en_5.pdf (accessed 30 March 2016).

Reay, David, Colin Ramshaw and Adam Harvey 2008. *Process Intensification: Engineering for Efficiency, Sustainability and Flexibility*. Oxford: Butterworth-Heinemann.

Reinhart, Carmen and Kenneth Rogoff 2013. 'Financial and sovereign debt crises: some lessons learned and those forgotten'. IMF Working Paper WP/13/266. Washington, DC: International Monetary Fund.

Reinhart, Carmen and Kenneth Rogoff 2010. 'Growth in a time of debt'. *American Economic Review: Papers and Proceedings* 100: 573–578.

Ridley, Matt 1996. *The Origins of Virtue*. London: Penguin Books.

Ridley, Matt 1994. *The Red Queen – Sex and the Evolution of Human Nature*. London: Penguin Books.

Ritzer, George 2004. *The McDonaldization of Society*. New York: Pine Forge Press.

Robeyns, Ingrid and Robert van der Veen 2007. 'Sustainable quality of life – conceptual analysis for a policy-relevant empirical specification'. MNP report 550031006/2007. Bilthoven: Netherlands Environmental Assessment Agency.

Robinson, Edward 1948. *Monopoly*. Cambridge Economic Handbooks, 1st printed 1941. Cambridge: Cambridge University Press.

Robinson, Joan 1955. 'Marx, Marshall, and Keynes'. Delhi School of Economics, Occasional Papers. University of Delhi.

Rockström, J., W. Steffen, K. Noone, Å. Persson, F. S. Chapin, III, E. Lambin, et al. 2009. 'A safe operating space for humanity'. *Nature* 461: 472–475. Online at www.nature.com/nature/journal/v461/n7263/full/461472a.html (accessed 18 December 2015).

Rogelj, Joeri, Michiel Schaeffer, Pierre Friedlingstein, Nathan Gillett, Detlef van Vuuren, Keywan Riahi et al. 2016. 'Differences between carbon budget estimates unravelled'. *Nature Climate Change* 6: 245–252. doi:10.1038/nclimate2868.

Rogoff, Kenneth 2015. 'Oil prices and global growth. Project syndicate'. Online at www.project-syndicate.org/commentary/oil-prices-global-growth-by-kenneth-rogoff-2015-12?utm_source=Project+Syndicate+Newsletter&utm_campaign= c9ff3f432f-Rogoff_Oil_Prices_and_Global_Growth_12_20_2015&utm_ medium=email&utm_term=0_73bad5b7d8-c9ff3f432f-104293997 (accessed 18 December 2015).

Rose, Hilary and Stephen Rose 2000. *Alas, Poor Darwin – Arguments Against Evolutionary Psychology*. London: Jonathan Cape.

Rosenbaum, E. 2015. 'Zero growth and structural change in a post-Keynesian growth model'. *Journal of Post Keynesian Economics* 37(4): 623–647.

Rothman, Dale 1998. 'Environmental kuznets curves – real progress or passing the buck? A case for consumption-based approaches'. *Ecological Economics* 25(2): 177–194.

Rousseau, Jean-Jacques 1754. *A Discourse upon the Origin and the Foundation of the Inequality of Mankind*, reprinted 2004. New York: Dover. Online at www.bartleby.com/168/605.html (accessed 15 November 2015).

RSA 2015. 'Creative citizen, creative state: the principled and pragmatic case for a universal basic income'. London: Royal Society for the Arts. Online at www.thersa.org/discover/publications-and-articles/reports/basic-income (accessed 14 May 2016).

Rutherford, Jonathan 2008. *Wellbeing, Economic Growth and Recession*. London: Sustainable Development Commission. Online at www.sd-commission.org.uk/publications.php?id=779 (accessed 19 January 2016).

Ryan-Collins, Josh, Tony Greenham, Richard Werner and Andrew Jackson 2012. *Where Does Money Come from?* London: New Economics Foundation.

Sabin, Paul 2013. *The Bet: Paul Ehrlich, Julian Simon, and Our Gamble Over Earth's Future*. New Haven and London: Yale University Press.

Sandel, Michael 2013. *What Money Can't Buy: The Moral Limits of Markets*. London: Penguin.

Sandel, Michael 2009. 'The new citizenship'. 2009 Reith Lectures. London: BBC. Online at www.bbc.co.uk/worldservice/specialreports/2009/06/090612_reith_ lectures_2009.shtml.

Sardar, Zia 2008. *Prosperity: A Transmodern Analysis*. London: Sustainable Development Commission. Online at www.sd-commission.org.uk/publications. php?id=739 (accessed 19 January 2016).

Schwartz, Shalom 2006. 'Value orientations: measurement, antecedents and consequences across nations', in R. Jowell, C. Roberts, R. Fitzgerald and G. Eva (eds), *Measuring Attitudes Cross-Nationally – Lessons from the European Social Survey*. London: Sage.

Schwartz, Shalom 1999. 'A theory of cultural values and some implications for work'. *Applied Psychology* 48(1): 23–47.

Schor, Juliet 2010 *Plenitude: The New Economics of True Wealth*. New York: Penguin.

Schor, Juliet 1998. *The Overspent American: Upscaling, Downshifting and the New Consumer*. New York: Basic Books.

Schumacher, Ernst 1973. *Small is Beautiful: A Study of Economics as if People Mattered*, reprinted 1993. London: Vintage Books.

Schumpeter, Joseph 1954. *History of Economic Analysis*, reprinted 1994. London: Routledge.

Schumpeter, Joseph 1950. *Capitalism, Socialism and Democracy*, reprinted 1994. London: Routledge.

Schumpeter, Joseph 1934. *The Theory of Economic Development*, reprinted 2008. London: Transaction Publishers.

Scitovsky, Tibor 1976. *The Joyless Economy*. Oxford: Oxford University Press.

SDC 2006a. *I Will If You Will*. Report of the UK Sustainable Consumption Round Table. London: Sustainable Development Commission/National Consumer Council.

SDC 2006b. *The Role of Nuclear Power in a Low-Carbon Economy*. London: Sustainable Development Commission.

Sen, Amartya 1999. *Development as Freedom*. Oxford: Oxford University Press.

Sen, Amartya 1998. 'The Living Standard', in Crocker and Linden (eds), pp. 287–311.

Sen, Amartya 1984. 'The Living Standard'. *Oxford Economic Papers* 36: 74–90.

Sen, Amartya 1985. *Commodities and Capabilities*. Amsterdam: Elsevier.

Shaw, George Bernard 1903. *Man and Superman*, reprinted 2000. London: Penguin.

Sigurjónsson, F 2015. 'Monetary reform: a better monetary system for Iceland. A report commissioned by the Prime Minister of Iceland'. Online at www. forsaetisraduneyti.is/media/Skyrslur/monetary-reform.pdf (accessed 9 March 2016).

Sippel, Alexandra 2009. 'Back to the future: today's and tomorrow's politics of degrowth economics (décroissance) in light of the debate over luxury among eighteenth and early nineteenth century utopists'. *International Labor and Working-Class History* 75: 13–29.

Skidelsky, Edward and Robert Skidelsky 2013. *How Much is Enough? Money and the Good Life*. London: Penguin.

Smith, Adam 1776. *An Inquiry into the Nature and Causes of the Wealth of Nations*, reprinted 1937. New York: Modern Library.

Smith, Pete et al. 2016. 'Biophysical and economic limits to negative CO_2 emissions'. *Nature Climate Change* 6: 42–50. Online at www.nature.com/nclimate/journal/v6/n1/full/nclimate2870.html (accessed 12 July 2016).

Sober, E and D Wilson 1998. *Unto Others – The Evolution and Psychology of Unselfish Behaviour*. Cambridge, MA: Harvard University Press.

Soddy, F 1931. *Money Versus Man*. London: Elkin Mathews & Marrot.

Solomon, Sheldon, Jeff Greenberg and Tom Pyszczynski 2014. *The Worm at the Core: On the Role of Death in Life*. London: Penguin.

Solow, Robert 1956. 'A contribution to the theory of economic growth'. *Quarterly Journal of Economics* 70(1): 65–94.

Soper, Kate 2008. 'Exploring the relationship between growth and wellbeing'. London: Sustainable Development Commission. Online at www.sd-commission. org.uk/publications.php?id=780 (accessed 19 January 2016).

Soros, George 2008. *The New Paradigm for Financial Markets: The Credit Crisis of 2008 and What it Means*. London: PublicAffairs.

Sorrell, Steve 2007. 'The rebound effect: an assessment of the evidence for economy-wide energy savings from improved energy efficiency'. A report by the Sussex Energy Group for the UK Energy Research Centre. London: UK Energy Research Group.

Stahel, W. and T. Jackson 1993. 'Optimal utilisation and durability: towards a new definition of the service economy', in Jackson (1993), chapter 14.

Steffen, Will, Katherine Richardson, Johan Rockström, Sarah E. Cornell, Ingo Fetzer, Elena M. Bennett et al. 2015. 'Planetary boundaries: Guiding human development on a changing planet'. *Science* 347(6223). Online at www. sciencemag.org/content/347/6223/1259855.abstract (accessed 20 December 2015).

Sterling, Peter 2016. 'Why we consume: neural design and sustainability. A great transition viewpoint. Great transition network'. Online at www.greattransition. org/publication/why-weconsume.

Sterling, Peter and Simon Laughlin 2015. *Principles of Neural Design*. Cambridge, MA: MIT Press.

Stern, Nicholas 2007. *The Economics of Climate Change: The Stern Review*. Cambridge: Cambridge University Press.

Stiglitz, Joseph 2013. *The Price of Inequality*. London: Penguin.

Stiglitz, Joseph, Amartya Sen and Jean-Paul Fitoussi 2009. 'Report by the Commission on the Measurement of Economic Performance and Social Progress'. Online at www.insee.fr/fr/publications-et-services/dossiers_web/stiglitz/doc-commission/RAPPORT_anglais.pdf (accessed 20 January 2016).

Stuckler, David and Sanjay Basu 2014. *The Body Economic: Eight Experiments in Economic Recovery from Iceland to Greece*. London: Penguin.

Summers, Lawrence 2014. 'US economic prospects: secular stagnation, hysteresis, and the zero lower bound'. *Business Economics* 49(2): 66–73.

Sverdrup, Harald and Vala Ragnarsdottír 2014. 'Natural resources in a planetary perspective'. *Geochemical Perspectives* 3(2): 129–341.

Swan, Alan 1956. 'Economic growth and capital accumulation'. *Economic Record* 32: 344–361.

TEEB 2012. *The Economics of Ecosystems and Biodiversity: Ecological and Economic Foundations*. London: Routledge.

TEEB 2010. 'The economics of ecosystems and biodiversity: mainstreaming the economics of nature: a synthesis of the approach, conclusions and recommendations of TEEB'. Online at http://doc.teebweb.org/wp-content/uploads/Study%20and%20Reports/Reports/Synthesis%20report/TEEB%20Synthesis%20Report%202010.pdf (accessed 30 December 2015).

Teulings, Coen and Richard Baldwin 2014. 'Secular Stagnation: facts, causes and cures'. London: Centre for Economic Policy Research. Online at www.voxeu.org/sites/default/files/Vox_secular_stagnation.pdf (accessed 17 October 2015).

Thaler, Richard H. and Cass Sunstein 2009 *Nudge: Improving Decisions About Health, Wealth and Happiness*. London and New York: Penguin.

Timmer, Marcel, Mary O'Mahony and Bart van Ark 2007. EU KLEMS growth and productivity accounts: overview, November 200 release. Groningen: University of Groningen. Online at www.euklems.net/data/overview_07ii.pdf.

Townsend, Peter 1979. *Poverty in the United Kingdom – A Survey of Household Resources and Standards of Living*. London: Penguin.

Tukker, Arnold, Gjalt Huppes, Jeroen Guinée, Reinout Heijungs, Arjan de Koning, Lauran van Oers, et al. 2007. 'Environmental Impact of Products (EIPRO) – analysis of the life cycle environmental impacts related to the final consumption of the EU-25'. European Commission: Joint Research Centre. Online at http://ftp.jrc.es/EURdoc/eur22284en.pdf (accessed 23 July 2016).

Turner, Adair 2015. *Between Debt and the Devil. Money, Credit and Fixing Global Finance*. Princeton: Princeton University Press.

Turner, A. 2013. 'Debt, money and Mephistopheles: how do we get out of this mess'. Lecture to the Cass Business School. February 2013. Online at http://ineteconomics.org/sites/inet.civicactions.net/files/Turner%20Cass%20Lecture%202013.pdf. (accessed 23 July 2016).

Turner, Graham 2014. 'Is global collapse imminent? An updated comparison of *The Limits to Growth* with historical data'. MSSI Research Paper no. 4, August. Melbourne: Melbourne Sustainable Society Institute.

Turner, Graham 2008. 'A comparison of *The Limits to Growth* with thirty years of reality'. *Global Environmental Change* 18: 397–411.

UN 2015. 'World population prospects: key findings and advance tables, 2015 Revision'. New York: United Nations/UN Department of Economic and Social Affairs. Online at http://esa.un.org/unpd/wpp/Publications/Files/Key_Findings_WPP_2015.pdf (accessed 7 November 2015).

UN 2013. Inequality matters. Report on the world social situation 2013. New York: United Nations/UN Department of Economic and Social Affairs. Online at www.oecd.org/social/in-it-together-why-less-inequality-benefits-all-9789264235120-en.htm (accessed 8 November 2015).

UNCTAD 2007. 'The concept of odious debt in public international law'. Discussion Paper no. 185. Geneva: UN Conference on Trade and Development. Online at http://unctad.org/en/docs/osgdp20074_en.pdf (accessed 23 October 2015).

UNDP 2013. Humanity Divided – confronting inequality in developing countries. New York: United Nations Development Programme. UNDP 2005. *Human Development Report*. Oxford: Oxford University Press.

UNEP 2016. 'Global trends in renewable energy investment 2016'. Paris: United Nations Environment Programme. Online at http://fs-unep-centre.org/sites/default/files/publications/globaltrendsinrenewableenergyinvestment2016lowres_0.pdf (accessed 29 May 2016).

UNEP 2015. 'International trade in resources – a biophysical assessment'. Paris: United Nations Environment Programme. Online at www.unep.org/resourcepanel/KnowledgeResources/AssessmentAreasReports/TRADE/tabid/1060710/Default.aspx (accessed 6 January 2016).

UNEP 2011. 'Towards a green economy. Pathways to sustainable development and poverty eradication: a Synthesis for policy makers'. Paris: UNEP. Online at www.unep.org/greeneconomy/Portals/88/documents/ger/GER_synthesis_en.pdf (accessed 15 October 2015).

UNEP 2008. 'Global Green New Deal – UNEP green economy initiative'. Press release at London launch, 22 October 2008. Online at www.unep.org/Documents. Multilingual/Default.asp?DocumentID=548&ArticleID=5957&l=en (accessed 11 July 2016).

UNFCCC 2015. 'Adoption of the Paris Agreement'. UN FCCC/CP/2015/L.9. Draft. Online at http://un'fccc.int/resource/docs/2015/cop21/eng/l09.pdf (accessed 14 December 2015).

UNICEF 2014. 'Levels and trends in child mortality – report 2014: estimates developed by the UN Inter-agency Group for Child Mortality Estimation'. Online at www.unicef.org/media/files/Levels_and_Trends_in_Child_Mortality_2014.pdf (accessed 24 January 2016).

US Congress 1973. 'Energy reorganization act of 1973: Hearings, Ninety-third Congress', first session, on H.R. 11510: 248.

Veblen, Thorstein 1898. *The Theory of the Leisure Class*, reprinted 1998. Great Minds Series. London: Prometheus Books.

Victor, Peter 2008a. *Managing without Growth – Slower by Design not Disaster*. Cheltenham: Edward Elgar.

Victor, Peter 2008b. 'Managing without growth'. Think-piece for the SDC workshop 'Confronting Structure'. April 2008. London: Sustainable Development Commission.

Victor, Peter and Tim Jackson 2012. 'A commentary on UNEP's green economy scenarios'. *Ecological Economics* 77: 11–15.

Wachtel, Paul 1983. *The Poverty of Affluence – A Psychological Portrait of the American Way of Life*. New York: The Free Press.

Wall, Derek, 2014. *The Sustainable Economics of Elinor Ostrom*. London: Routledge.

Wall, Derek 2008. 'Prosperity without growth: economics beyond capitalism'. London: Sustainable Development Commission. Online at www.sd-commission. org.uk/publications.php?id=771 (accessed 19 January 2016).

Walsh, Catherine 2010. 'Development as buen vivir: institutional arrangements and (de)colonial entanglements'. *Development* 53(1): 15–21.

Washington, Henry (ed.) 1871. *The Writings of Thomas Jefferson*, vol. 8, reprinted 2010. Nabu Press.

Weber, Max 1958. *The Protestant Ethic and the Spirit of Capitalism*, trans. Talcott Parsons. New York: Charles Scribner's Sons.

Webster, Ken 2015. *The Circular Economy – A Wealth of Flows*. Cowes, Isle of Wight: Ellen McArthur Foundation Publishing.

White, Allen, Mark Stoughton and Linda Feng 1999. 'Servicizing: the quiet transition to extended producer responsibility'. Report to the US Environmental Protection Agency Office of Solid Waste. Online at www.infohouse.p2ric.org/ref/17/16433.pdf (accessed 24 March 2016).

WHO 2012. 'All for equity'. Report of the World Conference on the Social Determinants of Health. Geneva: World Health Organisation. Online at www.who.int/sdhconference/resources/Conference_Report.pdf?ua=1 (accessed 25 January 2016).

Whybrow, Peter 2015. *The Well-Tuned Brain: Neuroscience and the Life Well Lived*. New York: W. W. Norton and Co.

Wiedmann, Thomas, Heinz Schandl, Manfred Lenzen, Daniel Moran, Sangwon Suh, James West et al. 2015. 'The material footprint of nations'. *Proceedings of the National Academy of Sciences* 112(20): 6271–6276.

Wiedmann, Thomas, Heinz Schandl and D. Moran 2015. 'The footprint of using metals: new metrics of consumption and productivity'. *Environmental Economics and Policy Studies*, 17(3): 369–388.

Wiedmann, Thomas, R. Wood, Jan Minx, Manfred Lenzen, D. Guan and Rocky Harris 2010. 'A carbon footprint time series of the UK – results from a multi-region input–output model'. *Economic Systems Research* 22(1): 19–42.

Wilhelm, Richard 2003. *I Ching or Book of Changes*, 3rd edition. London: Penguin.

Wilkinson, Richard 2005. *The Impact of Inequality: How to Make Sick Societies Healthier*. London: Routledge.

Wilkinson, Richard and Kate Pickett 2009. *The Spirit Level – Why More Equal Societies Almost Always Do Better*. London: Penguin.

Williams, Tennessee 1954. *Cat on a Hot Tin Roof*, reprinted 2010. London: Methuen Drama.

Wilson, Edward O. 1975. *Sociobiology – The New Synthesis*. Cambridge, MA: Harvard University Press.

Wolf, M. 2015. *The Shifts and the Shocks: What We Learned from the Financial Crisis and What We Still Have to Learn*. London: Penguin.

Wolf, Martin 2014. 'Strip private banks of their power to create money'. *Financial Times*, 25 April.

Wood, W., J. Quinn and D. Kashy 2002. 'Habits in everyday life: thought, emotion, and action'. *Journal of Personality and Social Psychology* 83: 1281–1297.

Wray, R. 2012. *Modern Money Theory: A Primer on Macroeconomics for Sovereign Monetary Systems*. New York and London: Palgrave Macmillan.

Wright, Robert 1994. *The Moral Animal – Why We Are the Way We Are*. London: Abacus.

Zeebe, Richard, Andy Ridgwell and James Zachos. 2016. 'Anthropogenic carbon release rate unprecedented during the past 66 million years'. *Nature Geoscience*. Online at www.nature.com/ngeo/journal/vaop/ncurrent/full/ngeo2681.html (accessed 22 March 2016).

INDEX

post-growth economy 224; and
wages 175–8
progress 2, 50–5, *54 see
also* novelty/innovation;
technological advances
progressive sector, Baumol's cost
disease 171
progressive state 185, 220–2;
contested 186–9; countering
consumerism 202–5; equality
measures 205–7, *206*;
governance of the commons
190–2; governance as
commitment device 192–5;
governmentality of growth
195–7; limit-setting 201–2;
moving towards 197–200; post-
growth macroeconomics 207–8,
224; prosperity 209
prosocial behaviour 198 *see also*
social contract
prosperity 1–3, 22, 121; capabilities
for flourishing 61–5; and growth
3–7, 23, 66, 80, 160; and
income 3–4, 5, 66–7; limits of
67–72, 113, 212; materialistic
vision 137; progress measures
50–5, *54*; relative income
effect 55–61, *58*, 71, 72; social
perspectives 2, 22, 48–9; state
roles 209 *see also* capabilities
for flourishing; post-growth
macroeconomics; sustainable
prosperity; wellbeing
prudence, financial 120, 195, 221;
financial crisis 33, 34, 35
public sector spending: austerity
policies 189; countercyclical
spending strategy 181–2, *182*;
welfare economy 169

public services/amenities: common
pool resources 190–2, 198,
199; future visions 204, 218–
20; investment 155–6, 204;
ownership 223 *see also* private vs.
public; service-based economies
public transport 41, 129, 193, 217
purpose *see* meaning/purpose
Putnam, Robert 122
psyche, human *see* human nature/
psyche

quality, environmental 12 *see also*
pollution
quality of life: enterprise as service
142; inequality 206; sustainable
128
quality to throughput ratios 113
quantitative easing 43
Queen Elizabeth II 25, 32, 34, 37
quiet revolution 127–31

Raworth, Kate 141
Reagan, Ronald 8
rebound phenomenon 111
recession 23–4, 28, 81, 161–3 *see
also* financial crisis
recreation/leisure industries 143
recycling 129
redistribution of wealth 52 *see also*
inequality
reforms 182–3, 222; economic
structures 224; and financial
crisis 103; financial systems 156–
8, 180 *see also* alternatives; future
visions; post-growth economy
relative decoupling 84–5, 86;
historical perspectives 87–9,
89; relationship with absolute
decoupling 96–101, 111